Talent Abounds

D1715249

Talent Abounds

Profiles of Master Teachers and Peak Performers

Robert F. Arnove

Paradigm Publishers
Boulder • London

Copyright © 2009 Paradigm Publishers

Published in the United States by Paradigm Publishers, 3360 Mitchell Lane, Suite E, Boulder, CO 80301 USA.

Paradigm Publishers is the trade name of Birkenkamp & Company, LLC, Dean Birkenkamp, President and Publisher.

Library of Congress Cataloging-in-Publication Data
Arnove, Robert F.
  Talent abounds : profiles of master teachers and peak performers / Robert F. Arnove.
     p. cm.
  Includes bibliographical references and index.
  ISBN 978-1-59451-633-7 (hardcover : alk. paper)
  ISBN 978-1-59451-634-4 (pbk. : alk. paper)
  1. Creative ability in adolescence. 2. Teacher-student relationships. 3. Teachers—Attitudes. 4. Influence (Psychology) I. Title.
  BF724.3.C73A76 2008
  153.9—dc22

                                                                              2008027741

Printed and bound in the United States of America on acid-free paper that meets the standards of the American National Standard for Permanence of Paper for Printed Library Materials.

Designed and typeset in Adobe Caslon by Straight Creek Bookmakers

13 12 11 10 09   1 2 3 4 5

In memory of Julie and Isadore Arnove

Contents

Acknowledgments

Over the past thirteen years, numerous individuals have helped in bringing this study to completion. First and foremost, I wish to thank the 150 talented teachers and performers my research assistants and I interviewed. They graciously shared their life stories, many of which remain to be told in subsequent publications.

At each stage of the research and production process—interviewing, transcribing, editing—I received invaluable help. Margaret Clements interviewed dozens of Indiana public school educators selected to be Armstrong Teachers in the Indiana University School of Education. Ryohei Matsuda interviewed a sample of the most significant Japanese Living Treasures in the Arts and arranged for me to do so as well. These interviews were videotaped by my daughter, Anna Strout, who also interviewed the artists featured in the chapter on modern dance masters. In addition to work done by Clements, Matsuda, and Strout, the following former students undertook the exacting work of transcribing the interviews: Stephen Franz, Shabana Mir, Allen Kashewa Manjari Singh, and Amber Gallup. As always, my wife Toby Strout proved to be both my most demanding as well as constructive critic. My son, Anthony Arnove, provided valuable advice on writing style and marketing of the book. The editorial and production staff at Paradigm Publishers could not have been more congenial and helpful. They include Martin Hanft (copyediting), Carol Smith (production), Sharon Daughtery (design, artwork, and text of the book cover) as well as Beth Davis (initial editing recommendations) and Ann Hopman (contracts). I am especially grateful to Dean Birkenkamp, Paradigm president and publisher, for his enthusiastic support of the project from its early stages.

Finally, my thanks go to Jeff Alberts and the former Research and University Graduate School (RUGS) of Indiana University for providing initial funding for this study of master teachers and the development of world-class talent.

Introduction

How can youthful talent become world-class talent? *Talent Abounds* tells the stories of master teachers and their students who raise performance to peak levels in classical music and conducting, jazz, opera, modern dance, chess, mathematics, swimming and diving, and the culinary arts.

The outstanding teachers, coaches, and peak performers profiled in *Talent Abounds* are individuals who are internationally recognized as among the very best in their fields. Master teachers attract the most promising young talents and receive constant referrals from widely respected educators, artists, and coaches. Peak performers set world records and win Olympic medals, take top prizes in international music competitions and chess tournaments, receive the most prestigious national awards accorded young and well-established artists, and make seminal contributions to the development of a particular field, whether it be swimming and diving instruction or the range of repertoire for a musical instrument.

In addition to describing the characteristics of master teachers and their prized protégés, as well as the interactions between them, I document how the profiled teachers form part of a continuum of knowledgeable and skillful educators going back for generations. For example, cellist Janos Starker and pianist György Sebok represent the culmination of a long line of teachers extending back to Franz Liszt; saxophonist Eugene Rousseau to Marcel Mule and Adolphe Sax, the inventor of the instrument; tubist Harvey Phillips to John Philip Sousa and the Ringling Brothers & Barnum and Bailey Circus Band; jazz composer and instrumentalist David Baker to the origins of jazz in New Orleans and Chicago; symphony conductors Michael Barrett and Michael Morgan to the influence of Leonard Bernstein on generations of musicians; and modern dance choreographers and artistic directors Jennifer Muller, David Parsons, and Sylvia Waters to Isadora Duncan, Martha Graham, and Alvin Ailey.

Themes and Questions

Common themes and questions organize my chapters. The individuals I feature describe their early family experiences and formative years, the progression of teachers and coaches they had, their performance careers, educational philosophy and teaching practices, and their legacies. I explore a number of important questions throughout: Is exceptional talent an innate quality? Even so, does its fulfillment depend on the intervention of expert teachers? How do social class, gender, and ethnicity influence access to instructional and performance opportunities? Can lessons learned in one particular national and cultural context or in one performance field be extended to other societies and fields? To what extent is there a match between a given individual's talents and the state of development of a particular field or domain? How does public policy shape the recognition and development of talent? How can public education nurture the talent of all individuals?[1]

The thirteen substantive chapters group teachers and performers by particular domains: instrumental music (classical, jazz, and traditional), voice (opera), dance (modern), athletics (swimming and diving), chess and mathematics, and the culinary arts.[2] Each chapter portrays clusters of master teachers and performers. Many of the individuals grouped together have been close colleagues who have inspired one another and shared students. I pair teachers and coaches with some of their most successful former students: for example, James "Doc" Counsilman, who pioneered the science of swimming instruction, with Mark Spitz, winner of seven Gold Medals in the 1972 Munich Olympics; diving coach Hobie Billingsley with Mark Lenzi, winner of the Gold Medal on the springboard in the 1992 Barcelona Olympics; violin master teacher Josef Gingold with international virtuosos such as Miriam Fried, Joshua Bell, and Corey Cerovsek; opera diva Virginia Zeani with renowned sopranos Sylvia McNair and Angela Brown.

When to call it quits to adding another virtuoso performer, prodigious talent, phenomenal coach and athlete? That was one of the key problems I faced in writing about some of the most prominent artists, athletes, and chefs over the past fifty years. Talent abounds. How it is nurtured is what this book is all about.

Notes

1. The following articles and books have been particularly helpful in organizing this thematic structure: J. F. Feldhusen, "A Conception of Giftedness," in *Conceptions of Giftedness*, ed. R. J. Sternberg and J. E. Davidson (Cambridge: Cambridge University Press, 1986), 112–27; R. Subotnik, "Talent Developed: Conversations with Masters in the Arts and Sciences," *Journal for the Education of the Gifted* 18(4) (1995): 440–66; K. A. Ericsson, R. T. Krampe, and C. Tesch-Römer, "The Role of Deliberate Practice in the Acquisition of

Expert Performance," *Psychological Review* 100(3) (1993): 363–40; and K. A. Ericsson, ed., *The Road to Excellence: The Acquisition of Expert Performance in the Arts, Sciences, Sports, and Games* (Mahwah, NJ: Lawrence Erlbaum Associates, 1996).

2. Domains, as studied by Howard Gardner—*Extraordinary Minds: Portraits of Exceptional Individuals and an Examination of Our Extraordinariness* (New York: Basic Books, 1992)—may be considered to be large, loosely bounded communities of practice. Fields refers to the systematic organization of a domain with prescribed roles, well-defined norms as to what constitutes legitimate and respected practice, and supportive cultures. For the most part in this book, I use the term "field," which is more commonly known.

CHAPTER I

A Constellation of Stars
Gingold, Starker, and Sebok

At the February 1995 memorial service for Maestro Josef Gingold an overflow crowd of seventeen hundred people gathered from all over the world to honor a singular violinist, musician, educator, and human being. More than seventy former students—including concertmasters of leading orchestras in North America and Europe and prominent soloists—assembled on the stage of the Indiana University Musical Arts Center to play Samuel Barber's mournful "Adagio for Strings" as a final tribute to a beloved teacher and companion. Years later, these musicians still talk reverentially about this towering figure as if he were still present, inspiring them to be honest to the music they play and to render enjoyment to countless new audiences.

This chapter profiles three extraordinary master teachers and musicians: violinist Josef Gingold, cellist Janos Starker, and pianist György Sebok. Over three decades, they were close friends, members of an intimate family of world-class musicians and teachers who have influenced hundreds of professional musicians. Together, they have left a rich legacy of recorded works, publications, memorable performances, and master class lessons. Their careers exemplify many of the attributes of peak performers and master teachers and coaches in the arts and athletics.

These attributes include a profound knowledge of the fields in which they work. Gingold, Starker, and Sebok mastered not only the skilled techniques needed to render beautiful music seemingly effortlessly but also a deep understanding of the very essence of music making—its historical, aesthetic, and even spiritual, dimensions. With this mastery, they developed the pedagogical skills and insights to communicate the fundamentals as well as the most refined elements of their field of practice to generations of students. Starting with a select group of talented individuals, they were able to rapidly diagnose strengths and weaknesses so as to challenge and assist their students to reach higher levels of performance in a never-ending quest for perfection. They personalized instruction, opened doors, unlocked inhibitions, and motivated their students continually to improve and eventually become self-directed learners, who, in turn, extend the boundaries of their profession.

Typical of many prodigious talents, the three started their careers at an early age, experienced a series of progressively more knowledgeable teachers who shaped their vision of music and their careers, and developed a lifelong love affair with their craft. Although their teaching styles differed, they all shared a passion for their life work, the goals they aspired to accomplish, and the legacies they wished to leave.

Brief stories from their formative years illustrate the intersection of historical context, family background, and exceptional teachers in shaping the distinct career lines that eventually converged in the Indiana University School of Music. Personal narratives blend with the remembrances of former students to highlight the enduring lessons that may be derived from studying the careers of Gingold, Starker, and Sebok. Insights from other musical personalities, including legendary violin teacher Dorothy DeLay, reinforce the identified patterns.

Formative Years—Precocity

Josef Gingold

The youngest of six children, Gingold had an older brother, who, lacking professional training, nevertheless was a gifted violinist. As Gingold recalls, wherever his brother played, "I would follow him, even though I was only four years old. I used to try and open his violin case when he was out of the house so I could play." Aware of Josef's keen interest, his father bought him a small violin while on a business trip. Thrilled by the present, he asked his father, "How does it play? What happens when I put a bow down?" His father responded, "There's a little man inside, and when you put the bow down, he begins to dance." The story continues: "And being four years old, I wanted to see the little man. I broke the violin in half that my father gave me. And my mother came to my rescue. 'Why are you telling him *bubbe-mayseh*? [Yiddish for "fairy tales."] Of course, he is a child of four. What do you want?'"

With the outbreak of World War I the following year, the members of his Russian town were given twenty-four hours to leave Brest Litovsk before the advancing German Army: "We walked, fifty families holding hands … in the fields, anywhere."

After two months of wandering to escape enemy troops, they were rounded up and put in an armory. Although they had to sleep on the floor, according to Gingold, they were treated humanely by the German soldiers.

One day, while he was in the recreation yard playing with children his age, he heard a violin. A guard was trying to play a tune his fellow guards were singing on the other side of the security fence: "Poor guy ... could not hear anything." And after hearing two or three failed attempts, Gingold pointed to a sentry to indicate that he wanted to have a go at playing the tune. Thinking the five-year-old child adorable, the sentry laughed and let him out: "I played to perfection. And, you know, to this day, I remember the tune."

At eight o'clock that evening two Germans came in with rifles, asking, "Where's little Josef who plays the violin?" Not knowing what had taken place earlier in the day, "My poor mother was so frightened, she thought I had planted a bomb or something. Then one of the officers said that 'they were having a party and someone said there was a wonder child from Russia. And we'll bring him back, don't worry.' So I went with them [even though he had already been asleep]. At the party, they asked me, 'Do you still remember the piece?' I said, 'yes.' An officer ask[ed] everybody to be quiet. Herr Schmidt [sang] the song again and they sang with so much fire [as he played the tune]." Then, the main officer, Oberleutenant Krock, asked him to play something alone, which he did—[a mazurka by Henryk Wieniawski]—that "I played not very well, but it was cute." Following that the officer removed his hat, took up a collection, and gave young Josef the money. But, "I pointed to my stomach. Ah ... he knew what I meant. I would rather have food. He sent me back with four soldiers with four big sacks. My mother thought that this was manna from heaven ... and the one thing I'll never forget is my first taste of a sardine. It was terrific. To me, it's still a big luxury." The rewards of his music making meant not only food but also that the lieutenant would bring Josef a small violin to play while he was interned with his family during the war.

Janos Starker

Like Gingold, Starker manifested his talents early. He began playing the cello at age six, and he gave his first public performance after studying only six weeks: "I was what is commonly called a child prodigy, except I did not become an exploited prodigy," as his family was protective. His first professional concert performance would wait until he was eleven.

Starker's family situation faintly resembles Gingold's. He had two older brothers who played the violin—and two were enough: "So with three boys, I had to play something else. There was no piano in the house, because my parents couldn't afford to buy one. So ... it was a little cello." At age seven he entered the prestigious Franz Liszt Academy, which he attended until age fifteen. One of his classmates was György Sebok. Another childhood companion and eventual colleague in the Indiana University School of Music was Eva (née Czako) Janzer, who was Janos's first student. She was six and he was eight!

Born in 1924, Starker did not suffer the vicissitudes of World War I as did young Gingold; but, being from a Russian Jewish family living in Hungary during World War II, he was interned in a work camp, as was Sebok. Conditions were harsh and did not allow for music making. Following the war, he left for France and eventually the United States.

György Sebok

Sebok "officially" began playing piano at age five. "Officially," because he played on his own even earlier: "That's why they took me to a piano teacher, because I knew many little pieces that I heard on the radio and I reproduced them on the piano. And then my grandfather said: 'Well, the child has started, let's take him to a teacher.'" According to Sebok, "we lived a very musical kind of life." His father, a lawyer, played the piano, and the family would often sit together listening to records or musical programs on the radio. Growing up in Szeged, Hungary, young Sebok benefited from the city's rich cultural life and easy train access to Budapest with its many exceptional teachers.

Progression of Teachers and Advanced Training

Benjamin Bloom, in *Developing Talent in Young People,* noted a common pattern in individuals who excel in the arts, sports, and other domains. In addition to having strong family support for their interests, these individuals progressively required and found teachers and coaches who would develop their talents to higher levels. Bloom identified three stages of development. Similarly, Dorothy DeLay, the renowned violin pedagogue of the Juilliard School of Music,[1] questioned whether innately talented individuals could achieve peak performance and acquire their own unique signature without the intervention of appropriate instruction:

> I don't think anybody can do that without a teacher. I think there are three very important stages, three types of teaching that are necessary in a very young person's life.... The first one would be from age whatever to about age twelve. That should be someone who supports the family, who helps the parents with their dealings with the child and who feeds the material to students in an orderly way.... Then when they start to be teenagers, children need a teacher who can really give them good discipline and see to it that everything is well organized.... And then, as they get older and are ready to go professionally, they need somebody who can help them toward really first-class performance.

The trajectories of Gingold, Starker, and Sebok, in part, conform to such a progression. Each of the three would pass through a number of teachers who would inspire them and shape their musical identities as performers and educators.

Josef Gingold

The outbreak of World War I interrupted his father's plans to take him to Warsaw to meet a professor "to see if there was anything there, talent, as he didn't know. We couldn't make the trip because all the trains were used for troops."[2] At the end of the war, Gingold's family moved to New York, where he attended the Third Street Music School Settlement: "I was there about six months and the director called me into his office one day and said, 'I think you've outgrown us. We have a wonderful teacher. He's Vladimir Graffman, an assistant to Leopold Auer.' And they even paid for my lessons. Just last year I got this diploma [pointing to it hanging on his apartment wall]."

Eventually he would return to Europe to study with an extraordinary teacher, the widely acclaimed Belgian violinist Eugène Ysaÿe. Above all else, Gingold recalls the great humanity of his teacher: "What a man he was. He was as great a man as he was an artist—a wonderful human being, a giant in size and in music." Not surprisingly, what Gingold's own students most strikingly remember about him are his great warmth and humanity.

Gingold went on to play in the NBC Symphony Orchestra of Arturo Toscanini and later became the concert master of the famed Cleveland Orchestra with George Szell as conductor. Gingold credits Szell, with his encyclopedic knowledge of music and insistence on perfection, as having greatly influenced his approach to teaching: "If I've amounted to anything as a teacher, it's largely due to him."[3]

Szell, like Toscanini, was a brilliant conductor and demanding taskmaster. According to Gingold, "He was a man who was so detailed in everything he did and … a tough guy to play with because when you played a dot for a dash and Mozart didn't write it … your life wasn't worth living after that."

Toscanini, more so than Szell, used *vergogna* (shame): "My God … I have a tape somewhere of maestro. You hear him scream and yell and you never knew what he meant. That was his worst problem, not knowing the English language [very well]. He spoke eight languages to perfection [but not English]. And he sometimes would scream, 'No, no, no, no!' and nobody would know [what]. One of the guys started calling him 'Toscan-no-no.'"

Unlike these masterful conductors and very much in the tradition of his mentor, Ysaÿe, Gingold's approach was never to shout or display anger. With Gingold's students, a sense of disappointment at expectations not being met was usually enough to send the students home to work on improving their performance.

Janos Starker

Starker, like Sebok, studied at the Franz Liszt Academy in the company of some of the greatest musical talents and teachers of the twentieth century: Béla Bartók, Zoltán Kodály, Erno Dohnányi, and Leo Weiner in a direct line of instruction originating with Franz Liszt.[4] It was the premier music conservatory in Hungary, if not Europe.

His first teacher at the academy was Adolf Schiffer, who was an assistant and then successor to the well-known David Popper. According to Starker, Schiffer was "an exceptionally daring and good teacher" who, although starting to play the cello very late and initially being self-taught, "happened upon the right principles." Those principles include physical ones on how to breathe and use the body.[5]

Schiffer and two other string teachers of the academy, Dezso Rados and Imre Waldbauer (the first violinist of the famous Waldbauer-Kerpely Quartet), who were considered to be scientific in their approach, "were not just teaching how to phrase something in a Mozart concerto, but what to do with your arms and legs and head and fingers and so on."

After leaving the academy, Starker conditioned his life "to find out what goes into the instrumental playing and the music making. I personally didn't have to alter anything. I simply had to find out why am I doing what I'm doing so as to be able to become what it requires to be a professional. Professional, meaning that you are consistent. . . . The professional knows what he does, so therefore he can do it when it's called for."

Another influence on Starker's performance and teaching career was conductor Fritz Reiner. At age twenty-five, Starker joined the New York Metropolitan Opera company as first cellist under the baton of Fritz Reiner.[6] When Reiner moved to the Chicago Symphony Orchestra in 1953, so did Starker: "I was extremely lucky because I happened to spend nine years with a man whom I consider to be the greatest conductor of all time. . . . His greatness was that he worked all his life so as to understand maximally the composer's intentions, what ensemble playing means, what balancing an orchestra means, and how to attain this with minimum physical effort." This approach to music making also is evident in the pedagogy and playing of his lifelong friend and colleague György Sebok.

György Sebok

Sebok was fortunate enough to begin his piano tuition, at age five, with a local teacher who had been a student of virtuoso pianist and composer Ferruccio Busoni. At age twelve Sebok's teacher left for another city, not, however, before finding someone from the Liszt Academy to come to Szeged (one hundred miles by train from Budapest) once a week to teach György and several other pupils.

That teacher was György Sándor, a student of Bartok's. Sebok studied with Sándor for four years.

When Sándor departed for the United States, Sebok's father urged his son to leave Szeged for Budapest and the Liszt Academy. There he studied piano, composition, and chamber music with Zoltán Kodály and Leo Weiner: "He [Weiner] taught us to hear.... For example, somebody played a Mozart quartet in the chamber music class, and one of the musicians played a wrong note. And then he stopped and pointed to one of us, and he said, 'What was the wrong note?' And if we said, 'Oh, I didn't notice it,' then he would say: 'You walk on the street. A brick falls on your head and you don't notice it?'" For Sebok, "He was music personified. His whole life was music. His method was music itself." Although Weiner was more a composer than an instrumentalist, when he did play short sections of pieces to demonstrate a point, it was a transcendental experience: "I never heard in all my life a piano touch like his. I had a feeling that if he played an F major chord, that's more F major than anybody else's F major. He played the essence of the music."[7]

Commenting on Kodály's impact, Sebok self-deprecatingly quipped: "Thanks to Kodály, I think, I did not become a composer." As a teacher, Kodály taught a small, select class: "He developed our musical understanding ... our musical mind. For example, for one year, we had to write in Palestrina style. He was expecting us to do all kinds of extremely difficult things like write a fugue for four drums, which means that the only variable is the rhythm, and there is no pitch. So this kind of mental training was extremely useful." In addition to being demanding, he never paid a compliment. When asked if being in the presence of such stern taskmasters was not intimidating, Sebok responded somewhat ironically, "No, we didn't have fragile egos there.... Our generation at the Liszt was different. Everybody thought of himself as a genius." When asked if "Kodály may not have respected your genius," the response was that "Kodály was just kind of floating above all that."[8]

What Sebok learned from his teachers was "absorbed and digested so deeply" that, when I probed him about specifics, he responded that the lessons operated at a subconscious level. Books on a wide range of subjects were another influence on his teaching because of his interest, "generally speaking, in how human beings function ... and that includes the physics, the physiology, the psychology of human movement. And I read with great interest, all the studies or philosophies related to that." This broad background, grounded in the ability to allude to poetry and philosophy as well as to physics, is what students and colleagues identify as the extraordinary ability of Sebok to diagnose a performance problem accurately and recommend strategies leading to improved musicality and self-expression.

What all three of these eminent teachers have done, in mastering their own performance fields, is to have found a way to communicate the very essence of music-making and to stimulate their students to peak performance and to be contributing members of their profession. The knowledge that needs to be taught and how it is taught with what impact form is the subject of the following sections.

Characteristics of Master Teachers

Mastering Music Making

What does mastery of a field of performance entail? Reflecting on his singular career, Janos Starker (then age seventy-three) observed "that he had played more than one thousand symphony performances, more than one thousand opera performances, and thousands and thousands of concerts, plus raised, or helped raise, hundreds and hundreds of students. And, in the meantime, [had] produced something like a hundred and twenty records ... [involving] three hundred hours sitting in the recording studios."

With this vast experience, he has developed an ideal model of instrumental playing. The elements of the model consist of what he calls "the principles, philosophies, and laws of music making." Once students have mastered these essential building blocks, the next step is to achieve "individual expression with each piece and with their entire musical existence." Students also must know the historical context and cultural traditions as well as the full extent of a composer's work in order to render a piece true to its origins. For Starker, "one cannot play Mozart unless you know his symphonies and piano concertos and his chamber music. So this means these principles are the result of a total view of the various composers' output. The style of these composers is what determines how a phrase in our literature has to be played." A fine balance needs to be achieved between adherence to basic principles and being "bold minded about how those principles are used.... The laws of music making have a great range which allows maximum freedom. I've been often quoted that I insist on discipline. What I teach is discipline, which in turn will allow, later on, freedom."

William Preucil, concert master of the Cleveland Symphony Orchestra, concisely summarizes a similar set of principles that characterize the instructional aims of Gingold, Starker, and Sebok. These principles involve "being able to understand the music that you're playing, to play in the proper style and the right context with expression, projecting the emotional experience of the music, and being able to play your instrument well enough to do that."[9]

For Starker, playing well necessarily means learning the "geography of the cello." Brant Taylor, cellist with the Chicago Symphony Orchestra, recalls how Starker taught him "how to get from one place to another, shifting positions, how the bow contacts the string ... and then being able to call upon those techniques when you are confronted with a problem musically.... He has certain things that he believes in. One of his underlying philosophies is that the better your technique is, the better you'll be able to express yourself musically. He teaches the craft of a profession."

Mastery of basic technique, of the workings of the instrument, is fundamental, but just the first step toward the achievement of musicality, the exquisite expression of the essence of the music being performed. Preucil, who studied with Josef Gingold for six years, had this to say about his teacher:

> We all knew he was not just a great teacher ... the greatest teacher, and he was so dedicated to his teaching. Looking back, after I myself have been teaching now for almost twenty years, I'd love to be a fly on the wall and see him take a student through from first lesson to a few years.... I think the way he was teaching was really remarkable because he taught us how to play the violin better and he taught us how to practice, and it was always in the sense that the music had to come to life.

Above all else, one cannot talk about Josef Gingold as an inspirational teacher without highlighting his great love for the violin and how he was able to communicate that love to his students. For Paul Biss, "There was a synthesis about Gingold, from his playing, to his personality, to his warmth, to his absolute two great loves in life—the violin and music. And every time he picked up the violin it was like a lesson." That love inspired both the beautiful golden tones that typified his playing and that of his protégés, who have gone on to internationally prominent careers, such as violin virtuosos Joshua Bell, Jaime Laredo, Miriam Fried, and Jean Piguet, who noted: "I must say that what I gained the most from Gingold was his incredible sense of sound, the warmth of the sound."

Communicating Technique and Musicality

Being an experienced, even virtuoso, instrumentalist does not necessarily translate into being a master teacher. One of the greatest violinists of the twentieth century, Jascha Heifetz, for example, could produce the most beautiful music; but when queried as to how a particular note or phrase was produced, often could not answer. One anecdote concerns a well-established concert violinist, who, while a student of the maestro, hesitatingly queried him after he exquisitely demonstrated the famous passage from the Glazunov concerto (which alternates the bow on and off the strings): "Mr. Heifetz, tell me, on the down bow, does the bow bounce too? Could you do it again or tell me ... ?" The response of Heifetz: "This is no place for questions. If you have questions, if you want answers, go to the Los Angeles Police Department." Most likely, the response was not uttered in meanness but out of frustration at not being able to answer the question.

Many great musicians, totally absorbed in music making, often perform at a level beyond immediate self-consciousness. As Biss noted about Heifetz's playing, "He was so naturally talented, he never had to think about how he did it." Another anecdote illustrating this point is that when young Heifetz was a student of the famed Leopold Auer, he asked a question concerning a particularly difficult passage. His teacher responded: "Jascha, play it with your feet. It will be fine." In other words, whatever he did, especially if done intuitively, would sound beautiful.

By contrast, if you had a specific, technical problem, Curtis Institute and Juilliard School violin teacher Ivan Galamian would be the person to visit. Gingold, to whom students were frequently referred by Isaac Stern, Nathan Milstein, and other leading violinists, sometimes recommended that his protégés work with Galamian on technique. Galamian was so good a "Mr. Fix-It" that his students would say that he could teach a person to play a broom and make it sound like a violin. Further confirmation: When Curtis Institute director and famed teacher and violinist Efrem Zimbalist was asked by some furniture movers what to do with an unwanted table, he quipped: "Give it to Galamian. He will make it sound."

Over the years, Gingold, Starker, and Sebok worked with many gifted young professionals. Their fame rests on their ability to develop and polish talent at the most advanced levels of performance. Despite their extraordinary ability to bring out the best in students from different backgrounds, mismatches involving the discrepancies between student needs and expectations and what a particular teacher can offer are inevitable. That occurs even as top-of-the-line teachers can selectively choose the limited number of pupils with whom they will work. As so many of my respondents observed, there is no ideal teacher for all students. These three master teachers, nevertheless, were able to reach and influence for the good an extraordinary number of novice musicians.

Tailoring Instruction

How was this possible? In great part, master teachers tailor their instruction to the specific abilities of their students, but without lowering expectations. The image of tailoring was first suggested to me by former Metropolitan Opera star and Indiana University Music School distinguished professor Giorgio Tozzi, who had this to say:

> For me a teacher is like a tailor who has just moved to another location. So he sends out notices to his customers. One customer lives on the northeast side of town; another, on the southwest side. Obviously, if he gives both customers [the same] directions on how to get to his shop, one is probably going to make it. The other is going to get hopelessly lost. So, he has to be able to know where the person's coming from. I feel that a teacher has to know where the student is coming from [in terms of personality, culture, and education].... Once he gets the customers to his store, he's got to make a suit. So, he has a pattern. The point is this—he can't cut the suit on one pattern and then just paste it on his customer and expect it to fit each one. Each one has to be individually tailored. One shoulder is higher than the other. One arm is shorter than the other. Who knows? Any

number of things. Same thing with a voice teacher. You have to sort of help tailor, make the technique that you're working toward suit the nature of the voice of each one.

As noted by former students, Starker, Gingold, and Sebok each personalized instruction in ways reminiscent of Tozzi's observations. Jean Piguet (concert master of L'Orchestre de la Suisse Romande de Geneva) had this to say about Gingold: "I think the most interesting part of his teaching was the fact that he taught every student individually. He knew what to say to such and such student, and what not to say. He would give completely different fingering and bowing [instructions] according to the idiosyncrasies of pupils he had. And he sort of nurtured the students as you would nurture a plant."

Discussing the expectations he places on students, Starker noted, "The most important [thing] is to assess the person's mental, physical, and musical ability. From then on, with this view in mind, I can help them in the following years."

Whether engaging in one-on-one instruction or teaching a group of diverse talents in a master class, Sebok was able to personalize instruction: "When I am listening … I have to understand the person; I have to understand how he feels or she feels; how he listens to music; how music is happening in his mind; and I have to compare what he dreams and what he is really doing. So I have to identify with the person."

Despite this finely honed empathic quality and his ability to draw on an impressive set of tools to remedy the specific problems each individual student presented, Sebok, nevertheless, was uneasy with the notion of tailoring if it meant cutting down or diluting the nature of what was to be acquired. If the instructional goal was that a student understand a particular piece of music or the genius [let's say of Mozart] who wrote the piece, then, as Sebok noted, "I have to help the student to find Mozart.... And if he or she needs to be transformed to understand Mozart, then the person should be changed."

According to Ada Pesch (first concertmaster of the Zurich Opera orchestra), this is exactly what happened as the result of students interacting with Sebok:

I've never seen anybody teach like Sebok. How he just sees the person.... He totally just focuses on the person and somehow realizes what he can do to change them. Because if you think about it, how much can you do in two lessons or in one lesson? But somehow he manages to change a person so much in one lesson so they have at least the feeling of how it could be. And the rest of it is up to them. But he somehow opens these doors. It's amazing.

Stretching Students

Very much in accord with the psychological and pedagogical insights of American educator and philosopher John Dewey and Russian psychologist and philosopher of mind L. S. Vygotsky, master teachers identify the specific stage of musical development individual pupils are at, and then find the means to challenge and assist them to the next performance level. Former pupils of Sebok, for example, equate this ability with an "x-ray vision," a capacity to identify problems and blockages immediately, and provide the means to overcome them.

This diagnostic ability is based on profound knowledge of a field of practice. According to Starker:

> Obviously, after you've taught hundreds and hundreds of students, there's very seldom a new problem that comes up.... As the years go by, it's much easier to find a concise statement of what's wrong. As recently as about forty-five minutes ago, one of my students came over and asked if I could help him learn how to play [a particular piece]. I watched him for two minutes and knew exactly what was wrong with it. So I set him on the road so he can now experiment, and probably, in about three years, he's going to write me a letter: "Thank you for that lesson, for I now understand how it works." It may take years, sometimes it takes seconds.

Providing Shortcuts

Starker, like so many other expert teachers, is able to accelerate and heighten the learning curve: "I give them all the shortcuts so they can reach their understanding of the things which took me thirty-five or forty years to reach. They can have it all at the age of twenty-four." Providing shortcuts and the keys to open doors constitutes the first steps in enabling students to begin the long journey toward being self-directed problem solvers, who critically reflect on their progress toward a continually elusive goal of ever more perfect expression of great works of art.

Discovery Teaching/Learning

In posing problems and providing challenges, these teachers consciously set out to develop self-reliant musicians. For Preucil, perhaps the most enduring impact of Gingold was this: "Sometimes he would give some clues [for example, an operatic phrase of a Mozart piece], and assuming that the student had a certain amount of curiosity, somewhere a little later down the line, maybe later in the week, maybe later in the month, maybe later by a couple years, some kind of discovery [would occur]." He continues: "If you have this curiosity, he could open a door that would lead you to opening many doors and ... you could actually learn a lot not only about what you were playing, but learn all this other music to put what you were playing in a context, a musical context, and learn things about style from that."

For Gingold, "The hardest thing about teaching is to teach someone not from lesson to lesson but for ten years ahead.... You try to work and show a student how he can be his own teacher too and what to look for and how to evaluate a piece of music. There are so many things, my God, I don't know where to start or stop."

Biss noted: "He lets students discover things much more on their own. And I think, perhaps with some, the process was absolutely perfect, and for some people, who needed necessarily a tighter rein, it worked less well." But for self-motivated former students like Biss, the results showed up years later when he became a university professor.[10] His stated goal as teacher is for his students "to think, to listen, and to improve their critical listening faculties" so that when they make a mistake or encounter a problem they can figure out how to remedy the situation.

This approach is based on an important assumption that students are self-motivated and can be turned on to learning and self-improvement, a belief held by Gingold: "I've never met a student who didn't want to learn. You open up the bulb and they see the light."

Overcoming Barriers/Bridging Gaps

A critical component of the process of turning on light bulbs, opening doors, and developing autonomous learners involves enabling students to discover their own shortcomings, inhibitions, and self-defeating behaviors. Many of the barriers novice musicians encounter are self-imposed. As Sebok was fond of saying: "The piano does not resist. The piano is willing." At age seventy-six, he told me: "If I play a recital now, I'm less tired afterwards ... and even less tired than I was thirty years ago. Because I think that I figured out more or less for myself how to function. So I overcome some inner frictions, or physical conflicts, or the contradictions between necessary movements and choreography. I think that today, physically playing the piano is easier. That means that what I hear and what I want to hear—the way music happens in my mind and the way it happens really—is now closer than it was before."

Commenting on Sebok as a teacher from whom any musician could learn, Piguet noted: "Not only does he know music like few people, but he also knows the common knowledge of how the body works to make music. And he can teach not only music, but instruments and instrumentalists [including] violinists [like himself] very fundamental things about playing."[11]

The case of French cellist Iseut Chuat illustrates how both Sebok and Starker can provide the insights and shortcuts to overcome physical restraints and enable students to bridge the gap between aspiration and execution. Recommended to Starker after she had met Sebok at the Banff Music Festival, Chuat decided to come to Bloomington in 1990:

> Let's say that Sebok pointed in the direction where I should go and what I'm looking for and Starker was there to help with that.... I was always searching for the link between the body and the rationality of playing, and none of my teachers before were

able to really explain it to me.... I was a rather intuitive player. And, it all worked [because of natural talent] until I was twenty. I had a feeling that I was fighting and using too much energy for what I wanted to get musically. I had the feeling that there was a big gap between what I wanted to say in music and what actually my body was expressing.

One year later, Starker, who was very pleased with her progress, said, "'You have to go back to France now and play,' because he was afraid that my phrasing was not as natural as before. He was afraid that I would lose my personality and that I would start to get conscious about everything." Yet Chuat decided to stay two more years because she felt "that [she] had not finished everything. And [she] needed to be more in his presence. And be more nourished by that."[12]

Guiding—But Not Imposing

A tension between dependence and independence, between nurturing and suffocating, frequently characterizes the intimate relationships between teacher and student, mentor and protégé.[13] In Starker's case, and this is typical of many outstanding teachers, there is no desire to create duplicates: "Once the principles are learned and adhered to, then comes freedom, which allows for the individualities. I want every student to play the cello as well as I do, but God forbid that they sound like I do, or that they play music the way I do! Because then it would be simply a cloning."

One important aspect of teaching is to know when to get out of the way and not impose a regimen or predetermined model on very talented students. Discussing child prodigy Joshua Bell, Gingold had this to say about his former protégé: "Joshua is an enormous musical talent. He just is incapable of doing something nonmusical. He's gold. Everything he does is just right. And I did not get in the way because of a dash or a dot."

According to Starker, Yo-Yo Ma, "the most famous cellist of today ... because of physical problems with his back ... and long fingers, plays in a way that's basically against all principles, but he plays terrifically." When queried how he could play terrifically if he started with all the wrong principles and techniques, Starker responded, "Because none of his teachers ever corrected anything he was doing. They let him go on doing what he was doing, because he was an incredibly gifted young man." Reflecting on his own teachers at the Liszt Academy, Starker ironically noted: "I'm simply lucky that they didn't teach me any bad principles."

Striving for Perfection

In addition to the tension between dependence and independence, there is the uneasy relationship between satisfaction and frustration. The challenges and problems are never ending for even the most accomplished of musicians, as well as for other world-class performing artists and athletes. In the case of musicians, as Sebok noted, "music is infinite.... I don't believe in absolute performance. Music has quite strict rules—a little bit like chess, you know, which has very strict rules and infinite possibilities." When asked if he ever heard a master class performance played so beautifully he could not recommend any improvements, he responded, "No": "Because then that would be accepting an absolute. I don't think that there is a performance which cannot be improved on." He illustrated his belief this way: "Improvement is not simply playing—it is not like a primitive kind of improvement. The pieces that we play are all pieces of geniuses. I don't think that any of us can put himself at the level of a genius. So we can approach it, but you can never give a *final* [emphasis his] performance of a Mozart piece. There is no such thing."

Starker describes the process of scaling the heights of musical expression as one of continual striving: "I always say that when you reach a certain point, you celebrate. But then you go for the next level, and you're at the bottom of the next level, so therefore everything stinks. And then you reach the next level of celebration, but it goes on because the levels never end."

Knowing When and How to Criticize

The more talented the student, the more demanding is Starker:

> I have those students who are astonishingly gifted. With them, I do things which can be called nasty, because they are not careful about those things that concern the next level of playing. If somebody does well with a limited ability, I'm invariably kind.... I've never been nasty to someone who is up to their level.... I only show displeasure if someone is capable of doing far more than what they are doing.

Certainly, negative comments by a world-renowned instrumentalist and teacher can have a devastating impact on novice musicians, even those who are very gifted. Starker, who on occasion can be caustic, has, according to those closest to him, mellowed over time. But, for Starker, toughness is a necessary attribute of musicians who wish to succeed in the highly competitive world of the concert stage.

The penetrating directness of Starker contrasts with the indirectness of Sebok. The experience of working with giants of the music world while at the Liszt Academy taught Sebok humility and a sensitivity to the effect of teacher comments on students. Throughout his teaching career, he cautiously avoided strong negative statements and, as noted by former students, tended toward analogies and poetic or philosophical examples to convey a lesson.

Because of Sebok's use of analogies from different fields of knowledge, Jean Piguet noted that he sometimes went "in a direction you didn't know where or what he's going to say and why." But then Sebok would get "through the chord or the musical problem ... to the point [he wished to make]. And it was amazing."

Gingold, who suffered under brutal teachers in public school, represents the extreme of gentleness to the point of never being overbearing.[14] He often would make a point by telling a story that invariably conveyed the history and context or unique characteristics of a piece of music. While occasionally displaying disappointment in a student's progress, Gingold would never shout or be scornful.

Being Self-Critical

Talented musicians are often their own harshest critics. Again Starker: "I don't think that more than a handful of people in this century are as hard on themselves as I am. There is a responsibility which has nothing to do with success, absolutely nothing to do with who thinks what of what I'm doing. If I am satisfied with my output, that's the only thing that matters.... : As recently as Saturday, I received a standing ovation and I felt like—well, I'm not going to use four-letter words, but certain things didn't work the way I wanted."

Former students, like Brant Taylor, carry on that tradition: "He teaches you to teach yourself, because we're not going to be in school our whole lives; and even when we are in school, you see your teacher for [only] an hour a week. So, if he was going to be my harshest critic, something was wrong. He wanted me to be my own harshest critic. So that when I was no longer working with him, I could still continue to work towards becoming a better cellist."

Envisioning the Future

As with athletes, musicians also need to visualize attainable goals and ways in which to reach them. For musicians, visualizing what one wants to play and how to produce the desired effect are two very different things. The crucial role of the coach or teacher is to enable novices to anticipate and be prepared for unexpected situations. Starker talks about using "preconceived imagination." He gives the example of someone playing for the first time in a concert hall, where the performance may decide that musician's fate. He believes that imagining oneself in that specific situation may help reduce the inevitable nervousness:

> It may sound a little bit complicated, but it comes back to the point when I made my debut in London. I knew that, not having performed for a number of years on the stage, I might become nervous. Therefore, for several months, in my practice process, I visualized my room, memorized my room where I was sitting and practicing, my own studio, so as to be able, when I sat in London in the concert hall, to close my eyes and imagine that actually I'm playing the same way I always do. It helped to totally

remove any of the unnecessary tensions of a real debut, or a debut in one of the major capitals of the world.

Concern for the Whole Person

A generosity of spirit and concern for the personal development of their students is a common characteristic of many of the profiled master teachers and coaches. Gingold, for example, is fondly remembered for the deep affection he felt for each one of his students and their general well-being. When asked what qualities he looked for in his students, Gingold responded: "To me, a human comes first. And then if he happens to play well, that's nice. But this is not what I look for in the young kids that I teach. I want to feel that any influence I have is backed by someone who has good qualities as a human."

This characteristic of Gingold is confirmed by Biss. He recalls first auditioning for Gingold during a visit to Bloomington with his parents: "I remember him coming into the room and saying in that gravelly voice of his, 'I'm so happy to be teaching Paul.' ... I don't remember the exact words, but the gist of it: 'I look forward to working with him as he develops as a violinist and as a human being.' And I think this really says a lot about him. Instead of, 'How fast do your fingers race?'"

Legacies

Preserving, enriching, and extending a performance field is a foremost concern for these teachers. Although he is considered to be one of the stellar virtuoso cellists of the twentieth century, Janos Starker views himself, first and foremost, a teacher, and he takes great satisfaction in that role. Reflecting on being in the enviable position of having played more than a hundred concerts a year for several decades, which is the dream of most professional musicians, he has reached this conclusion: "Now, more and more, I feel that what I've done and what I'm doing as a teacher is much more important. I set standards with my recordings and performances, but as a teacher I transmit the messages I've learned from those people I was exposed to since childhood, so it may last way beyond my earthly existence."

To his enduring credit, Starker does not actively seek out prodigies and extraordinary talents like Yo-Yo Ma. Rather, he derives satisfaction from developing competent young cellists into full-fledged professional musicians. For Starker, "the challenge has been to help people, who have some of the basic talents, to become important members of the musical community, whether they become orchestra members with principal positions within the orchestra, or whether they are going to be teachers, to make sure they know everything about it—that they can assess the students within seconds, so to speak."

Succeed he has, for when asked if there is any particular group of students that he has taken the greatest pride in, Starker responded: "Hundreds. My students are concertizing all over the world, they are principal cellists in major orchestras in Europe and Japan and South America and everywhere. And they are professors. Practically all the Midwestern colleges have my students as their professors."

Similarly, Ada Pesch recounted with great fondness the impact of Gingold on his students: "The unique thing about him is that instead of just having one famous soloist, he has a lot of students who have careers, like Joshua Bell and Bill Preucil.... There are concert masters all over the world who were students of his. Every orchestra's got students of his, and there are lots of quartets." As she noted, his former students are making significant contributions in all aspects of the art of violin playing as performers and teachers.

Although each of these three master teachers can count among their former students well-recognized soloists on the international concert scene, each was reluctant to single out a favorite student. Gingold perhaps summed up this position best in his response to my question concerning his greatest joy as a teacher: "That I've contributed something to a student. Someone asked me once, 'Who is your favorite student?' I said, 'The one I'm teaching at the moment.'"

Conclusions

The three featured world-class musicians and master teachers embody the characteristics of outstanding educators portrayed throughout *Talent Abounds*. These attributes include:

- Mastery of the knowledge, skills, and cultural traditions of a performance field;
- The ability to communicate effectively not only the technical skills but also the fundamental principles leading to artistry and masterful performance;
- Skill in diagnosing problems and individualizing instruction so that students are taught the precise set of tasks and challenges required to reach progressively higher performance levels;
- Knowledge of what set of incentives, both positive and negative, to use in motivating students to persist at improving their craft;
- An educational philosophy and pedagogy based on discovery learning that equips students to become lifelong problem solvers;
- The ability to help students envision what is required to succeed in a career while being contributing members of a profession extending across generations;

- A concern for the well-being and overall personal and professional development of their students;
- An abiding commitment to model the behaviors and values they wish to instill in their students.

These three extraordinary teachers increased many times over the universe of highly skilled and committed musicians. The vision, passion, and dedication they have inspired in generations of musicians perpetuate and extend the finest traditions of music making. The constellation of known stars in the firmament of music making is infinitely greater thanks to their teaching.

Notes

1. Her many former students include Itzhak Perlman, Shlomo Mintz, Midori, and Sarah Chang.
2. A memorable experience several years later was his father taking him to witness Leon Trotsky (then Bronstein) and the Russian delegation at the Brest Litovsk train station signing the treaty with Germany that ended hostilities between the two countries in March of 1918.
3. Cited from *New Yorker* article, "A Golden Coin."
4. The line of descent can be indirectly tracked back to Chopin and Beethoven.
5. The principles Schiffer taught in the cello pedagogy course he established for the academy, upon his retirement, derive from the late-nineteenth-century works of various doctors such as Adolf Steinhausen and Hugo Riemann, whose books are still used as source works on the proper functioning of the body. According to Starker, "They are elements of usage for the sake of instrumental playing."
6. Prior to joining the New York Metropolitan Opera company, he had played with the Budapest Opera and Philharmonic Orchestra and the Dallas Symphony Orchestra.
7. Starker published a book about Weiner, in which every former student who was then alive wrote about him.
8. Sebok's teachers were musical grandchildren of Liszt through a line of progression from István Thomán and Emile von Sauer.
9. Preucil, coincidentally, is the son-in-law of Janos Starker.
10. Biss taught violin and viola as well as conducted various ensembles in the Indiana University School of Music over a three decade period before joining the faculty of the New England Conservatory of Music in 2005.
11. This observation is reinforced by Andorran cellist Luis Claret: "I never met a teacher like that.... The incredible intelligence he has to listen to any music, instrument, or play. I mean he could teach clarinet, a singer."
12. During this period, Chuet studied and worked part-time as a coprincipal cellist of the Amsterdam Ballet. During her last year at Indiana University, she was a teaching assistant to Starker.

13. This point was first brought to my attention by Paul Biss.
14. For a description of his early schooling, see the story "The Gold Coin."

Sources

Interviews (in order of appearance)

Gingold, Josef. Interview by author. Bloomington, IN, May 26, 1994.
Starker, Janos. Interview by author. Bloomington, IN, May 7, 1997.
Sebok, György. Interview by author. Bloomington, IN, May 14, 1997.
———. Interview by author. Bloomington, IN, April 21, 1999.
Biss, Paul. Interview by author. Bloomington, IN, November 8, 1994.
DeLay, Dorothy. Interview by author. New York, April 24, 1999.
Piguet, Jean. Interview by author. Ernan, Switzerland (site of a music festival organized by Sebok), August 14, 1998.
Preucil, William. Interview by author. Ernan, Switzerland, August 19, 1998.
Taylor, Brant. Interview by author. Ernan, Switzerland, August 16, 1998.
Tozzi, Giorgio. Interview by author. Bloomington, IN, February 12, 1996.
Chuat, Iseut. Interview by author. Ernan, Switzerland, August 19, 1998.
Pesch, Ada. Interview by author. Ernan, Switzerland, August 14, 1998.
———. Interview by author. Ernan, Switzerland, August 19, 1998.
Claret, Luis. Interview by author. Ernan, Switzerland, August 14, 1998.

Article

Blum, David. "Profiles: A Gold Coin." *New Yorker,* February 4, 1991, 334–47, 350.

Book

Starker, Janos. *The World of Music According to Starker.* Bloomington: Indiana University Press, 2004.

Video

Janos Starker. Bloomington, IN: WFIU, Indiana University.

I'll Take You to the Moon and Beyond

Peak Performance in Swimming and Diving

Their coaching styles could not have been more different: one ("Doc") moving quietly along the side of the Indiana University outdoor swimming pool almost whispering to his swimmers; the other ("Hobie") yelling at the divers on the high platform. Yet together as a team, and in their own individual ways, they worked wonders in their fields. They produced some of the most talented swimmers and divers in history. James "Doc" Counsilman and Hobie Billingsley revolutionized instruction by introducing scientific principles to the biophysics of swimming and diving. In doing so, they were able to nurture innately talented, but often relatively untrained, individuals to achieve the previously inconceivable. Metaphorically, they were able to take swimmers like Mark Spitz and divers like Mark Lenzi to the moon—and beyond.

In swimming, speed measured in hundredths of a second determines world records. In diving, perfection of body movement in space will determine who wins Olympic Gold Medals. As with other extraordinary teachers, Doc and Hobie mastered knowledge in their fields and learned to communicate it so that rough talent was hewn into peak performance. They also were able to create a vision of what these individuals were capable of achieving, even though they themselves at first were skeptical. Counsilman and Billingsley proved things to the world and made a lasting mark, driven by unfulfilled needs that gnawed at them from their childhoods and early adulthood. Their personal narratives illuminate the makings of exceptional teachers and coaches. Their stories are reinforced by the testimony of two of their protégés, Mark Spitz and Mark Lenzi.

Inauspicious Beginnings

For a national swimming champion and the oldest person to swim the English Channel (at the age of fifty-eight in 1979), "Doc" Counsilman's first encounters with large bodies of water were disastrous. He nearly drowned twice, at the age of seven and again at twelve. Like his longtime colleague Hobie Billingsley, his first swimming lessons occurred at a downtown YMCA. Both came from families hard strapped for income during the Depression. At age thirteen, Counsilman began swimming at the St. Louis YMCA two hours a week, when pool charges were waived. Billingsley, who first learned to place his head under water and swim at the large fountain in a downtown park in Erie, Pennsylvania, was initially given a scholarship to the local YMCA at age seven: "Six dollars for a year's membership. I went to the Y for a year, and when the membership ran out, they didn't renew it. So I just snuck in for the next ten years.... They used to call me peanuts, because I was so small. They'd throw me out and I'd go through the window. And they'd throw me out and I'd go through the back door. They'd throw me out again and I'd go through the roof. They couldn't keep me out. I had no place to go."

Counsilman initially started as a diver, and Billingsley as a gymnast. Counsilman, after learning to swim, was placed on the Y's diving team. However, he was "a bit big for a diver. At the time, you had to be really small to be a diver. So, one time they entered me on the relay team in one of the meets. I swam faster than the kids that were swimming in the event. From then on, I was a swimmer." Billingsley started in gymnastics as a tumbler. His opportunity to become a diver, as well as a more-or-less welcome member of the Y, occurred at about twelve years old. When a member of the Y's diving team became ill at the last moment, the coach told an assistant, "Why don't you go get Hobie, that kid up there in the gym that does all that tumbling. I bet he could dive." So I came down to dive in their meet. And I won [as it wasn't very different from what he was doing in somersaults]. We didn't do many dives—about five. So I started diving for the team."

The desire to succeed and prove one's value came almost immediately afterward. The attraction of joining a competitive squad was that Billingsley would be able to venture beyond Erie: "They said, 'We're going to take you to Buffalo for a big meet.' Buffalo? Buffalo was ninety miles down the road. I thought, God, this is great, because I'm the best diver [better than the kid he had replaced]." The story turns out differently: "They put the names of the kids that were going to make the trip to Buffalo on the bulletin board on Friday. Boy, I was excited. All week I was saying, 'This is going to be great.' So Friday comes up and I walk up to the bulletin board and my name isn't on it. It affected my life." When Billingsley asked the coach if this wasn't a mistake, the coach cuttingly responded, "I just don't think you're a very good diver." Undeterred, the next day Hobie went down to the Y: "I'm standing there as kids are getting on the bus with their sneakers and lunches and bags. They were all excited ... and I'm standing there crying as they drive off. I'd never forget him [the coach] as I walked away from there."

The challenge had been laid down to Billingsley. From that point on he worked out at the Y three to four hours daily, consistently skipping school on Thursdays to spend the whole day practicing on the diving board: "As it turned out, after a couple of years, I probably was the greatest diver in the world on that board. You'd never beat me on that board." The nature of the board? "The diving board was about 5 inches thick, 10 feet long, about a foot and a half wide. You could hardly get your feet on it. Right off the deck of the pool. It couldn't be springy or you'd go right through the ceiling."

Counsilman, like Billingsley, had not been a serious student. He graduated 113 out of 116 in his high school class—the last one to get a diploma rather than an attendance certificate. Although he would become an accomplished coach and respected scholar, considered by many to be a genius, "Doc" passed his early years with very little sense of his ability. In truth, he suffered from a lack of self-esteem. A dismal high school academic record was compensated for by his success as an athlete: "I thought I was the dumbest mother that ever lived.... Swimming gave me some self-respect. I figured maybe I'm not smart, maybe my English and grammar are bad, but I'll beat anybody who can get in the pool. They were terrible years for me."

Influential Mentor-Coaches

College did not follow immediately upon high school graduation for Counsilman. It took Ernie Vornbrock, his coach and mentor from the St. Louis YMCA, four years to move him in that direction. Vornbrock brought novels, mostly classical literature, along for the leisurely breaks and fishing trips they took, when Counsilman was not working at odd jobs or swimming competitively: "Ernie Vornbrock got me thinking in terms of going to college. He would try to bolster my ego. He worked on my self-esteem. Pretty soon he got me convinced that I was smart enough to go to college.... One place where they accepted me with the poor academic record I had in high school was Ohio State." The first year at the university, he received a room and board scholarship to the International House, which paired U.S. students with overseas students to assist with their transition to campus life. His second year, the university found him a job in the state building: "So, I worked and paid for my meals and got money for operating the elevators; and I worked in the summer and saved enough for my tuition."

Vornbrock saw academic ability that remained hidden to Counsilman until he took the aptitude test to become a pilot during World War II. In 1943, his sophomore year at Ohio State, Counsilman received his draft notice. The results from the aptitude test were shocking. Despite a rather unspectacular 2.3 grade point average, he scored at the ninety-ninth percentile!

These scores were a boost to Counsilman's self-confidence. Moreover, the regimen of "self-education," begun under Vornbrock and reinforced by Doc's swimming coach at Ohio State, sparked a desire for learning that would continue throughout his life as a coach and educator at Indiana University.

Billingsley's career early on also was influenced by an excellent coach. Although extremely poor—his family was living on less than $10 a week—he talked his mother into moving from the "wrong side of the railroad tracks" to the more upscale north side of Erie so that he could be coached by Art Weibel, considered to be the best in the city for his age group: "I talked my mother into it. We moved over to the other side when I was in tenth grade or eleventh grade. I missed a year, because I got transferred. In twelfth grade, I won the state championship."

Comparing Weibel to the legendary Vince Lombardi of the Green Bay Packers, Billingsley recalled him as a "hard-nosed son of a gun. There's two of us sitting there drinking milk shakes at the drug store. This is during the war. He comes walking in and sees what we were drinking and he goes up and—*WHACK!*—there goes the milk shakes down on the floor. He says, 'You're not training.' He walked out the door and that was it." Weibel would stay on the case of his divers until they overcame the most difficult dives on truly terrible boards.

John Boyd was a classmate and close friend of Hobie on the school swim team. Robert Coram, in his biography, *Boyd: The Fighter Pilot Who Changed the Art of War,* provides further description of Weibel's qualities as a coach: "He was firmly grounded in the old-fashioned principles of strong work, individual accountability, and duty. He had a national reputation as a coach, in part because he accepted only the best boys on his team—not just the best swimmers but the best in everything. His swimmers were known for their character, their determination, and their desire to excel at whatever they did."[1]

At Ohio State, where Billingsley attended college, Mike Peppe was the coach of a world-class diving dynasty. Between the team's first national championship, in 1937, and 1958, Peppe had gathered the best divers from around the world. Billingsley describes his first sight of the university's swimming pool: "I'll never forget. I walked in the pool. It looked like Yankee Stadium. I'd never seen a pool like that. I went, 'Oh, my god.' And the coach said, 'I can't give you any money. I don't have any scholarships. But if you come here, I'll guarantee you'll be a national champion.'" Peppe promised to find Hobie work so he could meet his expenses. Billingsley took the coach at his word, both with regard to getting through college and becoming a winning diver: "I went in as a freshman and won the NCAA championship high board and low board, won the Big Ten championship right off the bat. Again, the war was on. The better divers were in the service. Then, I got called."

Becoming Educator-Coaches

Counsilman, who also was drafted, served with distinction as a pilot. Yet, there was something gnawing at him. At the time he was inducted into the U.S. Army Air Corps, he was a national champion in the butterfly: "And when I went into pilot training I had to quit swimming. I couldn't get into the pool, just pilot training. The guy who was second to me in the nationals went on to win the Olympics in the 200 butterfly, and I could have beaten him.... They wouldn't even let me go swim in the nationals [which were two months after his induction into the armed forces]." But several years after the Olympics, Doc met the man who had taken what he considered to be rightfully his. Doc was running a fitness program in Philadelphia. His erstwhile opponent? "Oh, I've been doing some bullshit." What was that? Selling insurance. At that point, according to Doc, "My whole concept changed. I said, 'If I had to be the Olympic champion to be in his shoes, I'll take what I'm doing.' I think I've got to convey to the kids [how to prepare for success and the aftermath of their swimming careers]."

Counsilman, after the war, went on to receive his baccalaureate degree at Ohio State in education and coaching, followed by a master's degree at the University of Illinois, and, finally, a Ph.D. at Iowa State University in physical education and physiology with a dissertation on movement mechanics. He coached at all three universities before coming to Indiana University in 1957. Billingsley came to Indiana University in 1959 as head diving coach, after receiving his degree in coaching at Ohio State University and serving a stint there as assistant coach. The lessons learned from their early mentors were to influence their approaches to coaching. Among them were the importance of teaching the whole student, establishing a caring relationship of mutual trust, and building up the self-esteem and confidence of their protégés. Although there are significant differences in how the sports are taught, the two coaches shared similar traits: an intellectual curiosity and willingness to be lifelong learners, as well as an ability to learn from their own students. Inspired by their early-stage teachers, they further shared a commitment to personalizing instruction, challenging students to the highest stages of performance, and providing a vision of a desired end state.

Research and Innovation

Among the many accomplishments of these two coaches are dozens of national championships and Olympians, world records set in swimming and diving, and numerous former students who have gone on to become prominent coaches and teachers. Yet, their most significant contributions reside in revolutionizing instruction in swimming and diving by applying a scientific basis to the mechanics of movement in their sports. Counsilman, with the 1968 publication of his book *The Science of Swimming*, turned taken-for-granted assumptions in swimming instruction upside down. The standard Red Cross text taught a stroke that was inconsistent with what Counsilman was observing and filming in his best swimmers: "Probably the biggest contribution I made to swimming was to get away from pulling straight through.... The Red Cross taught everyone to pull the straight arm right down the middle. When I got into coaching, I found out that none of the good swimmers did that type of thing. The big champions were doing this crazy zigzag." In fact, it was Mark Spitz, considered by Counsilman to be the greatest swimmer of all time, who revealed this pattern:

> We recruited Mark. I had a policy that if I got a real good swimmer, a world record holder, before I screwed up his stroke, I photographed him. Then, if I had any time when he wasn't doing well, I could get that underwater movie of him. I found that Mark Spitz did this.... So, I started coaching that.... I've done quite a bit of research on swimming—so much that I published 140 articles and three books. I tried to do research to substantiate the theories that I've tried to develop.

In an interview with Bloomington *Herald-Times* sportswriter Bob Hammel, Counsilman confessed that the "most important thing in my life is to constantly do research.... I'm trying to answer questions. I've always had a tremendous curiosity about swimming. I watch a dog running along, hop in the water, and I watch his stroke. I've got a reputation as a kind of nut." One humorous incident involves Doc's curiosity about what role a cat's tail plays in its landing on its feet. While driving one day, he spotted a tail-less cat. He immediately stopped his car in the middle of the street and chased the cat down an alley. When he finally caught up with it, as narrated to Hammel, "It was so scared it ran right up my shirt and perched on my bald head" ("A Tale with a Tail, and Then Without").[2] As it turned out, the tail had nothing to do with the cat's balance. Instead, Counsilman decided, "It's in the feet, tucked in front, extended in back, or vice versa, whatever is needed for the corrective contortion," that, as Hammel noted, and that we will see below, "sounds offhand highly applicable to Billingsley's field, diving."

Doc's research had led him to a 1788 treatise by Swiss physicist Daniel Bernoulli entitled *Hydronomica*. As described by Counsilman in his manual, "The Application of Bernoulli's Principle to Human Propulsion in Water":

> This principle of law states that fluid pressure is reduced wherever the speed of flow is increased. For example, an airplane wing is so designed, and its pitch so inclined in relation to its direction as to produce a greater speed of air-flow traveling over its upper surface than over its lower surface. This difference in the speed of flow causes a greater pressure on the lower surface and a lesser pressure on the upper surface ... and results in a lift or upward push on the wing.
>
> The propeller of a boat acts in the same manner and uses lift to supply forward thrust to a boat.

Similarly, the hand of the swimmer, if it is pitched in the proper manner in relation to its path through the water, can also serve as an air foil or propeller to provide forward propulsion to the swimmer.

The manual then goes on to explain the application of this principle in overcoming problems related to (1) "evolv[ing] a stroke pattern that, once he [the swimmer] has started the water moving backward, will allow him to get away from that water and work with still water, and (2) how to pitch his hands so they will serve as a propeller and not as paddles—that is, so they will not create a wake."

Counsilman proved equally adept at applying the three laws of motion of Sir Isaac Newton—for example, the principle that every action has an equal and opposite reaction—to achieve the type of propulsion in swimming that characterized the motion of steam engines. With these principles applied to swimming, his teams became unbeatable over a period of two decades.

Similarly, Billingsley photographed his divers to determine what they were doing right and wrong and to discover principles that would perfect their movement in space. By a strange and tragic twist of fate, his best friend, Bruce Harlan, died (right before Hobie's eyes) in an exhibition dive off a high platform. At the time, Harlan was the coach of the U.S. diving team for the 1959 Pan American Games. Billingsley, in honor of Harlan's memory, was asked to replace him. He describes how he prepared for his new role:

> A month later I had to coach this team. I knew them all. But, I didn't know enough about their diving. So, how am I going to coach them? What I did was I got a big Bolex camera and 800 feet of film, and I said, "I want to take a film of each of your full workouts separately." So, I took one guy, took all of his dives. I took another guy and all of his dives. Then, I took them into a room separately and said, "Let's watch your films and let's see what you want to change." ... Brilliant way to coach. We don't do it to this day. I mean I learned more from that one time. If every coach had any sense at all, they would take each individual and show them what they're doing, and then say, "What do you want to change and what don't you want to change?" If they don't want to change it, you can explain to them, if you know anything about biomechanics, why they have to change it. Now if they still are against it, then you're going to have to live with that.

When Billingsley moved to Indiana University to become only the second college diving coach hired as such, he brought his films. The following incident describes the breakthrough that occurred when one of his students pointed out a biomechanical principle that had eluded him: "When I moved over here [Bloomington], a couple of divers came with me. I had these films out one day; and one of these guys in this film was Bob Webster, two-time Olympic champion who is now teaching down at the University of Alabama. He's doing an inward dive layout. An inward dive layout is like doing a swan dive, but you're standing on the end of the board diving in toward it, pulling your arms out like this and then layout." Using close-up shots of Webster, Billingsley wanted to show that every diver goes under a strain at the explosive moment of lifting off the board. The face usually contorts in an *"Ugh!"* But Webster's face didn't even change—in fact it was effortless. Billingsley concluded that he had legs that were unbelievably strong. However, one of the divers watching the film concluded differently. As Billingsley recalls, this exchange ensued: "[Diver] 'He's not doing it with his legs.' [Billingsley] 'What's he doing it with, air?' 'No, he's doing it with his arms.' [Billingsley] 'What are you talking about? You get your strength from your legs.' He says, 'You get your strength from your legs, but the direction is being changed by the way he is using his arms. By pulling his arms down, because he's at an angle, he's getting a reaction from his arms that pushes his feet to the board and the board pushes back at his feet.' [Billingsley] 'Oh my God. I'd never guess.'" According to Billingsley, "From that kid making that remark, I saw it differently. From that time on, 1962, we developed the greatest divers in the world."

Billingsley's attitude toward coaching changed dramatically: "Well, I couldn't get into the pool fast enough. Up until then it was a boring sport. How would you like to just stand there seven or eight hours a day, yelling at kids doing things?" He also couldn't wait to get home at night to research nagging questions. No longer would he depend on trial and error to learn what works and what doesn't; he would use the insights of biophysics to change the field of diving. One principle based on the physics of Newton involved lengthening the radius of your body (by changing the ways in which the arms were held) in order to increase inertia and slow a diver's spin. Certain questions involving the biomechanics of diving would haunt him for as long as five years before a flash of insight might occur in as unlikely place as a taxicab in Chicago.

According to Billingsley sometimes the insight was "nothing to change the world. But, [it] satisfied one small part of my curiosity. One thing Doc and I had, we both had a tremendous abundance of curiosity about what makes it work and how can you make it better if you do know how it works. That was the secret of it all for both of us. I couldn't have worked with a better guy, because he was the top at what he did."

In our interview, Billingsley credited Counsilman with first discovering the laws of physics that enabled them to win twenty Big Ten Conference (1961–80) and six National Collegiate Athletic Association (1968–73) consecutive swimming and diving competitions—the longest record of university championships in any field. But, then, he changed his mind, believing that he may have made the breakthrough earlier. In any case, he described Counsilman's similar reaction to finding in science the key to a geometric leap in performance: "I can remember when he came to me [around 1963] and said, 'I'm going to change the world in swimming.' I'll never forget, he said, 'I just figured it out.'" For Counsilman it was the Bernoulli Principle as well as the physical principles elaborated by Newton; and for Billingsley, the transformation in his teaching was based specifically on Newton's Third Law: "Eighty-five percent or more of diving is based on one law."

They had nothing to hide. In fact, Counsilman in his various publications spelled it all out. Billingsley decided to tell everyone he could what he had discovered. But, at first, other coaches were skeptical: "We beat the world for ten years. They couldn't beat us. They wanted to know how we were doing it. I told them the truth.... I said, 'This is the way you do it if you're going to beat me.' And they didn't believe it."

Yet, coaches and teachers around the world would eventually follow their lead. Counsilman's *The Science of Swimming* has sold more than 100,000 copies in the United States alone, and it has been published in over twenty languages, well over 275,000 copies worldwide. The principles the text taught influenced all age groups and levels of swimming. For example, private correspondence from faculty at the Beijing University of Physical Education credits the Chinese translation of his book as a major contributor to the success of China in world competitive swimming.

Communicating Breakthrough Knowledge—Then the Results

Skepticism characterized not only coaches but swimmers and divers alike. One of the themes emerging from interviews with coaches is an initial reluctance by students to heed their counsel. By the time they have joined a university team and established themselves as winners, many have an "I already know it all" attitude. Long and tedious hours of practice further reduce their willingness to change behaviors. Coaches, whose job requires them to identify and correct flaws in performance, have to gain the trust of their athletes. The most effective coaches and teachers are able to accurately diagnose what is holding back a particular talent and what set of challenges will push that individual to higher levels of achievement.

Counsilman and Billingsley, as previously noted, had diametrically opposed styles. Hobie is a shouter; Doc, never. Despite those differences, both were able to establish control over a particular training regimen and communicate the knowledge that made possible the full development of talent.

The following story of the relationship between Billingsley and Olympic medalist Mark Lenzi illustrates many of the points about the ups, downs, and triumphs of coaches and their protégés.

The Education of Mark Lenzi

Lenzi first came to the attention of Billingsley in 1986. Paul Lenihan, a former Indiana University diver, called him with news that he had just seen someone on the East

Coast who was "right up his alley," a diver who "did somersaults like a son of a gun." Lenihan thought that Lenzi was just what Hobie was looking for. Billingsley wasn't so sure after seeing Lenzi dive during the first month of workouts in Indianapolis: "He hit the water like a bomb, like a human ball—*BAWOOM!* He couldn't point his feet. He had nothing. Nothing. And I'm going, 'Why me, God? How could I ever get myself into this?'"

But Billingsley persisted: "So, I kept working and working with him. I changed the tactics. I put him on a dry land board to see if he could get his board [skills] worked out, because he had none. And all of a sudden, he started responding to what I was telling him. It was just like digging for gold, and you hit it. It was that he was never in any kind of condition." Comparing Lenzi to the Frankenstein monster, Billingsley describes the magic moment when instruction, like a shock of electrical current, took hold: "Remember that old movie? He's lying there, they bring him down, and he's looking over at them like this. All of a sudden the hand goes like this. Doctor Frankenstein says, 'He's alive! He's alive!'"

At that moment, Billingsley told Lenzi: "We're going to teach you the toughest bunch of dives around. We're going to teach you the maximum list. We're going for the moon, baby." He was to repeat that promise a number of times, especially when Lenzi wasn't meeting expectations: "I was really on his case one day. I said, 'Mark, if you can just listen to what I tell you, I'll take you to the moon. Right to the moon. Do you understand?' Next year [1989] he won the championship."

In doing so, Lenzi achieved a world record for the highest number of points (between 103 and 104) for a single dive (a reverse three and a half somersault). The difficulty of the dive combined with the judges' scores on technique and form, ranging between 9 and 10, totaled more than a perfect 100. At the moment of victory, Billingsley ran over to Lenzi, gave him a hug, and whispered in his ear, "Welcome to the moon."

That was just the beginning of Lenzi's stellar flights. As he recalls after winning the Gold Medal on the springboard at the 1992 Olympics, "Hobie came up and hugged me and said, 'You're way past the moon, kid. You're beyond Mars.'" Lenzi also recalls another set of images that Billingsley used to describe the transformations that would occur: "He said to me when I first got here, 'Mark, now you are diving in a pair of jeans. When I am done with you, you're going to be diving in a tuxedo.'" But it was the image of reaching the moon that most impressed Lenzi.

Billingsley as Educator

Billingsley's ability to tailor instruction to the needs of his students and coach them to world-class levels is revealed in the following Lenzi quotation: "He's a great motivator, a great teacher, and a great psychologist. I mean, he doesn't just take one thing, he puts it all together and applies it to each individual. That's why he has had so many champions and why other coaches don't. They go with one formula, and it doesn't work for everyone."

According to Lenzi, Billingsley is a master not only in motivating people but also in getting them to believe in themselves: "He can take anyone and put them on the roof and get them to believe that if they jumped off the roof, they wouldn't fall. I mean that they would float. He's really good."

Lesley Bush's performance at the 1964 Olympics is an example of what Billingsley could accomplish. Bush, who was not a high platform diver eight weeks prior to the '64 Olympic games, won a Gold Medal with only five weeks of instruction and another three weeks of practice diving. According to Billingsley, when she made the team, he wasn't even coaching: "In fact, I had to sneak in to get into the meet" (something he had practice with from his youth).

For Billingsley, teaching is more concerned with the basic rudiments of an activity, while coaching focuses on advanced movements and physical problems more finite and individual in nature; teaching is directed toward self-satisfying objectives, coaching with obtaining goals related to competitive activity. Billingsley prefers to view himself as a teacher more than as a coach. His greatest satisfaction as an educator may come from developing in nonteam novices a greater self-confidence and a willingness to dive.

Like other exceptional teachers in this study, Billingsley had not only mastered fundamental tenets of his field but also was able to extend its boundaries. Counsilman and Billingsley were able to provide an advantage to their students by introducing new knowledge and techniques unknown to their peers and competitors. Lenzi notes, for example, that "Hobie taught me the physics of diving. In fact, when I went to flight school, where a lot of students were struggling with the physics of aviation, I knew it because it's the same thing in diving."

Another characteristic of master teaching—providing shortcuts by the use of analogies to drive home basic physical principles—is illustrated in the following example. When Lenzi was having difficulty swinging his arms all the way through to get a lot of somersaults, Billingsley responded this way:

> He'd say, "Mark, how are you going to hit a home run? Are you going to swing the bat half way and stop? No, you're going to swing all the way through so you get all the power. Well, if you want to get a home run in diving, throw your arms all the way through." And I always thought about that in my mind when I was diving. I was known as the fastest spinner in the world because I was always thinking about the physics and swinging my arms all the way through to get a lot of somersaults.

Mark Lenzi's story illustrates how Hobie Billingsley tailored instruction, diagnosed and corrected problems, taught basic principles and honed specific skills, enhanced self-confidence, and provided shortcuts to world-class levels of performance. These are defining traits of master teachers.

The Education of Mark Spitz

Billingsley was like a second father to Lenzi, someone he came to trust not only as a diving coach but also as a mentor in personal matters. A similar relationship characterized the bond forged between Mark Spitz and Doc Counsilman and his wife, Marge. Spitz, early on, had established a reputation as a world-class contender. But he came to Bloomington, Indiana, at a low point in his swimming career, lacking the self-confidence normally associated with great talent. His story, like Lenzi's, illustrates the significant role a coach can play in enhancing the performance of even the most naturally gifted individual in any performance arena. Unlike Lenzi, but much in keeping with the stories of other stellar performers, Spitz encountered a progression of increasingly significant mentors.

Formative Years

Spitz began swimming lessons in a YMCA program at age nine. His coach was a well-established figure, Paul Heron, who had swum the English Channel. Early that summer Spitz's talent was spotted by another coach, Sherm Chavoor, who told Mark's father: "Your son's got a lot of talent. I'd like him to come swim in my club." According to Spitz, "My father said, 'We don't have that kind of money to belong to a country club.'" He [Chavoor] said, "That's okay, I own the country club. I'd just like to have your son swim on the team." So my mother started to drive me across town, which might have been a thirty or forty minute drive, to go and practice."

Spitz's relationship with Chavoor, an Olympic coach, was to last on and off for a long time. He coached Mark when he was ten, during the summers when he was away from Indiana University and Doc Counsilman (1969–72), and during the last three years of his career (1973–76). Chavoor's coaching had an immediate impact on the fledgling talent—when he was ten years old, Spitz broke sixteen or seventeen national age-group records.

When he was eleven or twelve, Mark's father moved the family from Sacramento to San Francisco for work-related reasons. Spitz swam on several different teams over the following couple of year, unable to find a coach or swimming program that suited him. During a swim meet when he was thirteen or so, his father heard Mark asking his coach, "How come I keep getting beat by these three or four guys?" The coach's response—"Oh, that's okay, Mark, your times are improving"—didn't satisfy his father, who, in turn, remarked: "Yeah, his times are going to be coming down, but those other guys' times are coming down faster." Two of the swimmers who continually outperformed him came from the prestigious Santa Clara Swim Club, where George Haines directed the swimming program. At the time, Haines, who was an Olympic coach, had several outstanding swimmers on the Santa Clara team, including Don Schollander, who returned from the 1964 Tokyo Olympics with four Gold Medals. At the urging of Mark's father, Haines welcomed Mark to the team.

When asked what accounted for the success of the Santa Clara swimmers, Spitz noted first the characteristics of the swimming regimen and secondly the attributes of Haines: "The program was great. It was more conducive to swimming longer hours, better hours—in other words, it was a better time slot—than having to swim from 5:00 in the morning until 7:00 in the morning. You could swim from 8:30 to 10:30 [with this coach] in the summer programs. And then ... he knew how to coach better. He knew how to get more out of the athletes. If everybody was always the same kind of coach, you'd have everybody being a winning team—which is not the case, obviously."

Under Haines's tutelage, Spitz improved rapidly and dramatically: "Because I now had had one year of coaching from George Haines, and I was getting bigger and stronger, I started to beat those two guys that were beating me. Then in 1966, I won my first national championship. So now, I basically went in two years from being like twenty-eighth to first [in the 100-meter butterfly]." He also finished in the top three in the 400 and 1,500 free-style events. The following summer, in 1967, at a local swim meet with a variety of relay competitions and what Mark considered "crazy events" (such as an all-butterfly relay), something remarkable happened: he beat Don Schollander, who, until that point, had held the world record at 4:12.6 in the 400-meter butterfly. Jokingly, he told his good friend Fred Hayword that maybe he would break 4:30—his time the summer before had been 4:18. He finished the event at 4:10 flat, beating Schollander's world record by more than two seconds.

What happened next is important:

> My swim coach came up to me and said: "Congratulations!" He was all excited. About ten minutes later, he took me aside and whispered in my ear: "Listen, the whole world's going to know tomorrow what you did. Now comes the hardest time of your life. Before you were the hunter, and now you're the hunted." And he said, "Keep your mouth shut and keep working hard." I took that to heart. I worked out real hard, and I broke that world record a couple of times. I finally got it down to 4:07:06, or something like that. It gave me a lot of confidence. That summer, I went to the Pan-American Games in Winnipeg, Canada, where I won five Gold Medals. I broke the world record in the 200-meter butterfly and the 100-meter butterfly. So, I actually had three world records in that one year.

Success in the 1967 Pan-American Games was followed by both victory and defeat in the 1968 Mexico City Olympics. He received two Gold Medals (in relays), a silver, and a bronze. However, he missed an opportunity to be in the medley relay that went on to win a Gold Medal. That happened because he finished second in the 100-meter butterfly (even though he was the world record holder in that event). The American who beat him in that race left the Olympics with two Gold Medals. After not winning the 100-meter butterfly, Spitz, in his words, was "all bummed out." The last swimming event was the 200-meter butterfly. Despite qualifying first by a substantial margin, he finished dead last, "because I just didn't care. I just gave up."

Spitz does not blame his failure to garner more awards on the mile-high altitude of Mexico City; that would have affected everyone not adequately acclimated. Rather, he was not used to swimming all of his events in one competition. Usually, he would swim two different events, often overlapping ones. He also was suffering from a mild case of tonsillitis. Whatever the reason, the disappointment of the 1968 Olympics triggered a determination to do even better next time: "One of the compelling reasons that I continued in the sport of swimming."

Working with Doc Counsilman

Between 1968 and the 1972 Munich Olympics, where Spitz won an unprecedented seven Gold Medals while participating in seven record-breaking events, he was to attend Indiana University and come under the influence of Dr. James "Doc" Counsilman. What influence does he attribute to Doc? "You also have to understand that I—along with everybody else in college—was a maturing young man. I was nineteen, sowing my oats, left and right. I had no idea what I wanted to study, and ... I didn't have my parents telling me what time to go to bed. And he [Counsilman] was able to basically become that surrogate type of a father to all the kids on the team. And he was very special in that way, to everybody."

In addition to the parenting role, which figured in his coaching, Counsilman had an uncanny ability to know exactly what his swimmers were capable of achieving and what they needed to do next to reach an even higher level of performance. The *Herald-Times* sportswriter Bob Hammel recalls frequently interviewing Counsilman at poolside with swimmers bobbing out of the water to ask Doc where they were in their regimen, and Doc would instinctively tell them what their speed was and what they needed to do next.

According to Spitz, who already had established his stroke before coming to Indiana University, Counsilman was able to challenge him to even higher levels of performance: "Pushing us to the limit—the pinnacle of what was known in coaching was what he had to offer back in those days." Counsilman not only taught physical principles (in part learned from observing Spitz's stroke), but he also motivated his swimmers through the love he inspired in them. Reflecting on the influence of both Doc Counsilman and Sherm Chavoor, Spitz offers this unexpected insight:

> These people were the spot checkers.... They weren't [just] coaching me. They were
> babysitting me, encouraging me, inspiring me. And through the little nuances of the

friendship that ensued … I stayed motivated and keen on my sport, to want to stay in top form. So as minute as what their participation may have been as years waned, those little inspirations and sparks of brilliance were the whole reason that the catalyst effect took place…. Even if it is infinitesimal, it can make the difference of being the greatest or just an also ran, in all walks of life…. And, you don't know from an outside point of view that just a glimmer and a smile of recognition by the coach to the swimmer [for me] was the inspiration which pushed me to want to stay a little more attentive to my training hard for five extra minutes in a workout. You take five extra minutes here, and two extra strokes there, and one extra hard push-off there, and you start doing that over four years. I didn't win by four miles. I won races by strokes and fingernails—and sometimes more…. The point is that the sum of the parts is greater than the whole. It's hard to determine what little part was and could be left out and still maintain success. The element of somebody that's a guiding light can never be left out. That's how important a coach is.

Affection and Respect Expressed Differently

While Spitz never recalls Counsilman as ever shouting and rarely displaying any form of anger, Lenzi characterized Billingsley's style as "hard-nosed"—very much in the tradition of Hobie's high school coach. Billingsley admits to being a shouter and guilty of twenty-one of the twenty-three negative qualities that he taught coaches to avoid during his summer camps. He also noted that he had a number of positive qualities. Focusing the attention of the athlete is critical in the sport of diving: a seemingly simple mistake can cause a fatal or serious injury. For Billingsley, it was of the utmost importance to establish that he was in charge. He held his divers to a strict training regimen and code of conduct, which prohibited dating between members of the male and female teams. Two violations of the regimen and code were permitted. After that, to use one of Billingsley's favorite analogies, "Three strikes and you're out!" Very much in the tradition of renowned, as well as infamous, former Indiana University basketball coach Bob Knight, Billingsley's protégés learned to listen to the content of what he had to say rather than the form in which it was expressed. Despite his outbursts, Billingsley said that his divers knew that he loved them—and that love was reciprocated.

Counsilman could only play at anger. Mark Spitz fondly remembers a common routine between Doc and team members:

[A] workout was called, you had to be in the water at 1:30. We'd straggle in from class, get our suits on and jump in the water. But some kids would be milling around the pool yapping away, just having a hard time getting into the water. So, he would take off his belt and threaten to whip you. Of course it was a game…. You would jump into the pool. It was a cat and mouse sort of thing. He'd kind of swing the belt loopingly—never with the intention to hit you, because it was never in that direction…. So the big joke with us was, if you could run around the pool long enough … his pants would fall down.

Counsilman as Educator

Counsilman believed that his contribution to Spitz's achievement was this: "The main thing was to improve his self-esteem. That was so basic." He added, "I feel that I know enough about coaching and the kids and getting as close to them as possible." As a coach, Counsilman was able to instill in his athletes the belief that they could beat anybody. This was both noted and exemplified by Mark Spitz.

Doc's philosophy of teaching may be summed up as the need to be aware of one's own strengths and limitations, combined with systematic striving to perfect one's knowledge in order to be an effective coach and mentor to all students. Specific components of Counsilman's philosophy are illustrated in the quotations posted outside the entrance to the changing rooms at Indiana University's outdoor swimming pool:

- My first suggestion for mental preparation of swimmers would be better educational preparation of coaches.
- There is no easy way to coaching success. You must always do your homework so you at least give the appearance of being authentic, so the athlete has confidence in you.
- If your athletes don't like you, you should take time off to find out why.
- The philosophy of a coach must contain room for developing the abilities of all participants.
- A primary need is for love and affection—to like and be liked. I want the swimmers to know that I have a genuine affection for them and convey it when I can. If I see a former swimmer many years after his career with me has finished and I find that he has retained a strong tie with me and his former teammates, I am pleased. In many cases we have established lifelong friendships. I think this one of the greatest things going for us in athletics.[3]

Key elements of Counsilman's philosophy are further evident in the tribute he paid to his mentor Ernie Vornbrock: "His primary obligation was to his swimmers, to see that they achieved their potential academically, athletically, and socially. In other words, he tried to conduct his program in such a manner as to help his swimmers gain self-fulfillment. I feel the same obligations as a coach because of his example."

Students Honor Counsilman and Billingsley

Between Counsilman's retirement in the spring of 1991 and his death in 2004, there were a number of occasions that brought together hundreds of his former swimmers, colleagues, and friends to pay tribute to this man who had so greatly influenced their lives for the better. One extraordinary get-together, as described in the July/August

1996 issue of *Swim Magazine,* was "a swim meet, gala, bash, and family reunion all rolled up into one. Mostly, it was an opportunity for those close to legendary swim coach James 'Doc' Counsilman—the swimmers he coached at Indiana University during four decades—to honor a man most regarded as their second father." More than sixty of his former swimmers, ranging in age from thirty-one to fifty-eight, came to the Masters nationals held in Cupertino, California, "to swim one last time for 'Doc's Team,' many emerging from long years of aquatic retirement." Despite debilitating infirmities—including Parkinson's disease and arthritis, which required that metal supports be implanted in his ankles and a pull buoy be employed to help compensate for the inability to kick—Doc competed in the 50 free-style and 50 breast-stroke events for men in the age category seventy-five to seventy-nine. He swam slightly faster than his seed time, and, according to *Swim Magazine,* "in true swimmer fashion ... complained about his performance, noting 'I know I can do better; I've gone faster in practice.'" For the audience of three thousand spectators, none of this mattered, as "it expressed its love and appreciation with a five-minute standing ovation." The May 27, 1996, issue of *Sports Illustrated,* which also covered the story, cited one of the principal organizers of the reunion, Mike Troy (who won two Gold Medals at the 1960 Rome Games): "He gave life lessons we'll always have." The discipline and drive to succeed he imparted to his swimmers could not have been more evident than in Doc's performance that day.

Hobie Billingsley's retirement party in 1989 brought similar testimonials. His former divers still proudly refer to themselves as "Hobie's Heroes." Mark Lenzi recalled:

> The World Cup was going to be his last competition. He was going to coach me and that would be it. There was a reunion of divers and coaches that came into town. I don't know how many people there were, but it was a Who's Who of Diving. Everyone got up and made speeches about Hobie, and they were all emotional, crying left and right ... taking their own time to pay their respects to the man who molded them into some pretty decent human beings. I started to realize, "Wow, I am lucky. I'm in an elite group." You know, I hadn't really done anything. I won the nationals, big deal. I was interested in the World's, but I just realized that I would forever be a Hobie's Hero.

The following week, Lenzi won the World Cup in his first international competition: "Hobie came up to me and gave me a hug. And then I was like, wow, now I am really in the group."

National and International Honors

Honors for both Billingsley and Counsilman were to follow their retirements, respectively, in 1989 and 1991. In 1999, Doc was inducted into the inaugural class of the International Scholar-Athlete Hall of Fame, along with Arthur Ashe and Plato—yes, Plato, because of his advocacy of physical fitness and the life of the mind. Counsilman already was a member of the 1976 first class of the international Swimming Hall of Fame in Fort Lauderdale, Florida, for which he also served as initial board chairman. Prior to that, Counsilman had been named National Swimming Coach of the Year in 1969 and 1971, and twice was head coach of the U.S. Men's Olympic Team.

Hobie, during the 1996 Summer Olympics, not only served as a judge for the second time but also was picked to deliver the judge's oath at the opening ceremonies in Atlanta. Previous honors had included being voted Diving Coach of the Year from 1964 to 1971 and in 1982, being named the first NCAA Coach of the Year, coaching the U.S. Olympic women's diving team in Mexico City in 1968, and the men's diving team in Munich in 1972, as well as the Austrian Olympic team in 1976 in Montreal, and the Austrian and Dutch teams in the U.S.-boycotted Games in Moscow in 1980.[4]

Legacies

Although it is possible to tally up the number of world-record holders (fourteen) and Olympic medalists (twenty-two) that Counsilman coached, and the number of Olympic diving champions (at least four) that Billingsley coached, it would be nearly impossible to list all of the personal and professional accomplishments of their former students. Beyond the competitions won and the records broken is that spark of inspiration they ignited to enrich so many lives. In their distinctive ways, they personify the importance of a teacher who constantly seeks to learn as much as possible about a field of endeavor and to communicate that knowledge to as wide an audience as possible, while making instruction personally meaningful to each and every student, whatever their level of ability. Perhaps the most fitting way to end this chapter is to cite the inscription on James "Doc" Counsilman's gravestone. It mentions neither swimming nor coaching. It reads: "Sports Science Innovator."

Notes

1. Robert Coram, *Boyd,* 25.
2. Bob Hammel, "Out There Alone," B-1.
3. The quotations are taken from Counsilman's training manual and cited in sportswriter Bob Hammel's April 18, 2004, memorial tribute to Counsilman, who passed away earlier in that year.
4. Hammel, *Herald Times,* 7/20/96, B-1

Sources

Interviews

Billingsley, Hobie. Interview by author. Bloomington, IN, October 4, 1994.
Counsilman, James E. Interview by author. Bloomington, IN, July 8, 1994.
Lenzi, Mark. Interview by author. Bloomington, IN, October 7, 1996.
Spitz, Mark. Interview by author. By telephone, March 5, 1999.

Books and Other Writings

Billingsley, Hobie. "Teaching versus Coaching Diving." One-page personal memorandum, summer, nd.
Coram, Robert. *Boyd: The Fighter Pilot who Changed the Art of War.* New York: Back Bay Books, 2002.
Counsilman, James E. *The Science of Swimming.* Englewood Cliffs, NJ: Prentice Hall, 1968.
———. *Competitive Swimming Manual for Coaches and Swimmers.* Bloomington, IN: Counsilman Co., 1977.
———. "The Application of Bernoulli's Principle to Human Propulsion in Water." Bloomington, IN: Counsilman Co., ND.

Newspaper Articles

Hammel, Bob. "From Doc to Bernoulli to Spitz," *Herald-Times* (Bloomington, IN), April 18, 1991, B1, 4.
———. "'Out There Alone'—Doc, in Sculpture," *Herald Times,* April 22, 1991.
———. "A Tale with a Tail, and Then Without," *Herald Times,* April 28, 1991, B1.
———. "Billingsley Delivers Judges' Oath at Opening Ceremonies," *Herald Times,* July 20, 1996, B1.
———. "Respected IU Swim Coach Gets New Honor," *Herald Times,* May 20, 1999, A1, 9.
———."Innovator, Coach, Soldier and Friend: Counsilman Remembered at Ceremony on Campus," *Herald Times,* April 18, 2004, A1, 9.

Magazine Articles

McCallum, Jack, and Richard O'Brien. "Swimmin' for Doc." *Sports Illustrated,* May 27, 1996, 115–16.
Whitten, Phillip. "Doc's Family." *Swim,* July/August 1996, 29.

Other

Talk by Bob Hammel: "A Personal History Recounted by the Sportswriter at the Indiana University Emerti House on February 7, 2005."

CHAPTER 3

Jazz in the Halls of Academe

David Baker and Dominic Spera

In 1960, legendary band leader Stan Kenton predicted that the future of jazz would be secured in America's colleges and universities. How prescient he was. Just as collegiate sports teams have become the recruiting grounds for professional athletics, so has the world of performance jazz become wedded to the academy to provide an endless supply of talented musicians. These university graduates enter the performance world with a full complement of skills and knowledge that bridges the divide between the repertoire of classical Western music and the Afro-Latino traditions and rhythms of this distinctive American musical tradition.

This chapter profiles two outstanding jazz musicians and educators, David Baker and Dominic Spera. Over the past four decades, they have established jazz studies as a respected component of any world-class university music school. Each has contributed to jazz education from precollegiate to postgraduate levels, composed and arranged hundreds of pieces for a variety of ensembles, and extended performance opportunities.

David Baker

Just as Doc Counsilman is widely acknowledged as the founder of the "science of swimming," so may Indiana University's distinguished professor David Baker be rightly considered the doyen of the science of jazz instruction. Baker, over a fifty-year period of performing, teaching, writing books, composing, and arranging, has garnered just about every distinction possible for a jazz musician: his list of accomplishments includes composing more than two thousand works for every conceivable combination of musical instruments and styles, from classical to bebop;[1] writing more than sixty major publications on the history and teaching of music, particularly the art of improvisation; being a cofounder with Gunther Schuller, in 1991, of the prestigious Smithsonian Jazz Masterworks Orchestra and then its sole director, as well as serving as the president of the National Jazz Service Organization. He has served on panels and commissions of the John F. Kennedy Center for the Performing Arts, the State Department, and the National Endowment for the Arts (as a council member appointed by President Reagan during a particularly contentious period of national funding for controversial projects). A talented trombonist in his twenties, he played with the big bands of Stan Kenton, George Russell, Buddy Johnson, Quincy Jones, and many others. In 2001, the Indiana Historical Society named him a Living Legend. In March 2007 he was honored by the Kennedy Center for the Performing Arts, Washington, D.C., with the Living Legacy Jazz Award. Over a forty-year period as a professor and head of the Jazz Studies Department at Indiana University, he has mentored scores of musicians who have gone on to become jazz legends themselves.

The Precollegiate Years

Although a musical genius, Baker was not a child prodigy. An amusing story about his youth is found in this radio interview:

> I know I used to drive my stepmother crazy because we had a player piano, and I just loved to pump those keys all hours of the day and night if I could get away with it. I suspect I probably came close to causing a divorce because I started on an e-flat tuba.... My stepmother used to tell me that during the winter, when she would get within three blocks of home, coming from her sister's [where she frequently visited], if she heard me still practicing that e-flat tuba, she would go back. So Dad would get off from work and dinner wouldn't be ready. They survived despite my shenanigans as an e-flat tuba player.[2]

Baker's interest in his life calling as a music educator did not manifest itself until high school. As an African American growing up in Indianapolis, Baker attended a segregated inner-city high school. Here his story varies in another noteworthy way because, while attendance at such schools is often a disadvantage, that was not the case. As Baker retraces his biography—and this applies to a number of other prominent African Americans in the arts and sciences—the school he attended, Crispus Attucks, was characterized by high expectations, a sense of pride in African American history, and outstanding, caring teachers:

> I didn't opt for music until late. I probably was already in high school. I had the benefit of the same teachers that taught [famous jazz musicians] J. J. Johnson, Jimmie Coe, Pookie Johnson, and David Young, because we all went to the same high school at

different times.... All blacks went to Crispus Attucks High School and the various feeder schools into it. We had a treasure trove, basically because all the best black teachers available were in one school. There was nowhere else they could teach. We had perhaps as strong a teaching faculty as there was anywhere. Plus, we had a chance to study black history. I mean there was no such thing as a black history month, a black history week, or day. We had a good, nurturing kind of situation.[3]

Among the outstanding teachers Baker encountered at Crispus Attucks were his principal mentors, Russell W. Brown, Dr. Norman Merrifield, and Laverne Newsome, as well as James Compton, who supported the feeder system to the school.

Baker's interest in becoming a teacher, while a student at Crispus Attucks, is confirmed in this recollection: "I went back when we had our forty-fifth reunion. They had the yearbooks out. When I looked in the yearbook where it said 'ambition,' it said 'music teacher.' So, I guess I was on target, even that early."

Becoming a Teacher

Baker studied at Butler University in Indianapolis for a year before switching to Indiana University, where he received undergraduate and graduate degrees in music education. The training, as he notes, "then and now, was and still is predominantly [focused on] Western European art music." While preparing to become a teacher, he set his sights high: he aspired to play trombone, if possible, in a symphony orchestra, and he wanted to incorporate jazz as an integral and respected component of university music school programs. Realistically, he knew that he would have to fight both institutional racism in the performance world of classical music and the Procrustean bed of elitism in the academy:

I knew intuitively that I wasn't going to play in a symphony orchestra. I even did the round of auditions and people would explain to me—usually with great tact—that it didn't matter how you did what I did, their board of directors or the society that directs this orchestra is not going to have a black in there.

With the classical music route temporarily closed to him in the early 1950s, Baker toured with various jazz bands during summers. At the same time, he completed his master's degree. Following graduation, he did brief tours with Stan Kenton's band over a two-year period. When the band broke up after a West Coast tour, Baker landed his first teaching job.

Baker began teaching, in 1956, at Lincoln University, an all-black school in Jefferson, Missouri. One of his students, Julius Hemphill, would go on to a major jazz career as a prodigious composer.[4]

Baker returned to pursue a doctorate at Indiana University, going out briefly on the road with Maynard Ferguson, and forming his own big jazz band. While learning the language of classical music at the university, he was doing nighttime and weekend gigs with talents like Jimmy Coe and Wes Montgomery: "I was getting the best of all possible worlds here in composition, trombone playing, and all the things that are demanded of anybody who comes through Indiana University, even though those demands were considerably less than they are now. I'm not even sure if I could get into school now if I were auditioning, if I had only what I had when I came here then."

At the time, he mentored in the Indianapolis area his "first crop of really successful students": Virgil Jones (trumpet), Jimmy Spalding (flute), and Larry Ridley (bassist). Later on, the Brecker Brothers, Randy (trumpet) and Michael (saxophone), joined his band. All of them, like Hemphill, went on to become major performing and recording artists extending the boundaries of jazz expression.

Following work on his doctorate, Baker taught some classes at Indiana Central High School in Indianapolis, tutored students, and continued to tour with jazz bands. He alternated between his own band at a place called the Topper in Indianapolis, and New York City, where, in 1959, he joined the George Russell Sextet. Baker had met Russell, a teacher at the Lenox School of Jazz summer program, where David was studying musical theory, composition, and performance.

By 1962, a dislocated jaw from an old accident forced Baker to give up the trombone. He took up cello playing and by 1967 was proficient enough to record with Charles Tyler. But by then Baker had come to the conclusion that his destiny was tied more to teaching, composing, and arranging than performing full-time.

The turning point came in 1966, when the dean of the Indiana University School of Music, Wilfred Bain, invited Baker to join the Bloomington faculty.[5] At the time, there was no jazz department at Indiana University. According to Baker, "Buddy Baker (no family relationship) and Roger Pemberton had introduced jazz courses for credit, and Jerry Coker had furthered that pursuit. When Jerry got ready to leave, he recommended me to Dean Bain.... The result was that Dean Bain hired me with the proviso that I put together a jazz degree program building on earlier efforts of Coker, Baker, and Pemberton."

David Baker, like Buddy and Jerry, moved back and forth between being "classical people by day and jazz people by night" when they played gigs in city bars and clubs. They had learned the vocabularies of classical Western music as well as those of jazz, rhythm and blues, and rock and roll.

The question was how to teach the basic principles and language of jazz to a mass audience. Traditionally, learning to play jazz depended on listening to records, observing performing artists, and, on rarer occasions, one-on-one mentoring. More challenging was how to teach, if you could, improvisation. Drawing on his own background, Baker noted that in learning Western classical music one of the principles of teaching was "to enable the student to make intelligent choices, to know all the options." As with other master teachers, Baker was able to identify the fundamental principles of his field, systematically construct a coherent program with appropriate texts and lessons for teaching essential knowledge and skills, and actively engage students in the work of becoming professionals who would make their own contributions to their chosen line of endeavor. Moreover, Baker was passionate about what he was doing, and along with his many other time-absorbing roles he was a major advocate for the preservation and dissemination of jazz as a national art treasure.

Baker as Educator

In 2000, David Baker was one of three recipients of the National Endowment for the Arts American Jazz Masters fellowship. In the past the award had gone to a truly select circle of musicians, including Count Basie, Dizzy Gillespie, Ella Fitzgerald, and Lionel Hampton.

Most significant is the way Baker responded to the award. For him, the award was "particularly important because for the first time, it's gone to someone who is primarily an educator rather than an entertainer."[6] Despite the fact that he previously had been nominated for both a Pulitzer Prize and a Grammy for his compositions and more than seventy recordings, this statement is not surprising. Similar self-definitions of their primary role being that of a teacher—and their greatest satisfaction deriving from leaving a legacy of actively contributing professionals—are found in the statements of Janos Starker and Doc Counsilman and many other world-class performers.

Not surprisingly, Baker, since 1982, had been a member of the National Hall of Fame of Jazz Educators. In a 1986 interview in *Jazz Advocate*, Baker observed: "I find that what I do as a performer reflects itself in what I do as a teacher. Everything I do revolves around teaching." In 2008, at the age of seventy-seven, he is still teaching nineteen hours a week, in addition to writing, composing, and conducting. Moreover, he regularly subjects his courses to a substantial overhauling to be in sync with the changing landscape of jazz instruction and performance.

Codifying and Disseminating the Language of Jazz

Baker and his colleague Jerry Coker were among the first to publish textbooks acquainting a cross-section of the public with the fundamentals of jazz playing and composing. According to Baker, "The attitude until the mid-60s, when the ball started rolling for jazz education, was 'Either you got it or you ain't,' or 'You'll hear it.' He recounts how he would ask Wes Montgomery during rehearsals: 'How does that go? What are those notes?' And he'd say, 'You'll hear it.' Usually it was the best indication that I didn't have the chance of a snowball in hell of hearing it. I might as well put up the white flag or call 911, because I knew it was over at that time."

Baker decided that the only cost-efficient way to reach a larger audience was to write books: "There was mentorship, of course. But the ideal way to learn is still a problem, because first of all it denies the existence of the printing press for one thing.

You learn by trial and error. I tell students, 'Now I can tell you in a year what it took me thirty years to learn.' … It takes time for assimilation, for experimentation, the kinds of things that allow you to internalize that information. But I can give you the information."

Previously there had been very little in the way of teaching publications. Coker's book came out around 1964, and Baker's, on jazz improvisation, in 1969. According to Baker, "We were very fortunate because we were on the ground floor of virgin territory. A lot of that is purely serendipitous. Ain't no way you can plan to be somewhere. It's just good luck. It's when opportunity meets preparation. Later one of my students, Jamey Aebersold, came along. But now, people don't even know where those sources are." He goes on to explain: "I get so tickled when I'm talking to a student sometimes and words that I coined to take care of a phenomenon that had existed—but nobody had worried to teach about and name—will be used. A student will say something to me about trombone playing like, 'Well, what I'm using is a fretted approach.' And then they start explaining it to me."

When I interviewed him in March of 1996, Baker was preparing a new book on how to learn tunes:

I tell people that I know five thousand tunes or more. They look at me kind of strange sometimes. But what I'm saying, basically, is that I know probably ten tunes over and over. Because once formulaic things have been put in place, then we realize that it is no different really than the construction of language. Once I know roots and stems of words, I know how to use those. I also can look at these things contextually. And if I don't know the word, I can find out what it is by looking at what it is surrounded by. That's the same thing that happens musically.

Teaching Principles by Problem Solving

For Baker, the language of jazz involves a fixed set of basic harmonic formulas, which, once mastered, can serve as the basis for improvisation and creation. Baker cites the case of Duke Ellington: "I look at the whole Ellington repertoire and I see time and time again that he is using the same harmonic formula. The genius comes in how he obscures that formula and you don't even know what it is. You just know there is something very comfortable about it."

Baker asks his students to find the common element in a group of Ellington compositions:

STUDENTS: "They were all from 1940. Is that true?"
BAKER: "Nope."
STUDENTS: "They were all collaborations."
BAKER: "No—they were all blues."

Then, as recounted by Baker, "The light goes on and they say, 'Damn!'" As he continues: "Ellington is so skillful that he takes this very commonplace formula and imbues it with something that wasn't there before. And I say to the students that this is something we strive for.... I teach the principles."

Because Baker is teaching students to be self-reliant, he refrains from imposing his views on anyone: "We're going to take one person and transcribe his solos.... You're not going to transcribe the solo simply for the sake of transcribing the solo. What I want you to do is to try to find out how he solves problems. [For example,] how Miles Davis uses a whole tone scale. How do we do that?"

The students may then spend up to six weeks examining tunes in which certain chords seem to dictate the use of a whole-tone scale. The students are required to discover "the blemishes, the missed notes, everything they can" so that they know how Miles Davis plays. Then, Baker will give his students something that Miles never recorded. He tells them: "If I put you behind a screen, I'd like to think that you could play exactly what Miles would play. I mean, given the options." The students then tackle similar problems with other leading jazz musicians.

Baker further requires his student to pick a musician they don't like. The student has to find out what that musician may be doing wrong—or right. In this case, they have to probe techniques and styles beyond their own limited preferences or repertoire. The result of such exercises is that students discover a set of guidelines and criteria for determining "what it is they love and why they love it."

Baker wants the students to learn how to cope with the unexpected. Criticizing play-along records for their predictability, he (jokingly) prefers recordings "where the rhythm section continually speeds up, the bass player gets lost, they play the wrong bridge, the tempo changes, whatever. If you could do that, and have it happen in a capricious way, or some way where you hit a button and it would keep changing the variables, now you'd have a play along that would really get somebody ready for what's going to happen when they go out in the world."

In order to teach in what he calls a "mass setting," for example his improvisation class, Baker gives his students "parameters." He tells the students: "You don't have success with an art form until you limit what those options are or at least make some conscious decisions about where you're trying to go." Once those parameters are learned, students "can rise above them and make music." To sum up: "Music only happens on the basis of problem solving. I think that's the way the world works—constantly solving problems and coming up with efficient ways to do that."

Knowing History and Contributing

In conveying the fundamentals of jazz composing and playing, Baker is simultaneously teaching the history of jazz, and how traditions are passed on, refined, and extended:

We go back now and measure everything in terms of what the majority of the great players have done. So that Louis [Armstrong] says that he got a whole lot of what he did from King Oliver, who says he got it from Buddy Bolden. We have no way to verify that, because we don't have any recordings by Buddy Bolden. But we do know that through trial and error, we see Louis's playing change and become more confident, easier. And we can almost look at the evolution through Louis Armstrong as an improviser, and Jelly Roll [Morton] as a writer.... These are the first two giants [who set new directions for jazz]. Without Jelly Roll, I can't imagine Fletcher Henderson. Without Fletcher Henderson, I can't imagine Don Redman. Without Don Redman, I don't see Sy Oliver. Without Sy Oliver, I don't see Gil Evans or George Russell. The beautiful thing about jazz is that it progresses at the same time the recording techniques progress. So we have, in a sense, the entire history of jazz where we can view it in a way we cannot in classical music.

With jazz, unlike classical music, you don't have to imagine what a particular piece sounded like at the time of its playing: "I can listen to the first recordings of jazz in 1917 with the O.D.J.B. I can hear how all of a sudden they tried this, it didn't work. They tried this, it didn't work. I can hear this in big band writing." The musicians who made the right choices, perhaps intuitively, were Louis Armstrong, Lester Young, Coleman Hawkins, and Charlie Parker, even though their choices may not have been initially understood or appreciated. Sometimes, these major figures were able to find their signature without much trial and error; for others, like Dizzy Gillespie and Miles Davis, style evolved and often required venturing in new directions:

Dizzy we see evolve from a carbon copy of Roy Eldridge.... In the late 1930s and early '40s, you start to hear the stirrings of [the unique] Dizzy.... Miles Davis, in the American Masters Series, said something that was so profound. They were talking to Miles about Dizzy. "I never could play like Dizzy, because Dizzy was too hot. So, I had to do something else." And then he said, in his raspy voice, "You know, it took me a long time to learn how to be Miles."

To sum up, Baker's approach to jazz history not only resides in tracing the evolution of the art form but also in critically examining the choices that these musical giants made—which ones advanced the field and years later proved to be major contributors and which ones were not as good. Ultimately, it is his expectation that the students will find their own voices and leave their signatures on the field of jazz.

Dominic Spera

David Baker and Dominic Spera were Indiana University colleagues for more than two decades. Their relationship is reminiscent of that between Doc Counsilman and Hobie Billingsley. They complemented each other in producing generations of talented performers. According to Spera the division of labor roughly consisted of his providing the basics of the jazz experience, after which the students frequently graduated into Baker's band, where they learned sophistication with jazz charts. In terms of personality and teaching, the story-telling tough taskmaster Spera reminds one of Billingsley. The narrative of Spera's career as a performer and educator is noteworthy for not only his collaboration with Baker and the impact he has had on jazz programs for high school students but also for the insights he provides on the qualities of master teachers.

Early Interest in Jazz

Typical of his World War II generation, young Spera became hooked on jazz listening to the recordings of legendary greats like Louis Armstrong and Harry James. He began music lessons in seventh grade and by age fifteen was already teaching. At first he would help his fellow students—"this is what you do here, this is what you do there"—as few people at the time knew much about jazz. Then he began offering private lessons: "So I've been teaching for a long, long time. That's really what I do; my reputation throughout the country is as a troubleshooter, trumpet teacher, chop doctor, and so on and so forth."

He selected the trumpet, a very demanding if not punishing instrument, partially out of necessity: "I had extremely buck teeth. I was living with my aunt and uncle in Milwaukee. An orthodontist, he gave me two choices: either wear braces or play the trumpet. So it all came together pretty well; there was nothing magical about that." If not played correctly, however, the trumpet can cause serious lip and mouth problems, as Spera was to experience throughout his career.

Progression of Teachers

Like so many individuals who are motivated to go into teaching, a history of negative experiences with bad instruction was a driving force. Just about everything Spera was taught and what he did as a trumpet player was wrong, until he encountered a series of inspirational role models: Don Jacoby, Bill Adam, Carmine Caruso, and then Adam again.

Jacoby—known as Jake—spotted Dominic when he soloed with the Fifth Army Band in Chicago during the Korean War. Spera had just completed a six-month training stint at the Navy School of Music. Jacoby, who was a studio artist, must have seen promise in the young Spera because he offered to give him private lessons.

The following describes what happened when Spera visited Jacoby at his home in Waukegan, Wisconsin:

> So I went to his home.... He says, "OK, kid, play something for me." I played something for him. He says, "Sit down.... Now, don't take this personally, but you're playing all

wrong." So after six months at the Navy School playing twelve hours a day, this guy tells me I'm playing all wrong. The next thing he does, he looks at my Harry James Parduba Double Cup mouthpiece. He picks it off my horn and says, "Very interesting." As he's looking at it, he's walking toward the bedroom window. When he gets to the bedroom window, he opens the window and he throws the mouthpiece out the window and it goes *clankety clank* on the driveway. That was a sixteen dollar mouthpiece; back in the fifties that was a lot of moolah! So then he went and got a Bach 7C out of the drawer, popped it in, and said, "Now we're ready to start."

Rather than being intimidated by Jacoby, Spera was inspired "to practice like mad." He returned to Jacoby one week later much improved. Discovering that army private Spera could not afford even five dollars a week for lessons, Jacoby magnanimously decided not only to give him almost daily lessons but also to provide him with a free bedroom, as members of the Fifth Army Band were able to live off base: "Jake would come home from the studios and want to play duets and talk music and trumpet. He did that for about three, four months and never charged me another nickel. I said, 'Jake, what can I do to repay you for all this?' And he said, 'You can make me a promise that you will do this for somebody else when you get to be my age.' So he gave me an insight into what teaching was all about."

Around the same time, another significant insight came from "a wonderful Italian gentleman in Kenosha": "The teacher learns from the student, and that's why people teach, because there are some things about yourself and about your own playing that you'll never be able to figure out or come to grips with unless you try to teach someone else how to do it. And that's why great players teach. It's a two-way street."

At that point, Spera realized that his "main forte, besides playing, was teaching, that I was basically a teacher, a trumpet teacher." He continued his studies at the Chicago Musical College, followed by the University of Wisconsin, where he flunked out because he spent too much time playing music and having a good time. Eventually he completed his undergraduate and graduate studies in music at Indiana University, but not before spending many years playing with different well-established jazz bands, popular recording stars, Broadway musical orchestras, and even the Indianapolis Symphony Orchestra. Like Baker, he went back and forth between the academy and the performance world.[7]

Along the way, he had two other remarkable teachers: Carmine Caruso in New York City and Bill Adam at Indiana University.

Caruso. While performing for the Fred Waring TV show, Spera's lower lip gradually became paralyzed. He sought help from saxophonist/violinist Caruso, an internationally renowned teacher of brass instrumental players at all levels of accomplishment. When Spera asked him what it took to be a master teacher, especially of the trumpet, Caruso provided an excellent summary:

Well, that's easy. First of all, a master teacher must have an inquisitive mind. You have to ask yourself why this is happening. A master teacher has to have an analytical mind—you have to be able to problem solve. Thirdly, most important, is that a master teacher has to have a deep insight into human nature. You must know your subject, because the trumpet is an athletic event. As in coaching ... there has to be someone who observes what you're doing, analyzes it, and says, "Hey—don't you know you're doing this and that? Don't do that!" And they don't, and it solves the problem.

For Spera, this may be an oversimplification, but all the great teachers that he has studied with have been able do these things. Moreover, master teachers have "the ability to treat a person as a unique, one-of-a-kind individual ... to be able to tailor the exercises. Everybody does the same exercises—some people get better, some people get worse, some people don't move at all. Of course there's a reason. It's the adaptation of these exercises to fit individuals' physical and mental make-up."

How Caruso was able to do this with Spera is illustrated in the following vignette:

> Carmine knew more about me in two weeks than my own father did. That's why he could help me.... He knew, number one, that I destroyed myself when I practiced, because on the trumpet you're supposed to rest as much as you play, like a weight lifter. So what he did, he took my horn away from me. He would give me my horn three-quarters of an hour before the show started. At quarter after seven I went to his studio and he gave me my horn and my mouthpiece.... [Then] he said, "Here, now go warm up!"

As a result, Spera played better because he was more rested and less likely to make a mistake and ruin a number (which is possible because of the lead role of the instrument). Not only did Caruso withhold the horn from Spera but he also gave him this humorous and sage advice:

> One time he gave me my horn, he says, "Now wait a minute. You know what's in this bag?" I said, "My trumpet." He said, "No. Plumbing tools. You're going to fix a leak. Who the hell do you think you are? Heifetz? What do you think you're doing over there? For God's sake, you're making a living! What are you so *molto serioso* about? You're getting all emotionally involved in this stuff. Plumbing tools! You're going to fix a leak and then you'll go home and you'll forget about it."

For people who were playing "cold like a machine," Caruso might give this advice: "Man, you play like a plumber. There's a trumpet in that bag, not plumbing tools." With Spera, Caruso could use such analogies successfully, "because he knew the person he was teaching and had deep insight into what the person was doing."

Although Caruso's pedagogy was based on the biophysics of producing sound (for example, various forms of breath control), he also was into the psychology, if not philosophy, of music making. According to some of his former students and admirers, this approach resembled "Zen thinking" or "the ideas one finds in the *Inner Game* books."[8] According to one music writer: "Caruso advocates letting the brain take over to unconsciously do what needs to be done over a period of time as it learns to time all the necessary muscles to act together."

Adam. Caruso's educational philosophy and pedagogy resemble those of Bill Adam, with whom Spera first studied as an undergraduate before returning to Indiana University as a faculty member a decade later. A split lip threatening Spera's performance career, and the offer of a teaching assistantship with David Baker brought Spera back to Bloomington in 1966.

Adam, like Caruso, was very familiar with Zen philosophy, particularly as articulated in *Zen in the Art of Archery*. In his forty-two years of university teaching, Adam also drew upon the principles found in *Tennis and Psycho-Cybernetics*. As with the study of the martial art form *aikido*, according to Adam, students need to understand that "sometimes strength is your weakness and weakness is your strength. . . . I always used that business of putting my hand on a man's shoulder and demonstrating that if my arm were completely relaxed with no tension in it, it couldn't be pulled down." (This was an exercise Bill Adam had me undergo during my 1999 interview at his home in Bloomington. Sure enough, as he relaxed, I couldn't budge him.) His philosophy involves the achievement of a harmony between tension and inner peace.

Whether or not students accepted the Zen basis of Adam's teaching, they unquestionably admired him and were proud to be his students. For his eightieth birthday in 1997, they created a website "Bill Adam: Tribute to One of the Greatest Trumpet Teachers of the 20th Century."[9] According to Spera, Adam's students dominated the third floor of the music school and would literally throw out any other instrumentalist who ventured onto their turf.

Their devotion to Bill Adam was manifested in their practicing hours on end. When queried by one of his colleagues about how he got his students to be so dedicated, Adam responded that he honestly didn't know: "We just get together." For Spera, however, the answer was obvious:

> The way Bill Adam did it was, number one, positive reinforcement. There was never a negative word ever spoken in his lesson. No matter how big a bozo you were, he would always have something to say and encourage you. And on top of that, he would say, "Now look, if you do this, someday you're gonna make it—now do this!" And he'd play along with you. When you came out of his lessons you felt on top of the world. It was like, "Holy Cow, what a wonderful world this is I'm living in!"

Positive reinforcement was critical to achieving the self-confidence and discipline required to channel energy. From Adam, Spera learned what he called the three "Ds" that form the basis of his own approach to teaching: discipline, direction, and dedication. Furthermore, while not explicitly discussing the Zen or psycho-cybernetics of Caruso and Adam, Spera discusses the need to achieve a balance between drive and relaxation, so that neither the muscles, nor the brain, become "crammed." Like his mentors, Spera believes that it's necessary to demonstrate proper technique—"walking the walk."

Pedagogical Style

Although an advocate of positive reinforcement, Spera is not beyond shouting, show-ing anger, or chewing out his students. But, as he noted earlier, the teachers have to personalize their basic approach to the temperament of each individual student. You just can't "kick ass" with everyone: "We've got sensitive people who can't deal with this. So you've got to know who to do it to. Now I've got one student, I kick his fanny all the time because he's a space cadet. But he responds: 'Oh, OK.' And he doesn't care. I hug him after a lesson, he leaves, and everything's fine. But you have to know who to do it to, because some people you destroy."

One incident that bears repeating involves students being so accustomed to this style that they sense something is wrong when he doesn't criticize them: "I had a very talented young lady in the band. She came to me crying. I said, 'What's wrong?' She said, 'You've given up on me. You don't like me.' I said, 'Why do you say that?' She said, 'You haven't hollered at me in two weeks!' I said, 'Tomorrow I'm going to holler at you, OK?' She says, 'Good.' So the next day I said, 'What's wrong? You missed a key change here! Come on!'"

Spera then notes that to be successful, consistency is important. Number one for both him and David Baker is not to bring personal problems into the classroom or studio. Maintaining an even emotional keel is critical to the career of professional musicians. Although he may be demanding, if not harsh, at times, Spera also believes it is necessary "to joke and kid around." As he learned from playing with the Tommy Dorsey band, constant tension is harmful. Moreover, it's essential to know how to challenge students without discouraging them.

Preparing Youth to Be Professionals

Spera advocates the formation of good habits at all levels of education. According to jazz musician and educator Denis DiBlasio, "Practice does not make perfect, practice just makes things permanent."[10]

Spera's most significant contributions to jazz education may reside in the sum-mer music educator and youth programs he has played a critical role in establishing. At the Shell Lake, Wisconsin, summer camp, he offers an advanced jazz technique course to band directors, professionals, high school graduates, and college students.[11] The summer camp, which is the oldest ongoing program of its kind, hosts six full high school bands for three weeks with opportunities for precollegiate students to take master classes. Although many camp alumni pursue professional careers outside music, others establish successful performing and teaching careers. For example, Byron Stripling, a talented trumpet player and teacher in the Manhattan School of Music, claims to practice "the same things Dominic Spera gave me when I was in high school. I give everybody the same thing at the Manhattan School of Music. This is what he gave me, and this is what I use, because it works."

Although Spera takes pride in his former students who have gone on to become top performing musicians, his greatest source of satisfaction resides in those who have distinguished themselves as music educators. One of them is Lisa Fleming May, who, after being music director at Bloomington High School North, became the Jazz Ensemble director at Purdue University, and is now a professor at the Indiana University School of Music.[12] Spera: "These are the people that I'm really proud of, because they are making a continual lasting contribution to music. They're going to live through their students. The players, OK, but that's more of a selfish thing than teaching."[13]

Legacies

David Baker's and Dominic Spera's contributions are manifold. Their books, charts, and recordings have enriched the jazz repertoire. Their graduates have gone on to distinguished careers as performers and educators. They have shaped the content and pedagogy of jazz education while raising standards of excellence in university as well as precollegiate programs. They have employed problem-solving approaches to teaching that acquaints students with the fundamentals and history of the field. Although demanding in what they expect from their students, they also personalize instruction, taking into account the specific skills and knowledge that will enable them to make their own marks on the world.

In 2008, Baker and Spera, in their mid- to late seventies, are active as musicians and educators. Baker, still a full-time faculty member, talks about continually raising the bar for himself and his students so as to make even greater contributions to the understanding, appreciation, and dissemination of this American art form, which is now global in scope. His performance, conducting, and composing schedule would be grueling for someone forty years younger. Spera continues to give clinics, publish his arrangements and compositions, record CDs, and solo with high school and university jazz bands—but, at half the pace.

To return to the opening vision of Stan Kenton: "Universities," according to Dominic Spera, "are now the road bands, the smoke-filled clubs where a young fledgling jazz player learns what to do." In this process, universities and master teachers like David Baker and Dominic Spera have played instrumental roles in changing the international landscape of jazz performance and education.

Notes

1. Commissioned works include those for colleagues Josef Gingold, Janos Starker, Harvey Phillips, and Menachem Pressler and the Beaux Arts Trio.

2. Interview with the Indiana University public radio WFIU program "Profiles."

3. WFIU "Profiles" interview with Bob Willard, 2000.

4. According to his website biography, Hemphill "earned a reputation as one who broke down boundaries and defied labels ... [writing] luscious and shimmering sonorities with the ever-present tang of the blues.... [He] was as comfortable writing for full orchestra as he was for his Sextet or Big Band."

5. Bain previously had created the first jazz degree program in the country as the dean at the University of North Texas.

6. *Indiana Daily Student,* January 10, 2000.

7. The bands included those of Al Cobine, Lionel Hampton, Charlie Barnet, Tommy Dorsey, and Les and Larry Elgar; the popular recording stars, Burt Bacharach, Johnny Mathis, Andy Williams, and Henry Mancini; and the Broadway musical orchestras, "How to Succeed in Business," "Stop the World, I Want to Get Off," "The Roar of the Grease Paint, The Smell of the Crowd," and "On a Clear Day You Can See Forever."

8. "Carmine Caruso—The Master Teacher: A Conversation with His Longtime Student Charly Raymond."

9. The website was updated by his former students for his eighty-fifth birthday in 2002.

10. DiBlasio's comments were given at a jazz workshop at Bloomington High School North in the summer of 1999. The high school has one of the premier jazz programs in the country. Its longtime director, Janis Stockhouse, who has garnered national and state awards as an outstanding music educator, studied in Spera's Shell Lake summer camp.

11. Students may earn two academic credits through the University of Wisconsin–Eau Claire.

12. Former students of Spera's who are practicing professionals include West Coast trumpet players Charley Davis, Larry Hall, and Bob Slack.

13. Two other teachers mentioned by Spera with particular pride are Tom Dust, the head of music education at the University of Alberta in Canada; and Howard Lyman, band director at North High School in Eau Claire, who was one of three graduates honored at the seventy-fifth anniversary celebration of the University of Wisconsin-Eau Claire.

Sources

Interviews

Adam, Bill. Interview by author. Bloomington, IN, March 28, 1999.
Baker, David N. Interview by author. Bloomington, IN, March 4, 1996, plus follow-up review of chapter with him in 2005.

Spera, Dominic. Interview by author. Bloomington, IN, April 18, 1997.
———. Interview by author. Bloomington, IN, April 28, 1997, plus follow-up review of chapter in 2005.

Websites

"Julius Hemphill." http://www.aiartists.com/jhemphillsextet/juliushemphill.html.
"Carmine Caruso—The Master Teacher: A Conversation with His Longtime Student Charly Raymond." http://abel.hive.no/trumpet/interview.caruso/. At this website, there is the quotation from the *ITG Journal* (May 1985) about Caruso "letting the brain take over to unconsciously do what needs to be done."
"Bill Adam: Tribute to One of the Greatest Trumpet Teachers of the 20th Century." http://everythingtrumpet.com/Bill-Adam/.

CHAPTER 4

Opening and Extending a Field
Saxophone and Tuba Virtuosos

The careers of Eugene Rousseau and Harvey Phillips trace, respectively, the history of saxophone teaching in the academy and the popularization of tuba playing. Both had extraordinary teachers who were seminal figures in the teaching, playing, and arranging of music for their instruments. Each, in his own way, also achieved prominence for a number of "firsts." Rousseau gave the first solo saxophone recitals in Paris, Berlin, Vienna, London, and Amsterdam; offered the first yearly master course for the instrument at the prestigious Mozarteum in Salzburg; and premiered numerous works written for him by distinguished composers.[1] Phillips popularized tuba playing in various settings by being "willing to get his hands dirty," and initiated and franchised such seemingly off-beat events as "OCTUBAFEST," "TUBACHRISTMAS," and "TUBAQUILLAS."[2] A performance field is characterized by certain traditions, cultures, roles, forms of induction, and founding figures. Both Rousseau and Phillips have strengthened and extended a respected space for their instruments in university music programs and well beyond in venues ranging from concert halls to shopping malls.

Eugene Rousseau

The path from the Blue Island suburb of Chicago, where he grew up, to the Paris Conservatory and his eminent faculty positions at Indiana University and now at the University of Minnesota, began with Ms. Elda Jansen, a fourth grade teacher who liked music. As he recalls: They "would get together in the morning before school started.... I think she had a quality that runs through good teachers and that is enthusiasm. Obviously there are other factors, but that was something she always was encouraging and had a vitality that held things together."

Teachers Along the Way

En route to Paris, Rousseau would study at the Chicago Musical College for his bachelor of arts degree, a master of music degree at Northwestern University, and a Ph.D. in music literature and performance at the University of Iowa—but never specializing in saxophone. Typically, aspiring saxophone players had to major in another orchestral woodwind instrument. According to Rousseau, "The only specialist he ever had was Marcel Mule," the year he had a Fulbright Scholarship to study in Paris.

Mayer. At Northwestern University, Rousseau studied oboe with Robert (Bob) M. Mayer, who also played English horn in the Chicago Symphony and oboe in the Chicago Symphony Woodwind Quintet. Mayer was a special teacher because "he could explain things very clearly," and he was willing to work with Rousseau, who had no intentions of becoming a professional oboe player—he "just wanted to learn the instrument." Mayer said: "Fine, I'll take you wherever you are. If you have an interest, I have an interest. Let's go."

The Internet biographical sketch—"Bob Mayer: Teacher of Teachers"—reinforces the point made by Rousseau. It reads: "He has a strong conviction about teaching, believing that 'taking a youngster who has not played note one and carrying him through the beginning and middle stages of his instrument is as important as the advanced teaching of a more mature performer.' It is quite likely that Robert [Mayer] has started more young oboists of nine or over than has any other teacher."

At age nine Mayer began violin lessons, which were "three miserable years of life." Persuaded by a former clarinet teacher, he changed instruments. Then, because "the Grand Forks (North Dakota) City Band needed an oboe player, and there wasn't one in the entire state," Bob was persuaded to take up oboe, which he did "as a duck takes to water." His first oboe lessons were with the school band director, Leo Haesle, who soon "told Bob that he had taught him all he could."

An amazing odyssey began at that point: Every Friday afternoon he left his home in Grand Forks for a full thirteen-hour train trip to Minneapolis, where he had a long lesson with Louis Doucet, and a short stay in the city, and then take the return trip to have Sunday breakfast with his family in North Dakota. All of this was financially feasible because "Bob's father was a conductor on the Great Northern Railroad, and this got young Robert a pass good over the entire line."[3] The three hundred mile trip each way, however, was not spent in the comfort of a Pullman sleeper car but on the hard seats of a coach compartment.

As impressive as Bob Mayer's persistence was in learning to play the oboe, at any cost to comfort and sleep, even more so is the fact that within a few years of starting lessons with Doucet, he was invited to be the principal oboe player of the Duluth (Minnesota) Symphony. The demanding schedule required Mayer to leave Minneapolis, immediately following his Saturday lessons, to arrive in Duluth for a Sunday morning final rehearsal, followed by a concert that afternoon. He then boarded a train for home, arriving just in time to go to school on Monday morning.[4]

Soon thereafter, at age fifteen, the Mayer family moved to Minneapolis, where he studied with Alexandre Duvoir, whom he described as "a most marvelous teacher and player." In ensuing years, Mayer played extra oboe with the Minneapolis Symphony and was employed in various ensembles, including the Sousa Band. (Harvey Phillips's connection to the Sousa Band and its importance in popularizing band music throughout the country will be discussed later.)

It was Mayer's experiences with symphonic orchestras as well as studio orchestras and traveling bands that Eugene Rousseau found so valuable, Mayer's ability "to pass on what we would probably today call 'street smarts'—the nuts and bolts of what you need to survive." The multifaceted dimensions of a performance career also are what Rousseau and Phillips consciously set out to teach, and especially for Phillips, the business aspects of earning a living.

Voxman. Willingness to enter new fields and experiment with diverse woodwind repertoire is evident in the extraordinary teacher he then studied under at the University of Iowa (UI) for his doctorate. Himie Voxman, who was director of the Music School of UI for twenty-six years, is exceptional in many ways. He majored in chemical engineering (with high distinction) at UI, teaching clarinet to high school students to pay for his college expenses. After obtaining his B.S. and M.A., he joined the faculty of the school of music. When being named a Lowell Mason Fellow by the National Association of Music Education, his nominator, Herman Kroll, stated that "during his tenure at the Iowa School of Music, more heads of school of music and music department chairpersons were trained than at any other institution."

What impressed Rousseau most about Voxman was the breadth of his knowledge and his intellectual curiosity, more so than the instruction he received on the clarinet: "He had the biggest collection of woodwind instruments that I have ever seen in my life. It was one entire wall, shelf after shelf of these various instruments and combinations. . . . He was a scholar. There aren't many musicians really who would want to get into scholarly research, and can read German and French as he could."

Throughout his career, Voxman has exhibited the distinctive qualities of being a caring human being with the ability to stimulate scores of musicians to attain their individual potential.[5] Another remarkable quality is his vitality. In 2008, in his nineties, Voxman not only continues to teach but also still plays clarinet in the Iowa City Concert Band. Not a traditionalist, at age ninety-one he started to use a synthetic reed along with the more traditional cane reed, a fact that a manufacturing company has seized upon to advertise its synthetic product on the Internet.

Le Maître. Marcel Mule's life also was characterized by longevity. He lived to one hundred. But unlike Voxman, "Le Maître" ("maestro"), as all his students respectfully called him, retired from the Paris Conservatory at age sixty-seven, after teaching there between 1942 and 1968. He moved to Sanary in the south of France, where he hosted many of his adoring former students on their visits there. No longer teaching, Mule packed his saxophone away in a closet and left it to his protégés to continue the traditions he had passed on to them.

For his one hundredth birthday, former protégés came from around the world to pay tribute to this giant among musicians and teachers who had so profoundly affected them as individuals and artists. Six month later, he passed away. A memorial website contains the fond reminiscences of now many world-class musicians and distinguished teachers. As many recall, a turning point in their careers occurred upon first hearing one of his recordings, most commonly a piece by Jacques Ibert, or the Mule Saxophone Quartet playing Scarlatti, Tchaikovsky, Schumann, and Albéniz Sévilla.[6] They were so stunned by the beauty and purity of the sound, the incredibly expressive vibrato, and, according to Frederick Hemke, the "casually virtuosic technique over the entire instrument (the sound always staying relaxed and free)," that they immediately decided they needed to study with him in Paris. Several already had completed advanced woodwind studies and were professional musicians. For all of them, in the words of Rousseau, "he set an impeccable example as both artist and human being; he was a magnificent role model!"

Not only did his personal qualities and musicianship inspire, but Mule had the ability to know exactly what was required for each student to improve. One story evokes the first dramatic interaction between Dominic Spera and his mentor, Don Jacoby (in Chapter 3), when "Jake" threw Dominic's mouthpiece out the window. According to Paul Brodie, his first encounter with "Le Maître," began this way:

> [I] went directly into his music studio and I nervously put my alto saxophone together. He looked through the music I had brought with me and he asked me to play the Concerto by Glazunov. I got through to the end of the first section and he gently said, *"Très bien,* now I would like to suggest a few little changes." Within minutes some of these "little charges" would include a new metal mouthpiece, a different position for my embouchure, a complete altering of my concept for my vibrato and different ideas about the way I was breathing. He also began to suggest a new approach for me to developing much more facility on the saxophone to improve my technical ability, and he even introduced a new position for using my tongue. I was given several study books to work on and many saxophone compositions by French woodwind composers.

In addition to struggling to rapidly change his style of playing, Brodie's alto saxophone was in need of serious repairs. Realizing this, "Marcel Mule reached inside a cupboard in his studio and pulled out a beautiful silver lacquered Selmer alto saxophone and said to me, 'I will take your instrument to the … factory for a complete overhaul, and in the meantime, here is one of my own saxophones to practice on, while your instrument is being repaired.' I was overwhelmed by his generosity and great gesture of kindness to me."[7]

Mule's personalized approach to instruction, meeting students where they were and taking them to the next higher level, distinguished him from a clarinet teacher with whom Rousseau first studied in Paris: "It was a fixed routine: 'You're studying with me. It's your first lesson. Therefore … you will begin with a C Major scale.' After two months Rousseau tired of this instruction; he wanted to get more into repertory and ideas on interpretation"—which he was able to do after working with Mule.

The concluding sentences to the various eulogies for "Le Maître," typically French in style, read:

- *la légende continue* (the legend continues), by Marshall Taylor, lecturer in saxophone, Temple University;
- *Le Maître of the saxophone. Vive Le Maître! Vive Marcel Mule*! (The Master ["Maestro"] of the saxophone. Long Live the "Maestro!" Long live Marcel Mule!) Frederick L. Hemke, professor of music at Northwestern University;
- *Le Maître est mort, mais le saxophone vive* (The Maestro is dead, but the saxophone lives), Eugene Rousseau.

Rousseau's Philosophy and Pedagogy

The concluding thought of Rousseau's eulogy—"It remains for all those whose lives he touched (directly and indirectly) to uphold the principles for which he stood"—is very much evident in his educational philosophy and pedagogical approaches. These approaches concern what expectations are held for students and how they are communicated, and ethical ways in which to interact with each individual. They are summed up in the following statements:

- I believe, as teachers, we always must begin where the students are. That's the cardinal rule. One of my pet peeves about classroom teachers is to hear them say, "My class is two weeks behind." I have trouble with that. Because I think the class is where they are.
- Some students come in and you can tell from their background that they're from a very caring, loving family; and others come in and their parents couldn't care less what their kid is doing. You sense where they are. Therefore, I have to communicate a little differently with each one.
- I think that underlying everything that I believe is that I would like students to be on their own as soon as possible. I'm trying to make myself useless as soon as possible, to quote an old adage.

- I think more of self-discipline. I don't impose.
- I'm trying to lay a foundation so that you realize these are the things that you have to work on. Now, if in your junior year or senior year, I don't tell you next week, "Do this etude or this movement."
- Specifically, I'm dealing with the saxophone. But, in a broader sense, we're dealing with life. That's what I'm trying to bring to the students—that where does this all fit into the total picture? And how does one prepare?
- Mule always said, "*On n'arrive jamais.*" (One never arrives.) Getting there isn't half the fun, it's all the fun.
- I enjoyed the study [of various woodwind instruments] and their pedagogical aspects: how they differ and to be able to explain this to people. I get energized when I talk about these things.

Following my interview with Eugene Rousseau, I attended the class he gives to five first-year saxophone students. After each student performed, he both discussed and demonstrated on the saxophone ways to improve technique and capture the spirit of each piece. He modeled what he had articulated in the interview: "You have to be able to communicate. You have to motivate. You have to reinforce what you talk about. By example is very useful: by creative repetition, either statements or examples."

As with my other interviews, I queried Rousseau about how he showed his displeasure with students' work habits and what he looked for in selecting students. Although reluctant to shout at students, he admitted to losing his temper—actually, "blowing his top"—several weeks before with a group of sophomore and junior students: no one had voluntarily signed the posted sheet as to who would be performing for the master class the following week. His response:

> I took the sheet down ... ten minutes before class. And I started to boil.... I just told them that I didn't approve of this and I said, "You don't show any responsibility." I raised my voice. I used a couple of expletives, which I don't normally use. It was effective. I left the room, I'd say after five minutes, and reminded them when the next class would be and then walked out of the room.
>
> I checked my email the next morning. There were several messages of apology for not taking responsibility and it won't happen in the future. So I think I got my point across.

Even the most mild-mannered teacher or coach will occasionally display anger or resort to shouting, which is cause for subsequent regret. Among the master teachers I have studied, the more common reaction to disappointment is to request that the student return when he or she is better prepared: "Sometimes I will simply—and this hasn't happened very often—just get up, go to the door, and open it. And I'll say, 'Come back when you're ready.'"

What Rousseau looks for in selecting students raises a comparison between being a student in a university music school and being one in a conservatory with its more specialized training:

> It's a combination of talent plus other qualities that I try to assess—their desires, their interest. Another factor that I try to take into account, especially at a school like Indiana University, is their academic background. Because our academic departments in the School of Music are demanding, I don't want somebody to get hurt because they can't meet them. They may be very talented, but they may be in a situation where the [academic] demands are just too great.

Whether or not a general university education with a major in music prepares students for making a living solely as a performance artist is problematic. Most graduates, whatever their instrument, will have to supplement performance with teaching. When asked what former students he takes greatest pride in, Rousseau, like others, mentioned three who had gone on to careers as university faculty.[8]

These educators are carrying on the tradition of a long line of musicians, traced back to Adolphe Sax in the mid-nineteenth century, who have established a space for the teaching of the saxophone at the highest level, expressing the unique voice of the instrument, just as Eugene Rousseau has done over four decades with a vast repertoire from the classical to jazz. What better way to sum up Rousseau's career than to quote the words of his teacher Marcel Mule, who described his former protégé as "a brilliant saxophonist and distinguished artist"—an appreciation that has been echoed by his students as well as by music critics around the world.

Harvey Phillips

Maestro Phillips has been called everything from the "Paganini of the tuba" for his virtuoso playing to the "Iacocca of the tuba." The reference to Iacocca, an incredibly successful marketer credited with turning Chrysler around between 1978 and 1983, is not off the mark. A tireless advocate for the tuba, Phillips has done more than any other person to commission new compositions for the instrument and create performance and job opportunities for tuba players.

The very first point made by Phillips in our interview emphasized his entrepreneurial role in expanding the performance field for the instrument:

> Well, I'll tell you quite frankly, my attitude has been that I can't justify teaching and passing on skills unless I work just as hard, if not harder, to place my students, or to create opportunities for their performance.... The good news is that every symphony orchestra has a tuba—a solo tuba. The bad news is that there's only one tuba in each

orchestra; and no euphoniums, no tenor tubas on a salaried basis. So, that's one musician out of a hundred.

Phillips attributes his interest in expanding performance opportunities for tubists to his mentors William J. Bell and Vincent Persichetti, with whom he studied at Juilliard. How Phillips ended up in New York City merits a recounting of his family background and early experiences with the euphonium and tuba, including playing for the prestigious Ringling Brothers and Barnum & Bailey Circus Band.

First Experiences

Like Doc Counsilman and Hobie Billingsley, Harvey Phillips grew up in the era of the Great Depression. Although he long wanted to play a brass instrument, his family could not afford to buy one. His father had lost everything in the Depression. According to Phillips, by the time he was ten years old, he had already lived in nine houses. His family worked as tenant farmers or at whatever jobs they could find.

Essentially self-taught on the tuba until adulthood, young Phillips would hang around a band, mostly consisting of junior and senior year high school students. He would take his father's fiddle to school and try to play along with them. There was plenty of music to be heard at home in Aurora, Missouri, as well:

> On many Saturdays, especially in the winter when there was less farm work to do, my mother's brother played guitar. Her half-brother was a terrific mandolin player. And then I had brothers-in-law who played guitars or mandolins. We'd get together: mom would make a big pan of popcorn balls and plain popcorn, and then get another big dish pan full of apples from the cellar, and we'd just play music all night.

He also credits his mother with a significant role in tutoring him on the family piano: "I would sit at the piano for hours playing hymns out of a hymnal. My mother would be out in the kitchen singing along, and if I hit a klinker, or played something out of tune, she'd come right in there: 'Now, that's not right, Harvey.' So, in a sense, she was my first teacher."

At age twelve, Harvey began to study the sousaphone under the direction of the high school band director, who, like so many U.S. hometown musicians, had played with the circus. The year was 1942, with the country at war, and many of the older band members enlisted. Harvey's chance came:

> They had no one to play for the graduation ceremony. So, my first assignment was to memorize Pomp and Circumstance.... I had no method, but I would go home with the sousaphone. It was with me all the time. I rode it on my bicycle to school. I worked at a funeral home before and after school. I'd take it there. It was just constant. Once it was assigned to me, very few people ever saw me without it.

The sousaphone, a brass-wind instrument, was a natural stepping stone to the euphonium and tuba. Phillips must have excelled at the instruments, for at age fifteen he was invited to join the King Brother Circus for the summer. After high school graduation, he attended the University of Missouri for one semester before receiving an invitation to join the premier circus band in the country:

> I got a telegram from Merle Evans [famed band director] offering me a job with the Ringling Brothers and Barnum & Bailey Circus Band. I went to George Wilson who was bandmaster at the University of Missouri, and he said: "Oh, don't do it Harvey, you'll never amount to anything. You'll never finish school.... That's much more important than going with the circus." So, I called my mother and I said, "Mom, I don't know what to do." She said, "Why don't you talk to Homer Lee?" [the band master from the high school]. So I called him and he said, "What? I don't believe it! Merle Evans! Harvey, read that telegram." So I read it and he said, "Oh, Harvey, you get out of that university right now and get with Merle. That's the opportunity of a lifetime!"

Like Dominic Spera, who interrupted his university studies to play with nationally prominent bands, Phillips went on the road with the Ringling Brothers Circus. While gaining valuable experience, he captured the attention of orchestral musicians, many of whom (like Bill Bell) had played with the circus. In August 1950, he received a telegram from Bell that read: "You have a four year scholarship at Juilliard ... you can live in my studio ... come to New York."

Studying with Master Teachers

William J. Bell. During our interview, Phillips talked at great length about the fascinating life story of Bill Bell. Recounting at great length Bell's background, Phillips had this to say: "He started as a young tubist at age nine with the town band. By the age of fifteen, he was working professionally with the bands and orchestras of W. W. Norton in the upper Midwest [sometimes known as the "polka circuit"]. At age seventeen, William Bell joined the 'Million Dollar Band' of Colonel Harold Bachman. At eighteen he was summoned by John Philip Sousa to be Sousa's First Chair Tuba!"

The year was 1921. Two years later, while the Sousa Band was resting in New York City between tours, Bell was told by a tubist friend that conductor Fritz Reiner was in town to audition musicians for the Cincinnati Symphony Orchestra. Phillips's story continues: "Bell, who had only performed on BB-flat and E-flat tubas, borrowed an orchestral CC-tuba. He stayed up all night learning the instrument and memorizing the two works in the audition, Richard Wagner's '*Die Meistersinger* Overture' and the '*Ein Faust* Overture.' Next day, during the audition for Reiner, Bell played only the opening of the '*Ein Faust* Overture' and was immediately engaged."

In 1937, Maestro Arturo Toscanini formed the renowned NBC Symphony Orchestra. William Bell was the third musician he selected, after his concert master and principal oboe. Once again the *"Ein Faust* Overture" is the basis of a memorable anecdote:

> The orchestra was set up in such a way that he knew where each musician was. During a rehearsal one day of the famous entrance to the overture, Toscanini requested that its first phrase be repeated four times. The phrase involves the tuba playing in unison with the contra-basses. Sensing that the four repetitions caused uneasiness in Bell—"What could I be doing wrong?"—Toscanini said with a smile, "Oh no, there is nothing wrong. It's so beautiful, play it once again just for me."

According to Phillips, "Of course, that made Bill Bell the darling of the NBC Symphony," whose members often quipped that "this was the only time the old man ever said something nice to a musician in the orchestra."

Bell subsequently went to the New York Philharmonic. In addition to performing with the symphony, he became a member of the faculties at both the Juilliard School and the Manhattan School of Music. One of the most important lessons imparted by Bell was the need to create performance opportunities for his students; this he did for Phillips while at Juilliard. The complementary need for a repertoire to play was driven home by his other mentor at Juilliard, Vincent Persichetti.

Vincent Persichetti. Phillips in our interview, as well as in his article "Low Brass Renaissance—Since 1950," recounted what may be considered an epiphany.[9] After performing a job one winter evening, he returned to the Juilliard School to take advantage of a practice room that had been assigned to him. While walking through the halls of the school he heard pianists playing Chopin and Tchaikovsky, violinists playing Paganini and Mendelssohn, flutists playing Bach and Handel, and horn players playing Mozart and Strauss concertos. After taking the tuba out of its gigbag, he reviewed the music that had been in his briefcase: "Asleep in the Deep," "Rocked in the Cradle of the Deep," "Down in the Deep Cellar," "Jig Elephantine," "Hall of the Mountain King," "Solo Pomposo," "Bombasto," "The Sea Gong," and so forth. Immediately discouraged with the selection, he put the music back in the briefcase and went home. The next morning he arranged a meeting for the very same afternoon with his theory teacher, Vincent Persichetti. At the meeting, Persichetti asked, "What's the problem, what can I do for you?" Whereupon, Phillips poured out his heart about the lack of quality solo literature for the tuba. Then, according to Phillips, "what this wise man said to me I will never forget":

> "Harvey, all the music ever written belongs to you and your tuba as much as to any other musicians. If you hear music you like, and can play expressively on the tuba, take

it, it belongs to you." Then he looked at me and with a tone of sarcasm in his voice said, "So you want better music for the tuba, now tell me Harvey, do you think violinists are going to do something about that? ... If you want better music for the tuba, you'll have to do something about it."

The meeting with Persichetti became the spark igniting Phillips's lifelong engagement with improving the tuba's solo literature and getting "the tuba involved with all styles of music" to the point that, by 1999, he had "commissioned, cajoled or inspired more than a hundred solo works for tuba in a wide variety of combinations and musical styles."

Expansion of a Field

Even as a student at Juilliard, Phillips's metaphorical plate of performance opportunities and managerial positions overflowed. According to his Indiana University biography: "From 1950 to 1971 he maintained an enviable freelance career ... performing, recording and broadcasting with famous artists, conductors, bands and orchestras. In 1954, he was a founding member of the New York Brass Quintet. He served as personnel manager for Symphony of the Air, Leopold Stokowski, Igor Stravinsky, and Gunther Schuller. He was New England Conservatory Vice-President for Financial Affairs, 1967 to 1971."

In 1971 he joined the Indiana University Music School faculty, occupying the position left by the retirement of his former mentor, Bill Bell. As a professor, Phillips proceeded to build on past initiatives to raise the public stature of the tuba and open up career opportunities for its practitioners. Previously, as one of the founding members of the New York Brass Quintet in the 1950s, he had expanded the tuba repertoire to chamber music. As he notes: "With the brass quintet there is one tuba out of five ... better odds than the symphony. Today there are hundreds of quintets, both student and professional throughout the world."

Following his foray into chamber music, he took an interest in brass bands. Typically, they consist of twenty-five instruments, including four tubas and four euphonium/baritones. For Phillips, that meant eight out of one hundred instruments, thereby improving substantially the odds for performance and employment. With an overriding interest in building public appreciation of all musical instruments, especially those that have been traditionally marginalized, Phillips also has promoted the euphonium-tuba quartet and larger euphonium tuba ensembles, which "provide one hundred percent involvement of [these] instruments."

In the spring of 1973, Phillips organized the first International Tuba Symposium Workshop.[10] In addition to the three hundred professional tuba players and students attending the workshop over two weekends, there were sixty-seven composer friends, many of whom were unaware that "there were a lot of fine players [besides Phillips] who could play their music." This was critical, for "when a composer writes music, he wants it played"—and Phillips could "guarantee that with the tuba." Moreover, the extant repertoire of classical music suitable for tuba with which his composer friends could possibly be conversant was limited by the fact that the instrument didn't come along until 1835, well after Bach, Haydn, Mozart, and Beethoven.[11]

As a result of their attendance at the workshop, all sixty-seven composers wrote at least one tuba piece. They also interested their students in writing for tuba. Phillips estimates that the conference generated close to a thousand new works over a period of ten years. By December 1975, music critic Whitney Balliett could note in the *New Yorker* "Profile" of Phillips that there were "almost four hundred solo compositions for tuba—for tuba and piano, for tuba and string quartet, for tuba and nine French horns ... for tuba and small orchestra—as well as tuba octets, quartets, trios, duos, and solos." To that point, there had been, in the words of Balliett, a "trickle of tuba compositions"; but, "in the seventies this freshet suddenly became a river."[12]

Phillips's efforts were having an impact. Among his many ingenious initiatives to popularize the instrument were "OCTUBAFESTS," the first one held in the fall of 1973, and "TUBACHRISTMAS," with the first one given in 1974 at the ice skating rink in Rockefeller Plaza with more than two hundred and fifty tubists from all over the country playing holiday carols. Displaying the business acumen that garnered him the epithet "the Iacocca of the tuba" among many other honorifics, Phillips licensed the use of those names. All performances must be approved by the foundation he established to benefit not only the tuba but also other lesser known instruments and musical repertoires.

The popularity of "TUBACHRISTMAS" grew to the point that the twenty-fifth anniversary party attracted close to seven hundred tubists to Rockefeller Plaza. At other celebrations, more than four hundred instrumentalists played at the Kennedy Center in Washington, D.C., and the CNN Center in Atlanta. Phillips started the event to honor his mentor, Bill Bell, who was born on Christmas Day in 1902. Musicians were first recruited from a list of people Phillips could remember who had studied with Bell. The initial list of 342 names has since grown to more than thirty-four thousand people who participate in the tuba-related events run by the Harvey Phillips Foundation, Inc.

Another example of how the foundation works is the 1993 "OCTUBAFEST" concert Phillips gave in Grand Central Station, New York, for José Cuervo Tequila: "They wanted me to have a smaller special group to do some things. ... I put together a thirty-five-piece ensemble of tenor and bass tubas. And they wanted a name. So I came up with "TUBAQUILLAS"; and the next day I filed for copyright and registration. I beat Jose Cuervo by about two hours."

Providing opportunities for tuba players is important; so is the quality of performances. By licensing events such as "TUBACHRISTMAS," Phillips controls who will play under this rubric. He looks for "potential—a nucleus of professional players."

Given the growing popularity of the instrument and its inclusion in university schools or departments of music, there are now, according to Phillips, enough majors to do a tuba and euphonium concert just about anywhere.

Audiences for this music were readily available. As recounted by Phillips:

> The Sousa band set attendance records in some places in spite of all the rock concerts and everything.... Every town had a town band and people took pride in it. An audience was already created for a touring professional band like Sousa, because they wanted to hear how it compared to their town band. It works this way now for the tuba and euphonium. For over twenty-five years now, if you totaled the number of people who have participated ... and added to that, the number of people who heard "TUBA-CHRISTMAS" concerts, and then the number who have read about it in the newspapers and magazines, the number who have seen it on television, or who heard it on radio, you're talking about a multimillion dollar ad campaign that cost nothing.

The result? Phillips:

> I can show you letters I get from high school and junior high band directors thanking me for "TUBACHRISTMAS" because now they don't have to recruit. They don't have to go convince their overload of trumpets that some should play tuba and some should play euphonium. These kids walk up to their desk on the first day of school and say, "I want to play the tuba. I want to play the euphonium."

A Tireless Advocate and Performer

Phillips's advocacy of his instrument includes more than promotional events. His world-class performances are legendary not only for their artistry and the range of musical styles mastered, from the classical to the contemporary, but for the stamina required by an impossibly demanding schedule. An indefatigable performer, Phillips, in January of 1975, performed five recitals in Carnegie Hall over a nine-day period featuring thirty-nine compositions, twenty-seven of which were commissioned by or written specifically for him. Eighteen world premiers should have been attention-grabbing enough.[13] But, Phillips reasoned, if he had played only one recital in New York, "It would be over before anybody knew about it.... But to do five, got me a nice article in *Newsweek*, one of the longest profiles ever to appear in the *New Yorker*, the *Post*, the *Times*—they all gave attention to the tuba."

His prodigious drive and stamina are described in Balliett's profile:

> While he was the assistant to the president of the New England Conservatory of Music, in Boston, he kept his chair in the New York City Ballet Orchestra. During the season, he'd finish a day's work in Boston and take the six-thirty flight to New York, arriving at eight-fifteen at Lincoln Center; then he'd catch the flight back.

If he had a recording session in New York, he would fly there in the morning, according to the profile, "fly back for an afternoon meeting at the Conservatory, take an evening shuttle for his New York Ballet performance, and be home in bed in his Boston suburb by one-thirty."[14]

Poet and Philosopher of the Tuba

Recognized for his tireless efforts in behalf of promoting the tuba and related brass instruments, he is internationally acclaimed as the world's greatest living tuba player. What has been called the "poetry" of his playing is an expression of his general philosophy of music playing and his specific approach to rendering the unique qualities of the tuba. Balliett, for example, observed that Phillips had played a seminal role "in shaping a new sensibility in all music."

Music, to repeat the insight of other international artists, is a language that expresses individual composer styles as well as historical and cultural contexts. Very much like his colleague Janos Starker: "I tell a student, the most important thing when he sits down with a piece of music is the nationality of the composer. 'Don't learn excerpts. Learn composers. Learn Prokofiev ... Berlioz ... Wagner.... Bruckner ... Tchaikovsky.'"

He continues:

If you sit in the orchestra, and you play everything like it was written by Wagner, you're not being musically sensitive. You realize once you listen to Glazunov, Tchaikovsky, Prokofiev, and all the Russian composers that there is a Slavic similarity in all their music. You listen to French music: Debussy, Ravel, and Berlioz, you realize that there's a character there—and [the same for] Italian, English, and Scandinavian music.

That language must be communicated effectively, honoring tradition but also reflecting the performer's own artistic talents and understanding of changing times. According to Phillips, "Once you put that mouth piece on your mouth, the only way you have to communicate to anybody is through your instrument." To emphasize the point, he suggested the hypothetical situation of a musician attracted to a woman in the front row: "I mean you have to get the message to her." Depending on their moods, musicians can make "an audience feel sad ... angry ... happy."

At a more profound level is the importance of musicality in the artist:

An instrument is 95 percent flesh. I don't care what instrument it is.... The great Stradivarius is a beautiful work of art in and of itself, but you can lay it on the stage and it won't make a sound. It will lie there for thousands of years. A human being has to pick it up and give it voice. Well, it becomes an extension of the skills, the sensitivity, the musicality of the human element. And it amplifies that. If I put something ugly—talk about garbage in, garbage out—into the tuba, something ugly is going to come out.

Unfortunately, for Phillips, that sound is often ugly because the special qualities of the tuba are not recognized. Many musicians mistakenly equate a big sound with a loud one. The important thing is to fill the instrument with sound, "like someone with a Stradivarius filling that box with sound. Not just scratching the string across the top of the bridge." He explains:

> To me the worst tuba sound is too much tuba. Most orchestral playing for the tuba is chamber music. There are times when the whole brass section is playing like a brass band sitting in the back of the orchestra. But more times than not, you're playing with a first horn or first and third horn. And then you may be doing something with the trombone section and something with the woodwind section. It's like a kaleidoscope, just constantly changing shape and colors. I think of Prokofiev, for example the 5th symphony, which is as close to a concerto for tuba that he wrote: tuba, flute, bass clarinet, and violin, a whole long section of that instrumentation. You're sitting twenty-five feet away from each other. It's chamber music. It's not orchestral music. No strings are playing.

The special qualities of the tuba, "at the tonal bottom of the brass ladder," to cite Phillips, are exemplified in Balliett's description of his playing:

> Phillips's sound is unique. His tuba suggests a graceful trombone, or a horn minus its nasal quality, or a baritone saxophone of the most velvet persuasion. His technique is astonishing.... Most of the composers who write for him purposely include passages of such complexity that is possible no other tubist could maneuver them.[15]

For Phillips, "The worst thing a tuba player can do is dominate an ensemble; the best thing he can do is blend and balance and affirm." His emphasis on blending is further evident in the single most important lesson he believes he can impart to his students:

> Every time you pick up your instrument, you're not auditioning. You're not trying to prove something. You're there to play your part. But your next most important responsibility is to make it possible for the other people in that group to play their best. That means to constantly listen to them, to blend, to balance, to complement what they are doing. And if you don't have the skills to do that, you're not going to make it. So, the one liner that I give is: "Always be aware of the needs of others."

This point of constantly being sensitive to fellow musicians is related to Phillips's notions of his students not only making people feel happy but being so themselves. On the very first day of classes, he tells them: "I want my tuba players to be known as the friendliest, the happiest musicians in the School of Music."

Lessons Imparted and Pedagogical Approaches

The lessons Harvey Phillips wishes to impart comprehend more than music making and being a functioning member of an ensemble. In addition to technical skills, musicality, an appreciation of the historical and cultural contexts of music making, they pertain to ethical commitments, personal development, and practical knowledge of how to land and keep a job. As he remarked to Balliett, "I teach them life, if you will." These lessons are found in the following quotes:

- I'm one of those people who feel that it's not good teaching if all your students sound like you.... I think it's much more of a compliment if someone comes up and says: "My, you gave an outstanding performance. Who did you study with?" Instead of listening and saying, "That sounds a lot like Phillips's teaching." I want them to be free to pursue their interests, not just my interests.
- Just having a great talent won't make you a great musician. What it takes is time. No matter how much talent you have, you have to invest the time.
- I tell them, they have to learn as much as they can about music because that gives you credibility. You learn all you can about theory, about music history, and the joys of making music.
- You have to learn as much as you can about the profession. You have to learn the unwritten ethics of the profession.
- If you want security, you have to learn the business of music, all the other aspects: what makes a good contract, what makes a bad contract, how do you handle yourself.

As a case in point, Phillips warns his students not to get too cute with their answering machine messages: "If I'm calling you on the phone, that's a part of your professional equipment, you better damn well say, 'You've reached the residence or the number of ___. Please leave a message and I'll call you back as soon as possible.' Because if I hear a drum roll start, and all this other stuff, I hang up and call someone else." He reinforces this point with the example of his having to put together an orchestra of 130 musicians, one of 87 musicians, and one of 76 musicians, in a week and having no patience for long messages.

In fostering the development of his students, he wants them "to stretch out—I'm not concerned that this student should play better than that student. This student should do the maximum that he can do and that one should do the maximum that he can do." Recognizing that students have different capacities and talents, he purposely arranges to have mixed classes and workshops consisting of seniors as well as less advanced students so that they learn from one another.

This practice started with the first "OCTUBAFEST": "I wanted my students to showcase.... I had all the upperclassmen doing the standard repertoire so that the incoming freshmen could hear what they were going to be studying and hear how good the advanced students were. And I had all the freshmen perform so the upperclassmen could see what a new crop is like."

Although necessity was the mother of invention in this instance—lack of rehearsal space for incoming students—one outcome of this exercise is that first-year students become immediately involved in public performances. During the "OCTUBA-FESTS" every incoming student has an opportunity to perform a solo. The event functions as a workshop that involves rehearsing over five nights more than forty major works. The "fest" part of the workshop, prior to Phillips's retirement, was the culminating party at his eighty-acre spread appropriately dubbed "TUBARANCH."

Perfection Is Never Achieved

Relentless in his drive to promote music making and the careers of his students, Phillips, like many master teachers, is a perfectionist. When asked if he had finally mastered the tuba, he drew upon an analogy from his circus background: "You never master an instrument. It's like they used to say in the circus: 'You can train animals, but you cannot tame animals.' You never step into that cage of lions thinking that you have tamed those animals. And because of that, you cannot take your attention off them."

The maxim he teaches to his students he consistently has applied to himself: "I tell each student he only has one musician to compete with the rest of his days—himself."[16]

Honors and Legacies

Phillips has garnered numerous national as well as international awards. The one that appears to have most impressed him is the Hall of Fame Circus Band selected by Merle Evans, the band master for fifty-five years with Ringling Brothers and Barnum & Bailey. As Phillips proudly recalls the letter he received from Evans: "The band he named was me on first chair, Johnny Evans on second chair, and William Bell on a third chair." This singular honor places Phillips in a tradition of circus, and more generally brass, bands that were a principal feature of American musical life for a substantial portion of the twentieth century.

Thanks to Phillips's distinguished career as a performance artist, educator, and impresario, a host of new traditions have become firmly rooted across the continent and abroad as well. Of the various legacies that already have borne fruit—the popularity of the different tuba festivals that, for example, are incentives for young people to play varied compositions for multiple ensembles—there is one that I believe is also a source of enormous significance for Phillips and his lifelong quest to elevate the status of the tuba as a serious solo instrument. That legacy is this: "In the early fifties, if a major orchestra came in to audition in New York City, at the most there would be five or six people auditioning. Nowadays, you announce an opening in the Kansas City Philharmonic, you'll have three hundred people ask to be auditioned for the tuba."

These musicians and the countless tubists will continue the traditions established by Phillips.[17]

Conclusions

Virtuosi Eugene Rousseau and Harvey Phillips personify the characteristics of the peak performers and master teachers/coaches featured in this book. They have achieved world-class levels of musicianship and influenced generations of students who have become competent and contributing professionals. They have in their own ways expanded the boundaries of their particular fields with regard to what can be played by whom, as well as where and when. The musical repertoire and performance opportunities for saxophonists and tubists have, thanks to their efforts, reached levels previously unimaginable. They, like other path-breaking artists, have respected their musical roots and their mentors' teachings while themselves inspiring their protégés to go further by leaving their own legacy of joyous music making.

Notes

1. These composers included Juan Orrego-Salas, Jindřich Feld, and Bernhard Heiden.

2. Quotation of Dominic Spera, who is featured in Chapter 3. Other Phillips novelties include "TUBASANTAS" and "TUBAJAZZ."

3. "Bob Mayer: Teacher of Teachers," http://idrs.colorado.edu/Publications/DR/ DR10.1/DR10.1.Rigg.Mayer.html. Last accessed June 25, 2005.

4. Ibid.

5. "Dr. Himie Voxman" website.

6. Examples of these recordings include Concertino da Camera by Jacques Ibert and the Quatuor de Saxophones (Mule's Saxophone Quartet).

7. Paul Brodie reminisces about his teacher: "Marcel Mule: Saxophonist and Teacher." http://www.dornpub.com/saxophonejournal/marcelmule.html.

8. The three educators are Kenneth Fischer at the University of Georgia, Eric Nestler at the University of North Texas, and Jean Lansing at Wichita State University and principal saxophonist with the Wichita Symphony Orchestra.

9. He wrote the piece for the "Big Brass Bass—July 10–11, 1999," get-together at the Washington State School of Music.

10. The workshop also was the first event held in the new Musical Arts Center on the Bloomington campus.

11. Adolphe Sax, inventor of the instrument that bears his name, also contributed to major improvement in bass-tubas as well as horns, trumpets, and bombardons by using cylinders (or chromatics) instead of pistons. Website: "Adolphe Sax." http://www.saxgourmet.com/adolph-sax.html.

12. Whitney Balliett, "Profiles: Goodbye Oompah," *New Yorker,* December 15, 1975, 1.

13. According to Phillips, one of the pieces was a tuba-and-string quartet by colleague David Baker, who, before an accident to his jaw caused him to switch to playing the cello, played both the trombone and the tuba. He also opined that Baker would seldom compose a piece that did not have a tuba in it.

14. Balliett, 2.

15. Ibid., 5.

16. Ibid., 3.

17. In November of 2007, Harvey Phillips was inducted into the Classical Music Hall of Fame, the very first wind player to be so recognized.

Sources

Interviews

Phillips, Harvey J. Interview by author. Bloomington, Indiana, March 22, 1999.
Rousseau, Eugene. Interview by author. Bloomington, Indiana, February 9, 1996.

Articles

Balliett, Whitney. "Profiles: Goodbye Oompah." *New Yorker,* December 15, 1975, 1–5.
Stafford, Tom. "The Iacocca of the Tuba: Harvey Phillips Is Transforming the Way We Envision the Brass Bass." *News Sun,* March 8, 1987.

Other Publications

"Profile of Harvey G. Phillips." Indiana University Honoring Retiring Faculty (1994). Indiana University, Bloomington, Dean of the Faculties, 1994.
Phillips, Harvey G. "The Low Brass Renaissance—since 1950," and his "Phillips's 'P's' for Low Brass Players." Papers prepared for the Big Brass Bash—July 10–11, 1999. Hosted by Keating Johnson and Washington State School of Music.

Websites

"E. Rousseau: Biography." http://www.erousseau.com/ER1_Biography.htm.
"Dr. Himie Voxman." http://www.uiowa.edu/~musicsax/Voxman.html.
"Himie Voxman—Clarinet." http://www.legere.com/Himie_Voxman.htm.
"Marcel Mule: Saxophonist and Teacher." http://www.dornpub.com/saxophonejournal/marcelmule.html.

Alliance of Distinguished and Titled Professors, Indiana University. "Harvey Phillips: Distinguished Professor Emeritus." http://www.indiana.edu/~alldrp/members/phillips.html.

"Phillips Foundation, Inc., are TUBASANTAS, OCTUBAFEST, SUMMERTUBAFEST, TUBACOMPANY, TUBARANCH, TUBAJAZZ, TUBAQUILLAS, ETC." http://www.tubachristmas.com/whatis.htm.

"Harvey Phillips, the 'Paganini of the Tuba,' Honored by Classical Music Hall of Fame." http://newsinfo.iu.edu/news/page/normal/6906.html.

CHAPTER 5

A Bevy of Divas

The careers of six internationally renowned divas illuminate both the glamorous aspects of operatic stardom and the difficult circumstances facing talented individuals determined to succeed in a highly competitive field.[1] The first two, Teresa Berganza and María Bayo, represent successive generations of Spanish divas with striking parallels in the seminal influences on their careers as well as interesting generational contrasts. The third, Virginia Zeani, represents an operatic talent who has successfully transitioned from performing to teaching to retirement and is now thinking of future reincarnations. The fourth, Martina Arroyo, has been a colleague of maestra Zeani, and is at a point in her career as an educator where she has created a foundation to assist the development of young opera singers.[2] Angela Brown, a former student of Zeani's, reflects on the personal contributions of her teacher. Finally, the late Margaret Harshaw, a colleague of Zeani, is remembered by pianist and voice coach Davis Hart, who notes similarities between the two and revisits a number of issues related to teacher expectations.

Teresa Berganza

The Formative Years and Influences

Living conditions were difficult in Spain in the post–World War II period, and a career in music was generally considered a little *loco*. But for Teresa Berganza, a dedication to music stirred at the very core of her being. From her earliest years, she was surrounded by music. Her father, a music aficionado, played the piano, trumpet, and saxophone. He would trace melodies on the piano keyboard with her fingers, patterns that she would then attempt to repeat. A strict task master, he taught Teresa solfeggio, requiring her to practice scales without the accompaniment of piano, because she had an excellent ear for music. (As Berganza recalls, her mother patiently stood by lamenting how she "suffered.") Although learning this way was demanding, the outcome was a well-trained voice. Prior to entering the Madrid conservatory at age twelve or thirteen, she joined a choral group with solo parts being her reward. During her adolescent years, she attended both a regular academic secondary school (*colegio*) and conservatory classes. Because she was such a good student, Berganza was offered a scholarship to become a teacher, something she turned down, as well as the prospect of pursuing a university education.

Over an eight-year period at the conservatory, she studied solfeggio, piano, organ, and cello, as well as the history of music, harmony, composition, and conducting. Among the conservatory teachers who most inspired her were Jesus Guridi, a famous composer with whom she studied organ for four years, and a professor Gamboa, who taught chamber music. Berganza describes Guridi as an incredible musician, whose compositons she often has sung, and who has said, "No one, but no one, sings my songs like you." She credits Gamboa's classes as providing basic building blocks of her musical career. He taught his students how to read an entire orchestral score, and then reduce the score to its essence on a piano. Berganza believes that these are skills all singers need but may not have. The first thing she would ask for when being offered an opera part was to see the orchestral score. If she liked the music, she would take the role.

Although she recognizes the contributions of Guidi and Gamboa to her professional preparation, Berganza claims that her most influential teacher was Lola Rodríguez Aragón, who was a major force in Spanish voice instruction, a principal founder of the National Choir of Spain (*Coro Nacional de Espaòa*) and the Madrid Academy of Voice (*Escuela Superior de Canto de Madrid*).[3] At age seventeen Berganza attended her voice class, thinking she was simply going to learn how to sing in order to accompany the piano or organ as a member of a choral ensemble. But the very first day after hearing Berganza, the *maestra* said, "You are going to become a singer." Until that turning point, Berganza had been thinking of becoming a pianist or, after listening to religiously inspired music of J. S. Bach and César Franck in the Church of San Francisco el Grande, where she had organ lessons, becoming a nun! In her words, "She wanted to go into a convent, to be in a spiritual world, to dedicate herself to God."

But once she began voice lessons, Berganza admits that she was not interested in anything else. She gratefully credits Rodríguez Aragón with playing a critical role in providing her with the techniques to turn her raw talent into a "voice with a beautiful color ... a musical instrument within her body at the service of music." A consuming passion for music led her to renounce a life of any other calling. Although she is an adoring mother and grandmother, music for this diva, as for many operatic stars with long international careers, is "her life"—in her words, she "lives for and through [her] music." In our interview, references were constantly made to her voice as a possessive "lover" who transports her beyond the realm of ordinary existence—an enthrallment expressed as well by María Bayo, who, in her own career, was encouraged and inspired by Berganza.

Being a Diva

The Madrid Conservatory awarded Berganza, at age nineteen, first prize in singing. Soon thereafter, Berganza captured national attention with a "daring concert" debut in the Ateneo of Madrid, with a program consisting of demanding pieces.[4] By age twenty-two, she had garnered international attention with critically acclaimed performances in Paris and the Festival of Aix-en-Provence, where she sang the role of Dorabella in Mozart's comic opera Cosi fan tutte. The following year, without even an audition, she debuted in La Scala in Rossini's Le Comte Ory. Over the next four decades, she would sing in the principal theaters and festivals of the world. Described as the most international of the Spanish mezzo-sopranos and one of the best voices of the second half of the twentieth century, specializing in the operas of Rossini, Mozart, and Bizet, she had a very keen self-awareness of her talents and the range of roles that suited her voice.

Berganza's approach to a piece of music was to study the score and the required technical skills. Then, as is typically characteristic of world-class artists, she immersed herself in the literature of the particular historical epoch of the piece and learned for whom the composer was writing and why. Then, drawing upon an Italian saying figuratively understood as "absorbing music into her voice and her throat" (la pongo en voz, la meto en gola), she brought her own interpretation to the composition. Although she admired the immense artistry of Maria Callas, who was a supportive "older sister," there is no question that from the very outset Teresa Berganza was determined to develop and express her own unique voice.

Like the other peak performers, Berganza is a perfectionist who knows that "perfection does not exist, but [nonetheless] seeks it." "Without remorse," she admits, "I'm a sufferer." But, perhaps, only when her voice did not measure up to expectations or her health was in question. Her children frequently saw her examining her throat with a larnyxscope to check her vocal cords. Depending on what she saw, her mood could range from being estatic to very sad and pessimistic. If in a good mood because of what she saw, Berganza would "run, jump, sing, invite ten people to her home, write, do it all." The most sublime moments of singing were described by Berganza in terms comparable to the joy of giving birth to a child.

Teaching

During her operatic career, Berganza, who had neither time nor energy to teach, also feared straining her voice by doing so. Later, when voice teacher and dear friend Alfredo Kraus died, the director of the Reina Sofia Music School contacted Berganza about the possibility of taking up the vacant position.

Her approach to teaching is infused with the philosophy she developed as a singer and very much reflects her own personality:

- "I like to discover each voice, human being, and personality, color of voice, and spirit, because the voice has a spirit. Each voice has a body, a resonance."
- "Within each person there is something more, but they may not be capable of drawing it out [that is the challenge for the teacher]."
- "I am not interested only in the technique. What interests me is that the students become artists, individuals."
- "I want to have a group of singers who are capable of singing recitals, to sing a wonderful orchestral piece, and to sing an entire opera."

The qualities she looked for in the eight students she was teaching in 2001 were the beauty of the voice and the intelligence behind it, something that takes time to discover. When rhetorically asked if intelligence is important in an artist, Berganza responded that it, along with "the instrument" (her metaphor for the human voice), is absolutely essential. Sentiment also came into play because one's heart must be in the singing. Furthermore, emotions as well as all aspects of the lives of her students were of concern—a characteristic trait, if not issue, with voice teachers.

Berganza's students call her "Mami Blue" after the song "Oh Mommy Blue, Mommy Blue," because she "is concerned about everything, how they dress":

> Don't wear these shoes with this outfit, don't wear this hair style, look at yourself in the mirror, I don't want that you hold your body in this position.... You have to use your hand this way, this arm that way.

She recalls that her lifelong teacher, Rodíguez Aragón, whom she constantly thinks of when teaching, also was a mother figure to her. At the same time, she had come to realize the need to be less of a "mami," less of a "mother hen with her chickens." As with her own children, for whom she wants to provide as much freedom as possible, there is, nonetheless, a lingering tendency to want to mother them affectionately. She found the resolution to this tension in the insight of an Indian scholar who said, "Children do not belong to us," to which she added, "Nor do our students." Then, she talked about the quality of personally caring, actually using the verb *querer* (to love), every one of her students for their unique attributes—"this one for being very intelligent, the other one for being more affectionate"—because "I cannot live without loving" (*no puedo vivir sin querer*).

Very much in accord with her wish to have her students performing an entire opera, in May of 2002, they were preparing to present the very opera that launched her career, *Così fan tutte*. To do this she was taking charge of conducting the orchestra, designing the sets, and coaching the individual roles—*todo*.

When asked if she might also be preparing her students for competitions, an ultimate goal held by many teachers in the performing arts, Berganza replied that she was not: the reasons being that there were not many prizes in the first place, and that she had come to realize there was a lot of injustice associated with them. Those who lost often were devastated, and it was not always the case that the most talented person won. Instead, she prefers to prepare her students for theater auditions—something that is easier to do while providing performance opportunities.

Concerning changing conditions in the field of opera, she noted, there are more highly qualified students competing for a limited number of jobs. Moreover, opera companies are looking at the "physiognamies" of applicants. It is no longer suffficient to have a beautiful voice; physical type and acting ability are similarly important. The heavy-set diva with a beautiful voice may now find job opportunities limited.

In addition to the advantage of being slight of build, Berganza knew how to work well with conductors of opera orchestras, an important determinant of a successful performance career.[5] The relationship between soloists and conductors can be a conflictive one, depending on the status of each and their interpretations of a musical score. Berganza claims, however, that she never had a problem because she "respected the score.... The maestros were happy [with me], saying, 'Sing like Señora Berganza.'" As she noted, even cellists, whose sound, according to Berganza, is closest to the human voice, would say the same.

Despite striving for perfection, which also brought its difficulties, Berganza noted that she had been very fortunate overall (*he tenido una suerte enorme*). To achieve this success, whatever her natural talents, she had to work hard. Along with the demands of balancing her family life (three children) and a taxing performance schedule, came the fame and glamour of being a diva—arriving at a city with a stylish hat and fur coat, being met with a Rolls Royce. She "lived this life as in centuries past," and she enjoyed playing the role of diva. But that was her artistic life, very different from her personal life, in which she is very family centered while luxuriating in moments of privacy, being able to live alone, to read, to walk in the countryside unrecognized.

Concluding our conversation at her residence in El Escorial, she declared that, at age sixty-six, she felt this to be an excellent period of her life (*un momento bueno, buenisimo*): "I continue having concerts with a lot of Baroque music ... and recitals of all types of music ... Brahms ... [and the list goes on]." After five decades of performing, Teresa Berganza continued to exude the love for her vocation, the passion and commitment to music making that has sustained the distinguished careers of the artists in this study into their seventies and eighties. Maestra Berganza then repaired to her private quarters to prepare for a reception at the royal palace in Madrid that evening.[6]

María Bayo

The Formative Years and Influences

The career of María Bayo, the current reigning Spanish diva, has uncanny parallels with that of Teresa Berganza. Her father, also a music aficionado, sang traditional dance music (*jotas*) at home. In the small town of Fitero in the Narvarre region, her family would attend municipal band concerts, something that the Berganza family also would do on Sundays in Madrid. Her mother, who claimed to have a terrible voice, nonetheless declared that she liked singing. From an early age, María was bitten by the music bug, singing and inventing tunes by age five.

Her first formal music lessons were with a nun at age six. Like young Berganza, Bayo first concentrated on solfeggio and piano, but she soon became bored with piano. She switched to guitar, an instrument that more easily accompanied her singing in various settings. Her teacher, impressed with Bayo's voice, promoted her to the singing lessons for considerably older students so as to deepen her intonation. Young Bayo continued with these lessons for three or four years, while singing in the church choir.

A critical point in her career occurred with the arrival of a musically talented seminary student who took responsibility for church masses and voice lessons. He refined her singing as best he could. When, to her great disappointment, he had to to leave his post, he recommended that Bayo continue her studies at the Pamplona Conservatory.[7] At age fourteen she did apply but was not initially admitted because she first had to obtain a place in an academic high school (*colegio*) in the city. The school was reluctant to accept a student who would be enrolled at the conservatory at the same time. This was but a delay in her progression. Over the next two years, she sang in a choral group in a nearby town. The music, although largely classical Baroque, also acquainted her with a wide range of genres.

By age sixteen she reached the decision that she wanted to become a professional musician. She applied to the Pamplona Conservatory again, and this time she was admitted. Like Berganza, she was not initially interested in a career as a singer. Bayo was more interested in classical guitar. However, and here serendipity enters, there were no places open in the guitar program. So she decided to study voice for two years and sing with another choral group. At that time, she was unaware of "voice techniques." What she knew was singing (*el canto*). As with Berganza, upon first singing for her voice teacher, Bayo was immediately recognized as a promising talent.

She was assigned the solo part in a Bach cantata performed at an end-of-year benefit concert in which all of the students participated.

The teacher who would play such a key role in providing Bayo with the techniques she lacked was Edurne Averre. Over a six-year period, a mutually beneficial relationship existed. Bayo, who was indebted to her teacher for what she was learning, was, in turn, always available to substitute for singers who might have to cancel a performance. In her words, she was consumed by a "passion" to sing.

At around age twenty-four, Bayo came to realize that she had perhaps become too dependent on her teacher. Averre, like Berganza's mentor, also was a mother figure. As expressed by Bayo, there was a need to separate herself from this intimacy, "because at a certain point in your career and studies, you have to leave this mami." Bayo expressed the opinion that an important characteristic of a good teacher was a willingness to respect the individuality of each student, to guide but not impose, and to know when to let the student take wing on her own.

After graduating from the Pamplona Conservatory, Bayo received a scholarship to continue voice lessons in the Detmolt Music Academy (*Hoschule für Musik Westfalen Lippe*) in northwest Germany. For Bayo, however, Averre was her last influential teacher and mentor. Bayo describes that period in her life as the point at which she began to "fly" by herself—to know what it was to live alone and to be completely absorbed in her studies. While immersing herself in the classics of German lieder—Strauss, Brahms, Schubert—she also began to study opera, as there was no opera program in Pamplona or way to learn complete operas.

Launching an Operatic Career

One challenge of studying opera in Germany was that everything was learned and sung in German, including operas originally composed in Italian. The first opera she sang was *La Corona* (*The Crown*) by Gluck.[8] Bayo's next solo role was in Puccini's *Gianni Schicci*. To sing the legato phrasing for the one-act comic opera in the Italian style of Puccini, Bayo "had to work like mad." But, she had decided "that was what [she] wanted to do."

Although starting an operatic career at age twenty-seven might be considered late, Bayo immediately won first prize in the 1989 Belvedere Competition in Vienna and soon thereafter an unprecedented eleven more. At that very first concert, where she sang pieces by Mozart and Bizet, she met Teresa Berganza. Like Berganza, Bayo would go on to perform in La Scala (1991) and at the Metropolitan Opera (1997).

Bayo's response to my mentioning that I had interviewed Teresa Berganza earlier in the day was immediately to declare her admiration for the diva and their mutual respect. After their first encounter, Bayo, when opportunity provided, would meet with Berganza on interpretation, because "she already had developed the technical aspects of singing." For Bayo, as for other members of her generation, Berganza was a role model, "above all for the rigor and love of music she had." Moreover, Bayo affirmed Berganza's observation that without the necessary intelligence and technique it was impossible to render beautiful music, because "effectively the only instrument we have is here [in one's voice]." Yet technique was not enough, because other "factors are necessary to connect with the public."

I inquired about a comment that Bayo had made in a newspaper article that "fame did not last," and that she was a "slave to her voice." My question centered on the tension between the demanding public role she had and, at times, the need for a separate, private life. Her answer ran like this: "It's complicated to carry it off. It [singing operas and recitals] is a vocation. Because if you don't have this vocation, you cannot perform before the public. To do so is to enjoy making music and to share that joy with the audience." To emphasize her total commitment to this calling, she remarked that yesterday was her birthday and she did not celebrate it, because she was preparing for her recital.

When asked whether the all-consuming relationship of the singer to one's voice and career resembled that of having a lover (*amante*), Bayo added a deft twist by responding, "Rather like having lovers." She continued: "There is this difficulty of having a normal life like anyone else. You are limited by your voice." This observation accorded with her final words of advice to someone contemplating an operatic career: "You have to love profoundly music, because if not, it is a very complicated career, very difficult. You need a great devotion. It's as if you were preparing to be a priest or a nun. It's equal to that, because you have to dedicate all your energy to your voice."

Virginia Zeani

In 2001, when Teresa Berganza was just beginning her career as a teacher and María Bayo was on an upward trajectory in her operatic career, Indiana University professor and former diva Virginia Zeani could look back on a life well lived. As she colorfully declared in a 1996 interview, she would like to live three times—"one time, one life to learn; the second one to act; and the third to teach. Well, I had to do these three things in one life. And I hope my teaching life will be very, very long." Maestra Zeani retired in 2004 and moved to Florida, where she continues to give lessons. More than forty of her past pupils have gone on to major operatic careers, among them Metropolitan Opera finalists Sylvia McNair and Angela Brown.[9]

Formative Years

Virginia Zehan (her name was later Italianized) was born in Solovastru, Romania. By age four, as she recalls, "I started to sing in my house to everybody, melodies that I invented myself.... We had no radio at home. I was born [in the countryside] without electricity, so I never knew [opera]. But I heard people singing around—in the church and elsewhere." She would make up songs like "Mother, please be nice to me, give me a little bit of this." The story continues: "She saw her first opera, *Madame Butterfly*, at age nine: "And I thought, 'My God! I have to be a singer.'" Years later she would sing *Butterfly* at La Scala. As she admits: "So in the end, I never desired impossible things; everything that I desired, it was right."

At age twelve, her family moved to Bucharest to provide her with expanded educational opportunities. In her words, she was singing all the time. She also was able to pursue a classical education, eventually studying literature and philosophy at the University of Bucharest.

In the capital, she began voice lessons with a teacher whom she describes as very nice and with good ideas, but with limited international experience. The succession of teachers and coaches with whom she then had the good fortune to study reads like a who's who of legendary opera stars.

Life 1: Learning from Significant Teachers and Coaches

Lidia Lipkowska. The Russian diva Lidia Lipkowska, who was Zeani's first significant teacher, debuted in St. Petersburg at the age of eighteen before Czar Alexander. In the course of her career she would sing with the greatest talents of her generation, among them Enrico Caruso and Feodor Chaliapin. One of her favorite roles was that of Violetta in *La Traviata*, an opera that was to play an important part in Zeani's own career.

Suspecting that her first teacher had incorrectly identified her as a mezzo-soprano, Zeani sought out Lipkowska, who had relocated to Bucharest from Russia during World War I: "So I went to this Lidia Lipkowska and the moment she heard my voice, she said, 'My God! You are not a mezzo-soprano, you are a leading soprano with high agility.'"

As with Teresa Berganza and María Bayo, the intervention of a teacher at the right moment proved to be critical in discovering and nurturing the latent talent of a promising artist. Over the next three months under the tutelage of Lipkowska, Zeani's "voice took a high position, very crystal in sound." For Zeani, "it was phenomenal what she did with me."

Lipkowska, like other notorious teachers, was a very severe instructor.[10] This did not dissuade Zeani, "because at the same time I realized that she was a little bit like my mother, who was very severe with me. It was love because she believed in what I was doing." An enduring lesson Zeani derived from this experience, which she applied in her own teaching, is that being severe is only appropriate if a student has talent but lacks direction—"So you have to put them on the right track."

Zeani, with appropriate guidance from Lipkowska, was obviously on the right track. She also was highly motivated to find other instructors who could further refine her voice and performance. A distinction needs to be made here between voice teachers and coaches. Teachers work with "technique," the mechanics of breathing and cultivating the range and projection of a singer's voice in order to achieve a good sound. Coaches work on the interpretation of specific operatic roles. There is, of course, an in-between area where the two interact with and reinforce each other.[11]

Antonio Narducci. At age twenty-one, Zeani moved to Milan with approximately $500 dollars in hand, one suitcase with lots of music and two or three dresses, and "full of desire to conquer the world." She already had learned by heart four operas—two in French (*Manon Lescaut* and *Faust*) and two in Italian (*La Traviata* and *La Boheme*)—and was determined to find the best coaches. That she did. Her coaches included Antonio Narducci and Aureliano Pertile, who were close associates of none other than Toscanini. Narducci had been the teacher of Stella Roman, a well-established Romanian diva. He worked with Zeani for one year, at which time she was ready for her debut in Bologna. (It could not have come at a better time, as she had run out of money.) Zeani selected *La Traviata*, as she considered singing in a popular major opera to be a critical launching platform to a successful career. (Over the course of her career she would perform the role of the tragic courtesan in this opera 648 times!)

For Zeani, Narducci had the qualities of a great coach—"one who pays attention to the phrasing, to the musical direction—to be traditionally in time, to have great musicality weaving throughout the music . . . to have ideas about the diction in each language, and to correct the pitch in case you have problems." Narducci also arranged for the twenty-one-year-old Zeani to teach some of the less advanced students, even though some were considerably older, including his own wife. This was Zeani's first teaching experience.

Aureliano Pertile. Immediately thereafter Zeani sought out one of her idols, famed Italian tenor Aureliano Pertile (as it was commonly said, "There was Enrico Caruso, and then, there was Aureliano Pertile), whose recordings she had heard in gatherings of opera aficionados. Their first encounter merits repeating:

> I went to him and I knocked on the door. . . . He opened the door and I could not say anything because I started to cry . . . the emotion was so big. And he was saying, "I am a good person—why are you crying? You are afraid of me." His wife came near, and she took me inside. And I explained that I was a great admirer, that I was a student who came from Romania, and I'd like to study phrasing with him.

Pertile, like so many of the master teachers in this study, showed extraordinary kindness to a promising and impoverished student. He accepted her on a nonpaying basis, providing her with the opportunity to have private lessons as well as attend master classes. Zeani credits Pertile with perfecting her diction and phrasing based on his experience singing with the best operatic stars of the period and twenty-two years of performing with Toscanini. She describes the process of learning from Pertile in her own inimitable way: "I stole from him."

Zeani repaid her tuition by running various errands and helping with household chores. The benefits of that work, however, were perhaps even more important than the merely monetary. As in Japan, where carefully selected students routinely spend much time in the homes of master teachers and "living national treasures," Zeani found it educationally important, if not exhilarating, simply to be an intimate part of the life of a great artist—observing how these special individuals comported themselves in their daily round of activities.

What she learned on and off stage from her mentors and peers would be drawn upon in her long, successful operatic career, as well as in her two decades as a master teacher at the Indiana University School of Music.

Life Two: Being a Diva

Between 1948 and the early 1980s, Zeani sang in all the major opera houses of the world opposite the leading male stars from Beniamino Gigli and Ferruccio Tagliavini to Luciano Pavarotti and Plácido Domingo. During this period, she sang at least sixty-nine leading roles, performing in six languages, and moving "with agility among the coloratura, lyric, and dramatic soprano repertoires"[12]

The sheer quantity of accolades concerning the long career of the Romanian-Italian diva, as she is often described, is staggering. They include such superlatives as:

- "She has an uncanny ability to take a tiny phrase of line and produce a heart-wrenching effect" (Handleman);
- "[The] ability to bring precise meaning to her music, achieving that rare synthesis of *bel canto* and expression that drew praise for her interpretations, both for their dramatic sensitivity and intimacy and for her radiant singing" (Beaumont);
- "Soprano singing of the highest stratosphere—beautiful technique, dramatic awareness, keen musicality, faultless style" (Ciampa).

It is these qualities that Zeani was able to impart to her students, after beginning a full-fledged teaching career in the 1980s. But to get to this juncture in her life, it is necessary to return to a fortuitous set of circumstances in 1952. Only four years into her professional career, she was asked to replace Maria Callas in a production of Vincenzo Bellini's *I Puritani*. According to Leonardo Ciampa, in *The Twilight of Belcanto*, this fortuitous occasion "marked not only Zeani's Florentine début (and her first performance in a large, important house) but also the first time she met basso Nicola Rossi-Lemeni."[13] Four years later, at her début in La Scala, she played the role of Cleopatra in Handel's *Julius Caesar* opposite Rossi-Lemeni in the lead role. A week later he proposed marriage.

In 1980, Rossi-Lemni moved to Bloomington, to occupy a full-time faculty position in the Indiana University Music School. At the same time, Zeani accepted a part-time teaching position that permitted her to complete her performance schedule over the following four years.[14]

Life 3: Being a Master Teacher

Virginia Zeani personifies many of the distinctive characteristics of a master teacher who is able to tailor instruction to develop the unique qualities of each student. Similarly, her philosophy and methods of teaching reflect the wisdom gained from years of successful accomplishment in a particular performance field. The mastery of technique and skills—but also the artistry resulting from years of striving to perfect a talent—all contribute to the lessons that are imparted to novice artists and fledgling professionals. A common issue addressed by Zeani, as well as previously noted by Berganza and Bayo, relates to overly intrusive mentoring that involves not just the teaching of technique but also modes of presenting oneself to the world.

Although successful voice teachers, according to Zeani, need a "big experience" as well as good taste, those are not enough. Great artists who are retired and begin to teach often lack patience: "They forget that one time they were young. So they teach with anger and sometimes doubting all the time the value of the singer." Therefore, these qualities are required: "Certainly patience, instinct, a desire to become a psychologist, and the desire to observe the character of the voice and the personality [of the individual] who has this voice. We are all different. I have never seen in my life two identical persons, even in twins. . . . So are the voices. No one voice is like another one. You have to know how to track a new voice and personality."

Zeani prefers "to take young people and to form them little by little." As she notes, "This is my joy. Because normally when they come to you they are formed and with some defects, and it is so difficult to put them in order. Because a lot of times [the voice] is like an old dress, you have to unsew it, put it on the table, and then sew in another fashion."

In some respects, Zeani compares training the voice to the early stages of instruction of a child in basic skills: "So [with] the students in voice. We have to train them, first of all to speak in the right position, to have good diction, to have nice projection, and overall to breathe well. The breathing system is the basis of voice."

Two examples of how Zeani was successfully able to nurture two outstanding talents are Sylvia McNair and Angela Brown, both of whom came to her studio in their twenties.

Sylvia McNair. With regard to the internationally acclaimed McNair, Zeani observed: "Sylvia studied the violin a lot. Her musicality was so precise and so instrumental in direction that I tried sometimes to give her a little bit more of a flair in her sound. Not that she has an impediment, she's very colorful."

For Zeani, there are two kinds of artists—those who are predominantly cerebral (Mozart) and those who are "full of passion" (Verdi). Matching the temperament of the singer with that of the composer, Zeani noted that McNair's instincts were to prefer things more instrumental and cerebral with Baroque music, her natural repertoire: "In this kind of music she's the number one." Interestingly enough, McNair, within two years of working with Zeani, won the Metropolitan Opera national competition with arias from Mozart's *Abduction from the Seraglio* as well as Verdi's *La Traviata*—an enormous talent able to bridge the divide between the two worlds of music identified by her teacher.

Angela Brown. Another immense talent, newly arrived on the international opera scene, is Angela Brown. Her initial voice teacher, Ginger Beazley, was a former Zeani student.[15] Brown, along with several other students, accompanied Beasley over three summers to Zeani's classes. After completing her undergraduate studies in music at Oakwood, a historically black college in Huntsville, Alabama, Brown came to Bloomington to study for a master's degree.

If McNair is manifestly Mozartean, Brown, for Zeani, is definitely Verdian: "In Verdi she has something fantastic." Zeani, who had performed in a number of Verdi operas, was immediately impressed with the quality of her voice: "Certainly she sings as well as the best spiritual singer in the world today, but if you close your eyes and her voice projected on Verdi's music, it's absolutely unique."

Although Brown was considered to have a good fundamental preparation before coming to Indiana University, Zeani considered her to have "technical problems because she was young and without a lot of experience." While at Oakwood College, Brown wavered between careers in gospel and classical music. Although she was singing mezzo-soprano repertoires, Zeani correctly diagnosed her as being a dramatic soprano: "Maybe she won't be a dramatic soprano today, but she needs to be singing soprano repertoire." At this point, Angela changed. Brown began to learn entire opera roles, not just single arias. Whereas Beazley was described by Brown as being "kind and nurturing," Zeani "wanted you to have it right—she is definitely a polisher. She will polish you until you shine like a diamond, if you're worth it. She evidently thought I'm worth it.... And with her constant rubbing (laughter)—bless her heart—I'm finally turning from a lump of coal into a diamond."

Zeani saw her role as making Brown believe in herself because, at first, she seemed to lack the determination to succeed in the competitive world of opera: "So I convinced her little by little, saying, 'Look, you've got to develop this talent. And if you don't do something exceptional with this talent, then you will feel guilty all your life. You will have regrets.'"

Brown did indeed become a diamond, winning the Metropolitan Opera National Council auditions in 1997.[16] With her debut in the lead role of Verdi's *Aida* in November of 2004, Brown was acclaimed as the newest rising star in the world of opera. As *New York Times* reviewer Anne Midgette proclaimed, "At last an Aida!" Even more prescient was the assessment of the CBS News reporter who predicted that Brown's debut presaged "the future of opera."

Zeani's persistently high expectations for Brown may have been difficult for less confident students to bear. Accompanying Zeani's demands for the highest level of performance was her advice concerning posture, appropriate dress, and even what to eat. Being solicitous of the overall well-being of her students also meant providing financial support (much as she had received) when her protégés were short on funds.

When asked if she saw herself playing a parenting role with her students, Zeani responded: "Oh yes, I mother them all [laughing]. But not insisting too much, as I know that they have their mothers, and they don't like to have a second one. So I'm a mother who understands their problems.... And I put my experience at their service." As Brown astutely observed, students themselves determine through their own actions whether or not the relationship with a world-famous artist becomes suffocating or creates too great a dependency.

Years into successful careers, Zeani's students will return for further instruction, often staying in her home. At a certain point in their careers, some may experience panic when something goes wrong. In that case, the teacher may first have to reassure former pupils—"Oh, but this is nothing!"—and then proceed to calmly review a particular problem.

A Complete Life

A dilemma facing many divas concerns how to balance the demands of a glamorous career with the attractions of a stable family life. At a certain point in her career, Zeani decided to cut down on professional engagements in favor of a more family-oriented existence in Rome, where "she reigned as *prima donna assoluta* at the Teatro dell'Opera ... for twenty-five years."[17]

Zeani's exceptional talent drew comparisons to Maria Callas. But unlike Callas, who died at age fifty-three after a tumultuous off-stage life, Zeani decided, at age twenty-eight, to have a child and enjoy a more sedentary life. That decision was made against the advice of many of her peers. For Zeani, however, it was her "destiny"—a recurring theme in discussing her life, just as she believes it to be her role to help her students achieve their own destinies. As Angela Brown observed following her acclaimed debut at the Metropolitan Opera: "Miss Zeani told me to follow my destiny, that everybody's destiny is different," Brown said. "She also taught me to persevere, always to present myself well and to be a good finisher."

Whether or not there is a cycle of reincarnations, Virginia Zeani certainly appears to have lived three very full lives. If there is an immortality for teachers and artists, it is embodied in the enduring influence they have had on their students and those whose lives they in turn influence for the better.

Martina Arroyo

Martina Arroyo came to the Indiana University Music School in 1993 from a distinguished career. As her biography reads: "From the stages of the world's most prestigious opera houses ... the name of Martina Arroyo has become synonymous with music making of the highest order."[18] Her honors include opening the Metropolitan Opera three times, being appointed a member of the National Endowment of the Arts, serving on the board of trustees of Carnegie Hall, and, in 2002, being inducted as a fellow into the American Academy of Arts and Sciences. She also has made more than fifty recordings with leading conductors.[19] Like Virginia Zeani, she has balanced the competing demands of being an educator and opera performer. Yet, there are certain aspects of Martina Arroyo's career and her reflections on teaching that are distinctive in their nuanced interpretations of themes common to opera teachers.

Differences

The first differentiating characteristic of maestra Arroyo's trajectory is that she had but one teacher from age fourteen to her triumphant years as an international star. That teacher was Marinka Gurewich, who, according to Arroyo, "was more than a teacher ... she was as much a second parent in that she was totally involved in my life."[20] Gurewich, herself, differed from many of the outstanding opera teachers in that "she was not a singer who turned to teaching when either it didn't work out or at the end of her life. This is a lady who wanted to be a teacher from the beginning. Her performing skills, what performances she did, were for the sake of getting some experience so she could know what the performer would live through."

Gurewich, who first taught at a public institution, quickly realized that she would much prefer to run a private studio for reasons with which Arroyo empathizes: "It's a matter of having a certain number of people in the school and not necessarily top quality talent." Rather than giving equal time to every student, she would prefer to "have fewer students and give them an hour a day and feel that we are really working toward the building of special careers."

For the select few whom Arroyo calls "the prime talents of the world—the ones that you do recognize and who are few and far between"—a great amount of involvement is required. More than instruction is required: "Without becoming a stage mother … you make sure they take care of their clothes for concerts, their grooming, how they live—are they eating properly. You get involved with their private lives." She continues: "When they're not happy emotionally, they don't sing as well … even though you don't control it."

In our 1996 interview, she expressly preferred greater autonomy in deciding whom she would teach according to a more flexible schedule—something difficult to achieve as a full-time professor in a public university school of music. The norm for music school faculty at Indiana University is eighteen students—a situation many public school as well as college teachers would find to be ideal. But for Arroyo, that was not a satisfactory situation: "It's very much harder to be involved with eighteen people's lives than with the few that you think are really going to make it." Although she might give everyone equal time, she admitted, in all truthfulness, she could not say that "she gave everyone equal involvement."

Moreover, in a university music program, unlike that of a conservatory, there are likely to be more nonmusic graduation requirements: "Very often they [the students] get so involved in so many other subjects that they're not paying as much attention as they [should] to their voice. Many times they don't know if they want to commit their lives to this type of career this early."

Arroyo's honest expression of unhappiness with the above situation reflects reasons why certain extraordinarily talented artists may not wish to teach in a university, no matter how rigorous the selection process. As noted by Zeani, senior artists with no teaching background also might create problems by being very impatient with less talented students, often making discouraging demands inappropriate to their level of development.

Although certain students may not be well matched to her expectations, Arroyo does strive to individualize instruction as much as possible. She attempts to teach in the tradition of her beloved mentor Marinka Gurewich as well as other teachers whom she admires. This means that the teacher responds to specific problems and does not resort to "a general technique that just smears [the same thing] over everybody.… The teacher approaches that problem and works with that individual's ups and downs, failings, and good points." Moreover, "she doesn't try to make everybody sound alike and everybody do the same thing."

That is a point she has heard famed tenor James McCracken tell his students: "Don't do what I do, because what I do worked for me and just barely." Such advice might have seemed incredible to his students, who would have been more than delighted to sing like McCracken.

Another quality of an outstanding teacher, according to Arroyo, is a "great work ethic": "We have to keep studying. Even now that I'm singing maybe 15 percent of what I sang before. I still have to stay in shape."

Whatever Martina Arroyo's concern about her ability to be an effective full-time teacher in a highly structured setting, Indiana University awarded Martina Arroyo its highest honor in 1997, naming her a distinguished professor. The award would not have been possible without the input of her students and colleagues.

Whether maestra Arroyo would have scaled the heights she did without the intervention of an "angel" is an interesting question. She doubts that her continued studies in music and tuition at Hunter College would have been possible, if not for a generous donor who came to her financial assistance. The only demands made on Arroyo were to sing at the benefactor's yearly Christmas party.

Gratitude for such assistance at a critical period may be one of the principal reasons why this artist-educator established the Martina Arroyo Foundation in 2003. The educational mission of the foundation, however, is paramount and is indicative of Arroyo's vision of what is required to nurture world-class operatic talent. The foundation website reads: "A major problem with contemporary classical singers is a blandness in style. This was best articulated by Peter G. Davis in his book, *The American Singer.* Insights into an operatic role to include the background of the drama, the historical perspective, and the psychological motivations of each character are not provided in the institutions of classical music training in America."[21]

One final point concerns a fundamental question of this research undertaking: is it possible to achieve internationally recognized peak performance without the intervention of a teacher? This was Arroyo's reply:

> Most of the special people you're talking about have exactly that quality. Something in their voice itself ... the beauty of it ... the expressiveness of it that nobody has taught them. It's just there. Now, the point is to teach them so they don't lose it.... To help them know how to work with that great gift so that it stays healthy ... so that you can handle [over thirty-five to forty years] the pressures that will come into your life, onto that voice.

Virginia Zeani had a similar view concerning the important role of natural talent as expressed in a sign just outside her studio at the Indiana University School of Music: "Never try to teach a pig to sing. It wastes your time and it annoys the pig."[22] Notwithstanding this warning, Zeani, like the other profiled opera teachers, was able to polish metaphorical "lumps of coals" into diamonds of rare beauty and value.

Margaret Harshaw

I had heard so many people refer to the late Margaret Harshaw as an extraordinary talent and teacher that I decided to interview pianist Davis Hart, who had worked closely with her and her students over a period of more than ten years. Like Zeani and Arroyo, Harshaw joined the Indiana University Music School faculty after a long and accomplished career. Over a twenty-two-year period, from the time of her debut at the Metropolitan Opera House in 1942, at age thirty-three, she performed in more Wagner operas than any other singer in its history.

The distinguishing characteristics of Margaret Harshaw, as recalled by Hart, were that "she never accepted anything less than a person's absolute peak potential. She was the easiest person to get along with in the world as long as you worked and tried to live up to your potential. Otherwise, she could be extremely difficult, very demanding—not a perfectionist, but as close to it as a person could humanly expect to be."

This style of teaching bore resemblance to Harshaw's teacher at the Juilliard School, Anna Schoen-René, whom the students called "the Prussian general." Among a long list of Schoen-René's prominent protégés are Rise Stevens and Paul Robeson. Interestingly enough, Schoen-René did not teach by example, as she had contracted tuberculosis on a boat trip from Europe and never sang afterward. Whatever this drawback, Harshaw gained enough from her Juilliard experience to go on to win the Metropolitan Opera auditions.

Another Harshaw trait was her great sense of humor, if not sarcasm, in trying to teach a student to roll a double "r." In response to the student's futile attempts to accomplish this task, Harshaw responded, "My dear, that's not a rolled 'r'—it's a horse's fart." Whether or not such painfully honest instruction is well matched to the personality and talents of all students, as Hart notes, "When a teacher like Zeani or Harshaw says that something is good, there is a great sense of security that you know it is."

Conclusions

The biographies of operatic talents and master teachers featured in this chapter resonate with those of other extraordinary artists. The common features include:

- a supportive family environment
- an early fascination with music expressed in different ways
- the intervention of key teachers, at critical points in their careers, who identified their talent and helped them advance to a higher stage of development and self-expression
- a total commitment to their career as well as a resolve to balance what may be considered a "normal life" with the rigorous but glamorous role of being a "superstar"
- a desire to learn and constantly improve their technique and artistry
- a passion to communicate with audiences, and eventually a desire, at a later stage in their careers, to teach.

However, there is perhaps a subtle difference distinguishing opera artists from other musicians. The distinction resides in the human voice being the musical instrument on which one's career depends. A leitmotif running throughout the interviews of the various divas is the mystery of one's voice—its soaring possibilities as well as its vulnerability, if not fragility. It's as if the innately beautiful voice is a divine gift and therefore something mystical.[23] Technique, control over the voice, is something that must be mastered. Yet this is insufficient. Here is where exceptional teachers play such an important role in nurturing fledgling talent so that technical wizardry develops into true artistry of a transcendental quality.

Notes

1. "Diva," according to *Webster's New Universal Unabridged Dictionary*: "a goddess; a prima donna; a leading female singer, especially in grand opera."

2. "Martina Arroyo Foundation, Inc.," http://www.martinaarroyofoundation.org/.

3. My translations from Spanish to English are not literal. They are intended to capture the common-sense meaning of the words in everyday English.

4. The concert consisted of pieces by such composers as Max Reger, regarded as the heir to the piano music of Brahms.

5. Among the great conductors she had the good fortune to work with were Carlo Maria Giulini and Claudio Abbado.

6. The interview took place in her apartment in the historic Residence of the Queen (*Casa de la Reina*) in El Escorial, outside Madrid.

7. Pamplona, in addition to being famous for the running of bulls in the street during the July Fiesta de San Fermín, was also the birthplace of famed Spanish violinist and composer Pablo de Saraste.

8. Gluck, while residing principally in Vienna during his peripatetic career, was influenced by Italian musical traditions. Early in his career, he composed seven Italian operas.

9. Among Maestra Zeani's many graduates with successful careers are Nova Thomas, Marilyn Mims, Jeanne-Michèle Charbonnet, Stephen Mark Brown, Elizabeth Futral, Katheryn Krassovic, Vivica Genaux, Patricia Risley, Christina Pier, Andrea Atkins, Mark Bowman, Kirsten Gunlogson, Kendrick Jacocks, Tod Kowallis, Marina Levitt, Debra Mayer, Susan Patterson, Thomas Potter, Itzuki Shibata, and Peter Volpe.

10. One example is "Madame Sousatzka," on whom a book and Hollywood movie are based.

11. For example, Indiana University pianist and voice coach Davis Hart, who worked with Virginia Zeani, might tell students in rehearsal, "The tone [for a particular aria] is not good; fix it.' And theoretically, the teacher has taught them enough that without my getting involved in technique, they should know what to do to correct the vocal problem."

12. Indiana University distinguished professor profile of Virginia Zeani.

13. As told by Virginia Zeani, Rossi-Lemeni played a key role in launching the operatic career of Maria Callas by introducing her to the director of the Verona Opera House. From there she went with Rossi-Lemeni to perform in New York.

14. Her last performance was that of Blanche, the martyred nun in Francis Poulenc's *Dialogues of the Carmelites*, a role she had played in the opera's premiere in 1957.

15. Dr. Ginger Beazley is director of Ars Nova School of the Arts, and president of the board of Ars Nova School, Oakwood College.

16. Brown won on her fourth try, having come up just short in three previous competitions.

17. An interesting side note is that Virginia Zeani is officially listed with the Indiana University dean of faculties personnel directory under the name of Virginia Nicoli-Lemeni and not her internationally known name, suggesting the importance of her marital status.

18. "Martina Arroyo: Biography," http://www.martinaarroyo.com/bio.htm. Arroyo had given some lessons at Louisiana State University prior to coming to Indiana University, and since then she has been an invited professor at other institutions of higher education, including the University of California in Los Angeles and Wilberforce University in Ohio.

19. They include Leonard Bernstein, Zubin Mehta, Riccardo Muti, and James Levine.

20. Arroyo notes that Gurewich even took her to a dentist, much to the chagrin of her mother, who had not been consulted and most likely would have preferred a visit to the family dentist.

21. The website address is the following: http://www.martinaarroyofoundation.org/AboutTheFoundation.htm. The foundation's very first performance program took place in June 2005 in New York City with students from the United States and Europe.

22. Note of Davis Hart, who pointed out that a similar sign was posted outside the Indiana University studio of Margaret Harshaw.

23. Artistic talent as a divine gift, however, is not unique to singers. Child prodigies in instrumental music, and there are many, often are considered to be blessed by some inexplicable gift of nature or the gods.

Sources

Interviews (In order of appearance in the chapter)

Berganza, Teresa. Interview by author. El Escorial, Spain, May 29, 2001.
Bayo, María. Interview by author. Madrid, Spain, May 29, 2001.
Zeani, Virginia. Interview by author. Bloomington, IN, December 4, 1996.
Brown, Angela. Interview by author. Bloomington, IN, November 18, 1996.
Arroyo, Martina. Interview by author. Bloomington, IN, February 20, 1996.
Hart, Davis. Interview by author. Bloomington, IN, April 10, 1999.
———. Follow-up telephone conversation with author. December 9, 2005.

Websites (pertinent to appearance in the chapter)

Teresa Berganza: "Teresa Berganza." http://en.wikipedia.org/wiki/Teresa_Berganza; "Teresa Berganza." http://www.teresaberganza.com/indice.htm.

María Bayo: "Maria Bayo." http://www.operalive.com/english/maria/interview.html; http://www.mariabayo.net/html/engl/flashversioengl/home_fv.html; "Maria Bayo." http://www.andante.com/article/article.cfm?id=23222.

Virginia Zeani: "Virginia Zeani by Charlie Handelman." http://ourworld.compuserve.com/homepages/handelmania/zeani.htm; "An excerpt from the Twilight of Belcanto" by Leonardo Ciampa: http://www.leonardociampa.com/Zeani.html; biographical notes: http://ourworld.compuserve.com/homepages/handelmania/zeani.htm; http://en.wikipedia.org/wiki/Virginia_Zeani; distinguished professor: http://www.indiana.edu/~alldrp/members/zeani.html.

Nicola Rossi-Lemeni: "Nicola Rossi-Lemeni, Bass." http://www.naxos.com/artistinfo/Nicola_Rossi_Lemeni/5009.htm.

Angela Brown: "Angela Brown, Soprano with a Spellbinding Voice, Biography." http://www.angelambrown.com/bio.html; "Soprano Angela Brown Makes Promising Debut by Mike Silverman of the Associated Press": http://www.showmenews.com/2004/Nov/20041107Ovat018.asp; "Opera Star Angela Brown to Receive Inaugural Alumni Award from African American Arts Institute": http://newsinfo.iu.edu/news/page/normal/2101.html.

Martina Arroyo: "Martina Arroyo: Biography." http://www.martinaarroyo.com/bio.htm.

Margaret Harshaw: "Harshaw, Margaret, Encyclopedia Britannica." http://www.britannica.com/eb/article–9114724.

CHAPTER 6

♪ 𝄞 ♪

Symphony Conductors
The Legacy of Leonard Bernstein in Two Profiles

Now let us turn to two prominent midcareer symphony conductors who also are important educators, following in the tradition of their mentor Leonard Bernstein.

Michael Barrett is the cofounder and artistic director of the New York Festival of Song, cofounder with his wife, Leslie Tomkins, of the Moab Music Festival in Utah, and a past director of the Tisch Center for the Arts at the 92nd Street Y in New York. Since 2003 he has been chief executive general director of the Caramoor Center for Music and the Arts. Barrett first met Leonard Bernstein in 1982, and between 1985 and 1990 served as his assistant conductor with orchestras around the world.

Michael Morgan is director of the Oakland Youth Orchestra as well as the Oakland East Bay Symphony, the Sacramento Philharmonic, and artistic director of Festival Opera in Walnut Creek, California. While a student at the Oberlin College Conservatory of Music, he first met Bernstein during the summer of 1977 at the Berkshire Music Center at Tanglewood, while also studying with Gunther Schuller and Seiji Ozawa. In 1986, along with Michael Barrett, he conducted concerts of the New York Philharmonic under the tutelage of Bernstein. As a member of a generation of African American conductors who came to the fore in the United States in the 1980s and 1990s, he has pioneered a number of innovative educational programs that have attracted minority students to careers in music and acquainted the public with the creative work of nonmainstream composers.

The chapter also highlights the exceptional attributes and continuing legacy of Leonard Bernstein, appropriately named "America's Music Teacher." More than any other musician of his time, the "maestro" was not only the single most important mentor of American orchestra conductors but also the greatest force for educating the public about the joys of music and the importance of the arts in ennobling the human spirit. Through his televised young people's concerts and widely publicized lectures and best-selling books—and the very music he composed (from chamber music and symphonies to the score for "West Side Story")—he shattered the notion that only the classics of Western European music deserved attention.[1]

Michael Barrett

Formative Years

Born in Guam and brought up in California, Michael Barrett had parents who believed that he should "get music" but not necessarily have a career in music. His father played a key role in getting both Michael and his sisters started on musical instruments. As described by Barrett: "My father brought home a piano when I was six years old. He took six lessons on it and learned to play three dopey little tunes. He said, 'See how easy it is, kids?' Then he put my two sisters on the piano, and the next year I got lessons."

That was just the beginning, as several years later he brought home a ten dollar metal clarinet, saying that he always wanted to play the instrument. Shortly thereafter his father purchased a better instrument, giving the "old band instrument" to Michael. Father and son, most evenings, played the clarinet together for two hours. Unlike his less gifted father, Barrett had a natural talent for music, and within two years he was beginning to teach his father how to play, somewhat to his dad's consternation (humorously noted).

In addition to private piano lessons, young Barrett played clarinet in school orchestras. Opportunities began as early as fourth grade and continued throughout junior high in Piedmont, California, and senior high in Guam. The school orchestras played a diverse repertoire from Handel's *Messiah* to Gilbert and Sullivan operettas to big Broadway musicals like *My Fair Lady*.

While he played the clarinet competently, an interesting turn in his musical interests occurred at age fourteen, when the Barrett family moved back to Guam. Michael became seriously interested in the piano, under the inspiration of a "great teacher" from the University of Guam. Young and attractive, the teacher knew Barrett's strengths and weaknesses. The deficiencies were many, as right off she informed him, "We are going to start all over." After that "he never turned back" with regard to being a pianist. Soon he learned discipline, practicing up to six hours a day. Previously, he would often show up to music lessons without preparing, as he could read scores easily.

By age fifteen, Barrett had taken an interest in conducting. Living in the San Francisco Bay Area exposed him to nearby orchestras such as the Oakland Symphony, known for performing the avant-garde music of composers like minimalist Terry Riley.

Conservatory Years and Beyond

Back in the continental United States for undergraduate work, Barrett first studied at the University of California at Berkeley with his piano teacher and professor Harald Logan. Besides rounding out his education with courses in philosophy, art history, and language, he had access to a group of students interested in music. To practice conducting, he would "con everyone he knew" into forming orchestral groups. At the same time, he took conducting lessons with Berkeley music professor Michael Senturia, who is credited with building UC Berkeley's orchestra to the caliber of a professional orchestra.[2]

While an undergraduate, Barrett also met pianist and violist Paul Hersh, a distinguished professor in the San Francisco Conservatory and a member of the famed Lennox Quartet. Barrett found Hersh to be an inspirational teacher, not only for his passionate musical involvement and nondogmatic approach to teaching but also "his clear vision to make something really ring true when you are playing." Barrett considered him to be interpretatively brilliant, "a kind of renaissance man" with a profound knowledge of the Greek classics.

Under the influence of the two teachers, Barrett opted to study piano and conducting at the San Francisco Conservatory, where he completed his undergraduate studies and a master's degree. In reflecting on the value of a conservatory education, Barrett at times is critical, saying that it turned him into a snob initially interested only in highly abstract and mathematical music.[3] At first he was disdainful of American composers like Aaron Copland and conductors like Bernstein who championed Copland's music. He associated Bernstein with Hollywood, white suits, and paparazzi.

That was all to change and take ironic twists when he graduated from the conservatory. He was, like most aspiring conductors, stymied as to how and where he could get a permanent job as a conductor. Not finding work in the San Francisco Bay Area, Barrett went to New York, the epicenter for those wishing to become conductors, largely because of the magnetic attraction of Leonard Bernstein. His colleagues told him, "You have to go study with Leonard Bernstein if you want to become a conductor."

Bernstein as Mentor and "Liberator"

Barrett brought with him to New York the score of Marc Blitzstein's politically charged Depression-era musical *The Cradle Will Rock,* a piece Bernstein conducted while still a student at Harvard. This was to serve as the entrée to Bernstein. A mutual New York friend had arranged for Barrett to come to a Bernstein rehearsal.

Once inside the orchestra hall, Barrett had difficulty finding the rehearsal, ending up behind the double bass section, where he was in a position to view Bernstein's expressive face while conducting.[4] Moreover, "the unbelievable sound" of Sir Edward Elgar's "Enigma Variations" was so beautiful that it came as a "revelation" to Barrett. Bernstein was the "real thing," not some Hollywood stereotypic figure.

After the rehearsal Barrett introduced himself, admitting he was new to New York and needed help in finding a producer for Blitzstein's *Cradle.* Bernstein immediately arranged for his manager to help Barrett, inviting him to attend his conducting class that summer and the following one at the Los Angeles Philharmonic Institute. Here enters the irony: the institute and concerts with the Los Angeles Philharmonic were held in the Hollywood Bowl, exactly the type of glitzy place Barrett had once disdained!

Relationships between Bernstein and his students were close—an intense workshop experience for several weeks. After classes, Bernstein often would invite the students to his living quarters to relax and watch movies, such as *Tristan & Isolde.* Apparently, Bernstein took a particular liking to Barrett, as documented in a PBS film, *Leonard Bernstein: Conductor, Teacher, Composer.*

This was the beginning of a close relationship that would last to the very end of Bernstein's life. Bernstein would become a mentor not only in matters musical but also with regard to Barrett's general outlook on life. The education of Barrett, like that of other protégés, such as composer/pianist Craig Urquhart, involved a broad range of activities and topics. Bernstein introduced his assistants to the *New York Times* crossword puzzles, lectured about the history of the Sistine Chapel and other cultural sites, and urged them to read classical writers such as Plutarch. He even taught Barrett how to write sonnets. According to Barrett, Bernstein "had a compulsion to pass on everything he knew," patiently making sure that whatever knowledge or insights he shared were understood and internalized.

Barrett was not simply a passive receptacle for Bernstein's font of knowledge. On occasion, he would challenge Bernstein to break with routine. One such display of early independence and self-confidence involved rehearsals for a show Barrett was producing on the work of Marc Blitzstein at Alice Tully Hall with a "star-studded" cast, including Bernstein playing the piano and singing.[5] The story goes as follows:

The day of the concert, I remember I came over and I rehearsed him [Bernstein]. I said, okay I am going to make you go through this and get this right, because you always screw up the words. He couldn't believe I had the chutzpah to come to his house and make him run through it, but I said the concert is tonight and you've got to be good. He was impressed that I left no stone unturned. After that he started hiring me, from to time to time, on various projects when he needed an assistant conductor.

Barrett traveled the world with Bernstein, assisting with rehearsals and concerts of some of the most prestigious orchestras, such as the Vienna, Rome, and New York philharmonics.

Barrett described Bernstein, the teacher, as a "liberator" who skillfully helped untie the knots—physical, emotional, and musical—that often prevented young musicians from achieving their potential. Bernstein was masterfully able to "get inside people," and his goal was to enable individuals to have confidence in themselves and find the means of making their unique contributions to the world of music. He wanted musicians to have a deep personal and emotional connection to the music they were playing, a bond that would lead to authentic expression. Bernstein's outlook on music-making was, "Once you learned your music, and you got it in your ear, in your soul, and in your mind—now go out there and reinvent it."

Barrett offers the example of how Bernstein helped him overcome tension, which he describes as "being tied in knots." The situation involved rehearsing a youth orchestra in Fontainebleau, France, for a concert celebrating the centennial anniversary of the birth of legendary teacher Nadia Boulanger. There was a crowd of notables watching the rehearsal, cameras were rolling, and things were not going well with a slow movement of the piece. Barrett was "lurching" about. Bernstein told Barrett that he was too self-conscious, that he needed to relax. "Look at the musicians," he advised. Bernstein's mantra was "Forget about yourself. Go to the musicians and give them what they need. They will direct you to where there is a problem."

Bernstein often said he was conducting his best when he felt as though he "was composing the music on the spot. When it felt spontaneous and fresh." This lesson was passed on to Barrett, who believes that he achieves peak performance when least self-conscious: "Performing for me is a fun exercise. When I feel prepared or I know the music well, I usually forget that the audience is there. It just happens. I get absorbed in the music, and that's the best thing that can happen—that the only thing on your mind is what your next immediate musical goal is ... what's the specific expression you are going for in any given moment."

Preparation is the key to musicians achieving total identification with the music for which they are conduits. As Barrett notes, Bernstein was demanding with the musicians in his orchestras, meticulously going over every aspect of the score to achieve near perfection. Although the musicians might tire, he would not. At the same time, he showed great respect for his musicians. The result was a "synergy of interaction between the maestro and the orchestra." Before live audiences he would show his admiration for the musicians at the most climactic moments of a piece by barely gesturing and quietly encouraging them on—in dramatic contrast to his familiar pyrotechnics. His conducting was so inspiring that even jaded musicians said that he restored their faith in what they were doing. Barrett remembers on one occasion sitting next to the horn section of the New York Philharmonic: "Lenny was there teaching. This old guy said to his stand partner, 'Oh man, this can almost get me to like music again.'"

Carrying on the Tradition

Bernstein's compulsion to teach stimulated a similar drive in his protégés to be educators. Incorporating music education as an integral component of the public school curriculum, however, has been a challenge. Public funding increasingly has gone to the so-called basics of language and mathematics as measured by standardized tests. When I first interviewed Barrett in 1996 at the 92nd Street Y in New York City, he noted that music education had suffered neglect for at least fifteen years. The first programs to be cut were at the primary school level, something he lamented, as he first started playing in a public school orchestra in grade four.

In partial response to this problem, Barrett and his wife, Leslie Tomkins, started the Moab, Utah, musical festival in 1993. He is particularly fond of the festival, which brings as many as thirty-five professional musicians to play concerts over two to three weeks in this small desert town of five thousand. Barrett and Tomkins have transformed a situation in which "there was but one string teacher, teaching forty kids to play violin, cello, and viola in the county's lone high school" into a program whereby students have the opportunity to play with a professional orchestra for the final concert of the festival.

A principal feature of the festival involves "going into the public schools and working with the kids almost every single day." For example, Barrett describes introducing musical instruments to kindergarten classes with twelve children sitting in a circle on the floor. When a cello was brought into one class, the kids responded immediately—"It's so loud!" This response meant it was "good."

Assemblies are held for as many as three hundred, to acquaint students and parents alike with musical offerings. According to Barrett, "It's how we have endeared ourselves to the whole community."

His other commitments have included going every year to the San Francisco Conservatory to conduct Handel's *Messiah* with the student orchestra, and teaching at the Pacific Music Festival (Japan). The festival, founded by Bernstein in 1990, has an institute that attracts approximately 140 students between the ages of eighteen and twenty-six. Their concerts are held in municipal halls in Hokkaido, Osaka, Nagoya, and Tokyo.

Barrett's championing of new music represents a different form of public education. Since 1988, as cofounder and codirector with Steven Blier of the New York Festival of Song (NYFOS), Barrett has launched a series of innovative concerts with the commissioned work of dozens of notable American composers who have enriched the repertoire of American vocal music. In 1995–96, the festival started an Educational Outreach Program to develop future audiences and musicians. The program reaches approximately 450 students in public high schools.[6]

In 2003, Barrett was named chief executive and general director of the Caramoor Center for Music and the Arts, where he oversees the Caramoor International Music Festival. At the center, he has implemented a program characterized by "a wide variety of ambitious music rarely heard in a festival setting covering a wide range of new presentations that attract a diverse audience."[7]

Furthermore, Barrett, in collaboration with Jamie Bernstein Thomas, has been actively involved internationally in the creation of educational programs for symphony orchestras. He is a frequent visitor to the Indiana University School of Music, where he conducts and teaches.

A busy conducting, program management, and teaching schedule allows little time to perform as a pianist. An accomplished soloist, nonetheless, Barrett has recorded numerous compact disks, among them Blitzstein's "Piano Concerto" and the "The Joys of Bernstein."[8]

Philosophy of Teaching

Barrett's philosophy of teaching closely parallels the approach he observed with Bernstein. As an educator, his role is to identify and help overcome the technical and emotional blocks students experience so that they can achieve their potential. This requires individualizing instruction and finding means of putting students at ease: "The great teachers are the ones who say: 'Look, put down your instruments. Let's have a talk.' It's not like: 'No, you're going to do that until you get it right!' It's none of that. It's like: 'You have to be in a very quiet, calm, controlled place or you can't play those big chords in Opus 111 pianissimo because you are tied up in knots.'"

Once at ease, students are more likely to be attuned to the music they are playing: "A musician's job is to really find, in very specific ways, the character of the music he's playing at any time. I think that leads to clear and heartfelt, emotionally strong performances that audiences can respond to." According to Barrett, a musician's ability to express the spirit of a composition takes precedence over technical proficiency.[9]

Michael Morgan

Formative Years

From an early age, Michael Morgan was surrounded by recorded music of all kinds (classical, jazz, rock) and family encouragement for his growing interest in music. As Morgan explained, "While my mother's side of the family had the church musicians, it was my father's purchase of a used piano from a neighbor and his acting as my driver for so many years that really made music study possible." At age eight, he began piano lessons at a once-a-week after-school program. While he attended concerts with his parents, the visual aspects of orchestral conducting caught his attention. At the same time, he began reading Bernstein's popular 1959 book, *The Joy of Music,* which acquainted him with the structural patterns of compositions. By age twelve, Morgan was conducting public school orchestras in Washington, D.C.

In junior high school he had the good luck to benefit from both an exceptional teacher, Hermann Seush, and the opportunity to conduct the school orchestra. Morgan claims he has never encountered another public school teacher as knowledgeable as Seush (who eventually joined the music faculty of the University of the District of Columbia). For starters, he had a great background in all instruments. Taking a serious interest in the talents of Morgan, Seush taught him music theory and history, and the fundamentals of composition (for example, transposition of instruments) that were essential to conducting.

Morgan spent all his spare time studying with Seush, who, in turn seems to have benefited from having such an apt pupil. As with other public school teachers who tutored Morgan, Seush was able to "talk above and beyond what was normally expected of him."

Although Morgan continued with his piano lessons, he "never thought that the world would need another pianist." From an early age, he was set on conducting. While still in junior high school, Morgan rounded up a dozen or more members of his youth orchestra, as well as church congregation members and neighbors, to play in a community orchestra.

In high school, Morgan became the student conductor of the Washington, D.C., Youth Orchestra. The pieces they played were demanding, including, for example, Mahler's 4th and 5th symphonies and the major orchestral works of Beethoven. The orchestra's schedule routinely included European tours.

In high school, Morgan began private lessons with Murray Sidlin, at the time the number three conductor at the National Symphony Orchestra in Washington, D.C.[10] Morgan also studied theory and composition with his high school teachers in their free after-school hours. Totally absorbed with his music lessons, he had little time for anything else, including his regular school subjects. He would easily spend as many as twenty hours a week on his musical pursuits—and even more hours as concerts approached.

Following graduation, Morgan attended the Oberlin College Conservatory of Music. One reason for choosing Oberlin was the opportunity to major in composition. His principal mentor was Robert Baustian, who, according to Morgan, "imposed discipline" on what he was doing. Baustian, furthermore, was supportive of the "tremendous number of ad hoc concerts" he was conducting while at the conservatory.

Meeting Bernstein

The summer between his junior and senior years, Morgan was awarded a fellowship to Tanglewood, where he first encountered Bernstein. As Morgan recalls the meeting, he was scheduled to conduct Beethoven's 7th Symphony in a morning session that had been moved up to 9:30. He did not know if Bernstein would be present, as he was often late. The maestro nevertheless showed up on time. His body language initially suggested that he would rather be anywhere else in the world but there. Once the music began, however, his expression immediately changed to one of "intense concentration." After Morgan finished conducting the first movement of the piece, Bernstein rushed to the stage and placed his left hand with a lit cigarette on Morgan's shoulder, a few inches from his left cheek (a very vivid memory for him), and proceeded to tell the orchestra all the wonderful things Morgan had done with the piece. As Morgan would recall more than twenty years later, he would carry that "gold star moment with him the rest of his life."

Although many wanted to spend as much intimate time as they could with Bernstein, Morgan preferred something else—to place some distance between himself and the maestro. As he noted, when Bernstein focused his attention on you, it was "a lot"—you could be overwhelmed. Morgan believed that he could learn as much about the "mystery of what Bernstein was doing" by observing his movements as he could by specifically asking him to explain his actions. As he noted, you don't stop conductors in the midst of what they are doing. With "phenomenal" musicians like Bernstein, much of what they do is instinctive—a point made earlier, when Bernstein was describing his most inspired conducting.

Bernstein's and Morgan's paths crossed at various points in ensuing years. But it was only after Morgan's 1986 stint with the New York Philharmonic that he saw Bernstein on a regular basis. By that time, Morgan had established a solid reputation as a skillful conductor.

Shortly after graduating from Oberlin, Morgan, in 1980, won the prestigious Hans Swarovsky Competition for conducting. The following year, he was an apprentice conductor at the Buffalo Philharmonic Orchestra under the baton of Julius Rudel (past maestro at the New York City Opera). He went on to become assistant conductor of the Saint Louis Symphony Orchestra, under Leonard Slatkin, followed by a five-year tenure as assistant conductor of the Chicago Symphony Orchestra, under both Sir Georg Solti and Daniel Barenboim. While in Chicago, he also was conductor of the Chicago Youth Symphony Orchestra and the Civic Orchestra of Chicago (the training orchestra of the Chicago Symphony).[11]

In January of 1990, Morgan began his tenure as music director of the Oakland East Bay Symphony. Several years later he became the artistic director and principal conductor of the Oakland Youth Orchestra. Subsequently, he assumed the overall directorship of the Oakland East Bay Orchestra.

Conductor and Educator

As a protégé of Bernstein, Morgan had learned that to be a musician and conductor was simultaneously to be an educator. This meant not only nurturing talented young musicians but also fostering music appreciation in students and adults, particularly among nontraditional audiences. Moreover, Morgan had a special mission to encourage students of color to take up instruments and become competent enough musicians to play in school orchestras, a platform for future careers in music.[12]

To these ends, Morgan started a multifaceted music education program in Oakland and surrounding communities. A key objective is getting primary school students interested in performing. Nine primary schools feed into a public high school with special strengths in music. Youth concerts are organized on a year-long thematic basis: for example, one year will feature music by Latino composers; another year, female composers or unusual instruments (such as the e-flat clarinet, the contrabassoon, and the English horn). On weekends, the youth orchestra may join a local high school jazz band to visit schools and discuss similarities and differences between musical genres.

To make music available to a wider public, the East Bay Orchestra has kept prices at unusually low rates. A season's ticket for up to six concerts could be as low as $100 (in the "rafters"). Opportunities exist for everyone to attend concerts, regardless of ability to pay.

The Field: Opportunities and Constraints

Michael Morgan is one of very few prominent African American orchestra conductors. This list includes James DePriest (conductor of the Oregon Symphony Orchestra), Raymond Harvey (Fresno and Kalamazoo symphony orchestras and the El Paso Opera), and Andre Raphael (Philadelphia Symphony Orchestra). Morgan does not attribute the small number of prominent African American conductors to intentional racism or outright hostility. He believes that the problem is rooted in an historical, unconscious bias in favor of white European males on the part of boards of directors of U.S. symphonies, a prejudice shared by the general public. The bias may be even narrower: European males with a German accent. In 1993, D. Antoinette Hendry, director of the music program of the National Endowment for the Arts, observed, "There's still that old idea that anything other than American is better."[13] Catherine French, president of the American Symphony Orchestra League, found an even greater barrier to African American classical musicians becoming a symphony conductor or music director: "The symphony orchestra, as an institution, was assumed to be an organization for white people."[14]

Paradoxically, European orchestras are now recruiting American conductors, because, according to Morgan, the Europeans know that American conductors are currently as excellently trained as any in the world. Moreover, women have gained entry into the once closed society of conductors.

Remembering Maestro Bernstein

On April 11, 1999, Dean Charles Webb of the Indiana University School of Music held a panel session with Michael Barrett, Michael Morgan, and Craig Urquhart (former assistant conductor) to discuss "Leonard Bernstein, the Teacher." The second among many generations of conductors, they referred to themselves as "Lenny's kids."

There was strong agreement among the panelists with regard to what they had to say about Bernstein and about their own views on conducting and teaching. The first point emphasized was that Bernstein had a passion for teaching and sharing his knowledge. When he founded the Pacific Music Festival, just prior to his death, Bernstein, according to Barrett, "made the statement that he had decided to devote almost all of his time to education."

He was a teacher until the very end. Barrett recalls how he and his wife, Leslie Tomkins, visited Bernstein at his home in New York the last week of his life. On a respirator in his bedroom, Bernstein was unable to join them for dinner. They left the transpositions for a composition Tomkins was working on. One week later, while on the West Coast, Barrett received a call informing him of Bernstein's death. Shortly thereafter, Urquhart called with the same announcement, adding that he had just mailed to Barrett and Tomkins Bernstein's comments on the piece. "For God's sake, change your left hand fingering on.... " As Barrett quipped, "He couldn't stop teaching."

As much as he wished to share his vast knowledge and profound insights, Bernstein was anything but dogmatic. Typical of the most experienced master teachers, he had an ability to identify almost immediately an individual's abilities and problems, and where to go from there: "He was perceptive enough to be able to look at you and experience your work for a few minutes and then be able to just cut to the chase and get to the heart of the matter."[15]

Craig Urquhart, for example, recalled, "When I first met Bernstein in 1976, I sent him some of my academic atonal music and a few tonal songs. He asked me which of the pieces really reflected my soul. Well, it was my tonal music that rang true. So what I learned from him is to have confidence in my creative process, to listen to my voice and to honor it. I hope I have."[16]

As an educator, a principal concern was that his students be fulfilled as individuals, and that they be better human beings. A concern for the well-being of his individual students extended to humanity writ large. This was evident in his various charitable involvements as well as his support of progressive activist organizations such as Amnesty International.

For Bernstein, an intelligently designed music and arts curriculum was essential to a liberal education. In studying the fundamentals of music and the contexts in which music is created, students learn history and philosophy as well as mathematics and other basic subjects. Among his legacies is the GRAMMY Foundation's Leonard Bernstein Center for Learning. The center has developed a model, "Artful Learning," for all levels of public education based on the belief "that the arts and the artistic process reinforce teaching and learning in all subjects." The model is being implemented in schools from New York to California.[17]

Conclusions

A familiar pattern is observed in the biographies of these two prominent midcareer conductors. They enjoyed supportive family environments. Budding talent was recognized and nurtured by exceptional teachers at critical stages in their development as musicians. Especially noteworthy is the role of public school music programs in providing opportunities for the two not only to be instrumentalists but also, more important, actually to experience the role of orchestra conductor. That is one reason why they are so committed to public education. Like their mentor Leonard Bernstein, Michael Barrett and Michael Morgan manifest a total commitment to extending the joys of music making to an ever-expanding circle of audiences in powerful ways.

Notes

1. Here one is reminded of Duke Ellington's quip (frequently reiterated by Peter Schickele): "If it sounds good, it must be good."

2. David Bithell, "Review," *San Francisco Classical Voice*. http://www.sfcv.org/arts_revs/corodamici_4_20_04.php.

3. Barrett offers as an example the post-1950 atonal and rhythmically complex piece of American composer Elliott Carter.

4. As a student in London in the fall of 1959, I had an opportunity to purchase the very last ticket to a Bernstein concert at Royal Festival Hall. The seat, considered less desirable and therefore costing less, was right behind the orchestra, actually also behind the double bass section. To view Bernstein's conducting from the front was truly one of the most memorable musical experiences I have had. The exhilaration was almost enough to lift me off my feet.

5. Barrett already had coproduced, with John Houseman, "The Cradle Will Rock" a couple of years earlier, after returning to New York from Los Angeles.

6. For further information on the New York Festival of Song, see its website http://www.nyfos.org/index.php.

7. "Michael Barrett: Chief Executive and General Director," *Caramoor Center for Music and the Arts*. http://www.caramoor.org/html/biombarrett.htm.

8. The Deutsche Gramophon CD of "The Joys of Bernstein" features Barrett playing solo piano and Bernstein conducting. Other CDs by Barrett include *Lieder* of Robert Schumann with Lorraine Hunt and Kurt Ollmann. For a more complete list of discography, see ibid.; and Michael Barrett website.

9. Here Barrett offered the example of a pianist performing "an added ninth in a certain orchestration leading to this chord" (something apparent to a professional musician, but not to the average audience member).

10. Sidlin's distinguished career includes serving as the director and guest conductor of major orchestras and resident artist/teacher and associate director at the Aspen Music Festival.

11. Information taken from the website "Michael Morgan, Music Director," *Oakland East Bay Symphony*. http://www.oebs.org/page/michael.htm.

12. His educational philosophy, modeled on that of Bernstein, sounds similar to Barrett's. His pedagogy involves "climbing inside his students" to find out what the students need to do differently in order to be better. He emphasizes the unique attributes of each individual.

13. The quotation is from her 1993 article "Making Classical History—African Americans Who Have Become Symphony Orchestra Conductors."

14. Robyn E. Wheeler, in *American Visions*, February–March 1993, available on the Internet at http://www.findarticles.com/p/articles/mi_m1546/is_n1_v8/ai_13560610.

15. Barrett interview of April 10, 1999.

16. Jamie Bonk, "Conversation with Craig Burkhart." http://www.jamiebonk.com/conversations/craig_urquhart.html. The conversation with Bonk is almost identical to the comments made at the April 11, 1999, panel held in Auer Hall, Indiana University School of Music.

17. "Biography: Leonard Bernstein," *Leonard Bernstein*. http://www.leonardbernstein.com/lifeswork/biography/.

Sources

Interviews

Barrett, Michael. Interview by author. New York, March 12, 1996.
———. Interview by author. Bloomington, IN, April 18, 1999.
Morgan, Michael. Interview by author. Bloomington, IN, April 20, 1999.

Panel Discussion

Dean Charles Webb, Michael Barrett, Michael Morgan, and Craig Urquhart. Panel Discussion. Auer Hall, Indiana University School of Music, Bloomington, April 11, 1999.

CHAPTER 7

Modern Dance Masters

What do professional dancers have in common with other peak performers in the arts? How do they differ? A review of the life histories of a select group of modern dance masters (David Parsons, Tina Ramirez, Jennifer Muller, Sylvia Waters, and Moses Pendleton) reveals several strong similarities with the careers of world-class musicians who became master teachers:

- They evidenced a strong interest in their performance field at an early age, an interest that grew into a passionate commitment to a lifelong career.
- Family members as well as school-based programs awakened and nurtured their talents.
- They encountered inspirational teachers early on, teachers who could trace their teaching philosophies and methods back to the founders of their art form.
- They have had successful careers as performers before turning to teaching and establishing their own studios or directing programs in which generations of students have flourished.

These dance masters, however, also differ in several notable ways from the classical musicians featured in this book.[1] First, they—not unlike many of their peers—have studied and performed with many teachers. This pattern contrasts with the more familiar pattern of not studying with more than three significant teachers, each one entering at a major stage of the individual's life cycle: preadolescence, adolescence, and early adulthood.[2]

The reasons for studying and working with numerous teachers reflect characteristics of the performance field of modern dance. As a reaction to the formalistic constraints of late-nineteenth-century European ballet, modern dance can be traced, in the United States, to the 1920s and 1930s (notably to Isadora Duncan, Ruth St. Denis, Martha Graham, and Mary Wigman). It is an evolving art form characterized by experimentation and constant pushing up against the limitations of the humanly possible. Although there have been stellar companies, choreographers, and art directors since that time, there never has been anything equivalent to a European academy of the arts. Constant change characterizes the field.

Performance opportunities, moreover, are often transient. Many jobs last only a few months, for example, with a touring company or, at best, several years with a permanent dance/theater company. Depending on the artistic directors and choreographers with whom dancers are working, dancers will be exposed to differing aesthetic visions and teaching approaches.

In many respects, modern dancers are akin to jazz musicians performing in different ensembles whose founders have their own take on what music making is all about. Similarly, jazz musicians, who receive formal training in the academy in classical music as well as their own field, are not that different from modern dancers, who first study classical ballet. For example, Waters and Muller studied at the Juilliard School, where they necessarily received a strong grounding in all aspects of classical as well as modern music and dance.

But more than just performance opportunities accounts for the multiple apprenticeships they underwent. Being intellectually curious and wishing to expand their repertoire of skills, the profiled dancers eagerly sought out the best teachers and most influential artists of their time: Martha Graham, José Limón, Antony Tudor, Anna Sokolow, Alvin Ailey, and others. As a result of these experiences, they, like so many of their successful colleagues in dance and other creative fields, are eclectic in their views of what constitutes effective teaching. They are able to draw on various dance idioms and traditions (classical, folk, and modern) to achieve their own unique signature in the artistic works they create and the lessons they convey to their students.

Featured Artists

As the focus of this chapter is on similarities and differences across performance fields, only brief biographical sketches will be provided:

- David Parsons has had a distinguished career as a performer, choreographer, teacher, director, and producer. He has created more than sixty works for the Parsons Dance Company as well as choreographed pieces for the Paul Taylor Dance Company (in which he was a past lead dancer), American Ballet Theater, New York Ballet, and the National Ballet Company of Canada, among others. His creations have been performed by the Paris Opera Ballet, Netherlands

Dance Theater, English Dance Ballet, and the Batsheva Dance Company of Israel. Since 1987, when he founded his dance company, Parsons has been a dedicated dance educator in multiple venues.

- Tina Ramirez has made her mark on the national dance stage by founding the Ballet Hispanico, which has introduced American audiences to both traditional as well as Latino-inspired dance forms (Spanish and Latin American). Her various education programs, including "Primeros Pasos," acquaint public school students in the New York City area not only with traditional dance forms but also the cultural contexts that produced them. Her school offers dance education for students from age three up.

- Sylvia Waters, after graduating from the Juilliard School, danced with the Donald McKayle Company, joining the troupe for a seven-month European tour performing Langston Hughes's musical *Black Nativity*. She then spent three and a half years in Paris, where she worked with Paris TV and Michel Descombey, director of the Paris Opera Ballet. She performed with Maurice Béjart's dance company in Brussels as well as in the 1968 Mexico City Olympics. Later that year she returned to New York, where she joined the Alvin Ailey American Dance Theater. After seven years as a dancer, she was asked to assume the directorship of the Alvin Ailey Repertory Ensemble (now ALVIN Ailey II), which prepares talented young dancers for professional careers. For more than thirty years she has been a major force not only in dance education but also in the commissioning and presentation of new works.[3]

- Jennifer Muller is widely considered to have a unique visionary approach to dance performance based on Asian philosophy and innovative use of various art forms. She is not only a choreographer but also a playwright. As the artistic director of Jennifer Muller/The Works since 1974, she has toured internationally with her company, performing various of the more than eighty pieces she has choreographed and for which she has designed lighting, decor, and costumes. She has worked with Keith Jarrett, Naná Vasconcelos, and Yoko Ono among others. Companies that have commissioned her work include The Netherlands Dans Theater, Alvin Ailey, Lyon Opera Ballet, Ballet Contemporaneo, and Ballet Jazz de Montreal. In recognition of her more than thirty-five years of creative teaching, she was chosen as a founding member of the World Arts Council, one of thirty artists in six disciplines.[4]

- Moses Pendleton is best known as the artistic director of the Momix and Pilobolus companies, whose extraordinarily athletic dancers create a mind-bending world of dance-illusion. He came to dance at a later age than most of the other featured artists. His interest in dance arose, when as a student at Dartmouth College in the 1960s, he participated in anti–Vietnam War demonstrations. The protests combined poetry, theater, and dance as new forms of cultural expression. In works such as "Lunar Sea," he uses props, light, shadow, humor, and the human body to create surrealistic images, such as phosphorescent creatures emerging from the sea or bodies seemingly floating in midair.[5] His work is intended both to delight and amaze and also to educate the public into new ways of conceiving the relationship between movement, time, and space—much in the tradition of the most innovative masters of modern as well as classical dance.

Becoming a Dancer

For some of the featured artists, a desire to dance was almost inborn, or certainly a strong inclination developed very early in life. For some, other interests naturally led to studying and then becoming enthralled with dance. The latter is more typical of Parsons and Pendleton.

David Parsons

Parsons came to ballet from an athletic background.[6] He was a gymnast who specialized in trampoline, an exercise routine that gave him an "experience of freedom … being in the air, making shapes." As he reflects: "I didn't realize at the time, but it was dancing. I was putting together routines on the trampoline. I was building my balance and gymnastic skills, and that's basically where I think I started to dance."

His formal training would begin after attending a summer school for the arts, where he met Paul Chambers and Cliff Kerwin, who had worked with Hanya Holm, a dance pioneer, who in turn had studied with Mary Wigman, one of the founders of the field.

He joined a small dance group called the Missouri Dance Theater, which used the Hanya Holm technique.[7] Surprisingly, the technique appeared directly connected to his gymnastics training: "All of a sudden, I was doing double air turns, using double technique, experiencing the strength and resilience of the body. I was introduced to stretching." By the time he moved to New York, at age seventeen, to start a career as a professional dancer, he considered himself to be well prepared in the techniques of one major modern dance master as well as the physical skills required of a gymnast.

Tina Ramirez

A different, and somewhat unusual, set of actors favored Tina Ramirez's career as a dancer growing up in Venezuela: "In Hispanic culture, you start learning how to dance when you're born, because I can remember standing on my father's feet and even though he was pushing me around, I was already dancing at that age."

Her father, who was a bullfighter, further encouraged her dance-related abilities by inviting her to do workouts with him. Bullfighters, like prize fighters, build endurance by doing road running. Even when she was only two or three, she would try to follow behind him. Physicality, which is important for dancers, came early and easy to her.

The theatricality of bullfighting—"the sun shining at 4:00 in the afternoon, it hits those suits, the parading in, the music, the danger, the applause"—as well as the precise, graceful moves of the toreadors, awakened in her an early interest in theater. Then, when she saw classical Spanish dance and the discipline involved, she knew immediately that it was "everything she wanted to be a part of."

As fate would have it, she observed her first dance classes taking her younger sister to lessons, after the family moved to New York City. The classes, in the CBS building on 53rd and Broadway, were taught by Lola Bravo, who had been trained in the Madrid Opera House in classical ballet as well as various Spanish dance forms (classical, flamenco, and folkloric).

Jennifer Muller

As a child, Muller lived in the same household with her mother and grandparents. The mother, who had a degree in theater, directed approximately two hundred local productions in Westchester County, New York.[8] Young Muller's grandparents, however, were "very Victorian"; they kept trying to persuade her to pursue a more traditional career. But, for Jennifer, self-described as a "terribly shy child," acting, art, dancing, and singing in choral and a cappella groups was the means by which she could express herself. Dance eventually "took over because it took so much time." She had started to dance as early as age three, when Norma Liss, a teacher in Westchester, taught her creative dancing: "She was a tree, a color.... It was a very Ducanesque way of being brought into the field of dance. I didn't know there was such a thing as or being only a dancer. It was all about creation." This view of dancing is very much at the heart of Muller's teaching and composing.

A prodigious talent, she created and choreographed her first stage piece in front of an audience at age seven. At ten, she entered the Juilliard Preparatory School, where she studied with Pearl Lang and Alfredo Corvino. She also began lessons with Antony Tudor, with whom she would continue to study at the Juilliard School proper and afterward for a total of eleven years. While still a student at Juilliard she toured in Asia, an experience that played a seminal role in influencing not only her view of dance but also of human relations.

Sylvia Waters

Like so many musicians whose parents were not professional musicians, Sylvia grew up in a family that encouraged her to be musical. Her father had a "wonderful singing voice and had even performed on the radio." Her mother "somehow envisioned piano for [her]." In addition to playing piano, she was actively involved with sports, running track and playing basketball.

Her energies were initially channeled into dance by an "absolutely fascinating" junior high school gym teacher, who "wore a suit and high heels and was a strict disciplinarian." Ms. Maisel, who it may be surmised was a former dancer educator, required the students to have a "little bag sewn to their gym suits" that contained two sets of taps.[9] Two or three times a week, the students would put the taps on the bottom of their sneakers and do time stepping. Hooked on dance, Sylvia attended Ms. Maisel's after-school interpretative dance class, for which students could create and choose their own music.

Other early influences were at work. Waters had a close friend, who showed her exercises from the Martha Graham technique. She also took her piano teacher's two children to dance classes on Saturday, where she watched them go from tap to ballet and acrobatics. At Evander High School, she was given the option of studying dance in lieu of gym for forty-five minutes, five days a week. She benefited from a gifted teacher, who paid close attention to the individual characteristics of her students and used books to acquaint them with the history of dance, while instilling in them respect for the art. She singled out Waters to tell her: "You know, I have the feeling that you really like this and you have a very good jump." She took time, to show her pictures of major dance figures such as Pearl Primus, Katherine Dunham, and Martha Graham.

With her interest in dance enhanced, she and two friends signed up for classes at the New Dance Group, which had been created as part of the Works Progress Administration during the Great Depression. As described by Waters, it was "a haven in the late 1950s for some of the most wonderful artists I had ever seen in my performance life." At the same time, she began attending the New York City Ballet performances of the *Nutcracker* and *Swan Lake,* and taking in modern dance concerts at the YMHA and Hunter College, and seeing, for the first time, Alvin Ailey, who was dancing with Donald McKayle. Waters remembers these times as a period of "personal self-discovery as an adolescent."

When she graduated from high school, Waters's parents encouraged her to attend college. Her father had been a charter member of the Princess Anne Academy, which became the University of Maryland. Although few of the women on her mother's side had further education, all the men had attended college. Higher education was a definite possibility, as Sylvia was a good student, well suited for an academic career.

Serendipity enters here: invited by her closest friend to accompany her to an audition for the Juilliard dance program, Sylvia became entranced by what she observed: "The dancers were all in black, they all had buns, and they all moved and breathed together—it was like church service." What impressed her about the ballet classes was their nonaustere formality that "created a reverence.... It was serious and it was beautiful." So right off, she got an application. Sylvia was accepted at Juilliard with a scholarship.

At Juilliard, Waters studied with Antony Tudor, Alfredo Corvino, and members at the Martha Graham Company.[10] In addition to a summer scholarship at the Martha Graham School, she attended workshops and master classes with well-known dancers and choreographers, including Doris Humphrey, Pearl Primus, and Fiorella Keene. Her career had been launched.

Moses Pendleton

Unlike the other profiled dancers, who grew up in urban environments, Pendleton was the son of a dairy farmer: "My father's dream was to create the perfect Holstein-Freisian show cow, and I was part of that dream." Later, the black and white cows inspired one of Pendleton's dance pieces.

Growing up in Vermont, Moses typically started skiing at an early age. If Parsons describes himself as dancing on the trampoline, Pendleton recalls himself dancing on skies—"It was like the twist." (Skiing is another theme woven into one of his pieces.)

Whether or not it was a skiing injury that led him to a dance class or the desire, as he admits, to get his grade point average up at Dartmouth College is uncertain. Another attraction was the instructor, Alison Chase, whom he considered to be "beautiful and sexy." Another influence on Pendleton's interest in the performance arts was Don Cherry, described as "fantastic, a big mentor of ours." Cherry taught Pendleton and friends "how to improvise, how to drum, how to be musical, and how to be free." An important lesson Cherry taught was how to draw upon one's energy. The relationship between energy and movement is also a theme particularly important in the pedagogical theory and practice of Jennifer Muller.

By his senior year, Pendleton was beginning to evidence signs of unusual creativity, a signature of his later years as a choreographer and dance theater artistic director. His undergraduate major was English romantic poetry. For his senior thesis final examination with his advisor Professor Zach Finch, Pendleton performed Shelly's *Ode to a Skylark,* in, no exaggeration, the Baker Library's Wren Room. In his performance, he re-enacted the various draft stages the poem underwent before its final version. In doing so, Moses hoped to illuminate the poet's creative process: who was Shelly?; could you see him in the series of changing versions of the *Ode to Skylark?* To conclude his performance, Pendleton opened the window of the Wren Room and "dove out of it like a bird." Professor Finch, according to Pendleton, gave him an "A" on the project, as "he had nothing to compare it with." This point concerning the incomparable nature of young Pendleton's creative work aptly applies to his work as a mature artist.

Characteristics of Their Teachers: The Good and Not-So-Good

As the featured dancers had many of the same teachers at various points in their careers, this section summarizes the characteristics of the most prominent ones in a more synthetic way.

In discussing influential teachers in their lives, what most dancers talk about is a particular dance style or technique (basic approaches to movement) associated with the individual. The charismatic personality and awe-inspiring presence of a Martha Graham, José Limón, or Alvin Ailey are not traits that can be easily emulated, if it all; but the way these teachers approached their students, the extent to which they showed respect for their dancers, and the way they corrected mistakes and imparted basic lessons about dance as well as life were pedagogical and philosophical orientations they attempted to follow.

While some teachers can provide valuable technical skills, they may also destroy the self-confidence of their charges by general meanness and cutting remarks. For example, Antony Tudor of the Juilliard School was described by Sylvia Waters as "a very engaging person. He had an amazing eye for dancers and their facility, what they could and should do, what they should expect of themselves, and what he expected of you." As a choreographer, he provided musical dance steps that, according to Waters, "felt good doing them, you didn't feel like you were just doing an exercise. Even at the bar, it all made sense; it was building and layering movement." The exercises he designed not only "warmed up your body, but your temperament and your mind." Other dancers who extolled the valuable lessons Tudor taught also pointed out his downside: how he might not consider a lesson to be successful until someone left in tears.

Tudor also had an enormous influence on Jennifer Muller. From him, she learned "everything I know about phrasing, about subtlety of performance," as well as "awareness of being on stage." Other influential mentors were Louis Horst, Pearl Lang, and Anna Sokolow. Horst, who had been an artistic partner of Martha Graham's in the early years, emphasized the importance of form. He taught her both preclassical and classical forms. He particularly wanted her to be more expressive "dramatically." Muller admits that when she was "vague" in this respect, Horst "was very tough on me." Pearl Lang taught her not only Graham technique but also how to be "professional," which meant, among other things, "never missing a performance or a day of work in her life. I learned to show up—step up to the mark." (Lang, for example, required you to cross the floor in three steps—"That was something you somehow had to do.") From Sokolow (another former student of Graham's), Muller learned "honesty." What this meant is exemplified by the following exchange between Sokolow and her students concerning the "inevitability of movement":

> You would be in one position and she would say, "What would you do next?" And you would try something, and she would say, "No! I don't believe you!" You'd go back and

stay there for another five minutes, try something else, and, "No! I don't believe you!" So I learned the concept of inevitability, of what you have to do, rather than "decorate."

As Tina Ramirez noted, "Each teacher gives you something, if you know how to capture it. In any lesson you can learn." Her very first teacher was Chester Hale, who danced in Anna Pavlova's company. According to Ramirez, "He transformed the way she thought about the human body." Lola Brava, Ramirez's first Spanish dance teacher, used to take her students to Spanish clubs to see shows and also perform.[11] After only a year of lessons, they were given a theatrical experience. Ramirez admired Bravo so much that, at age thirteen, she declared to her, "I want to be like you." When queried by Bravo what that meant, whether she was going to be her competition, Ramirez responded, "No, I just want to teach."

From her next teacher, Alexandra Danilova of the International Dance Studios at Carnegie Hall, she acquired strengthening exercises and musicality. Ana Sokolow, who also was very musical, impressed upon her students the need to do research, read widely, and study music. Moreover, Sokolow, with a Mexican background, imparted an appreciation for the cultural roots of music and movement—something implicitly understood and used by Ramirez, especially in forming her own choreography and dance instruction.

Ramirez describes Carmelita Maracci, with whom she studied in Los Angeles, as a "fabulous dancer, a superb technician who could dance ballet on pointe" as well as perform Spanish dances. In addition to teaching technique, Maracci's classes related the history of dance to that of music in imaginative ways: "For instance, if you did an arabesque, she would say, 'The arabesque comes from the minuet and you have to imagine somebody across the room to whom you are extending your arm,' or she would say, 'And now do an arabesque as if you were standing on top of the world looking down.'"

Dance teachers, not unlike those who teach voice, often attempt to influence the overall well-being of their charges. Maracci, as a case in point, is not described as possessive, although she seems to have cast a spell over Ramirez and her sister (who was attending the same classes). Wishing to extend her students' horizons, Maracci would take them on various cultural and culinary trips. For example, one time she came over to Ramirez in class and said, "Dear, today we are going to lunch at the Farmer's Market." According to Ramirez, "You couldn't say, 'I can't go, Carmelita'— you went to the Farmer's Market, and you went to her home, where she cooked wonderful meals."[12]

Extraordinary acts of generosity are characteristic of many of the profiled teacher/ mentors. The very best teachers find their greatest fulfillment in preparing a generation of professionals who will continue, extend, and further refine an art form or craft. Although Lola Bravo was not particularly close to Ramirez as a young dancer, years later, when Bravo was ready to retire, she called Ramirez to ask her to take over her school. At the time it had about seventy-five pupils. After observing lessons at the school, Ramirez indicated that she needed a trial period of one year to see if she really wanted to accept the responsibility. At year's end, she decided that she loved the job and stayed. Even though Ramirez offered to keep her former teacher's name on the school, that was not Bravo's wish. What Bravo wanted was for Ramirez to continue working with her students, teaching the fundamentals of Spanish dance and the ways it had evolved into new forms of artistic expression. Moreover, Bravo's belief rooted in Spanish culture was that teachers, according to Ramirez, "largely assume the role of the mother to their students—this is why Bravo wanted a woman to continue her legacy." Ramirez has admirably met Bravo's expectations: over the past five decades, she has contributed significantly as performer, artistic director, choreographer, and educator to the evolving field of modern Spanish dance.[13]

Philosophies and Approaches to Teaching and Directing

David Parsons

Parsons credits his teachers with shaping his interpersonal relations and approaches to fostering creativity. Right off he notes that he started as a dancer and choreographer. Although people do not tend to think of choreographers as educators, they are, by their very nature teachers: "When I make up material, I have to keep in mind that the dancer will perform some movements one hundred to two hundred times a year. Any movement done that many times becomes a very important part of teaching the bodies. So, you create a movement that is going to actually shape the muscles of the people you are teaching."

Parsons describes his principal teacher and mentor, Paul Taylor, as a "much harsher teacher, very demanding ... he would raise his voice." Although that did not bother Parsons, it did others. By contrast, Parsons tends to follow the style of his other teachers, Hanya Holm, Cliff Kerwin, and Paul Chambers, who, while teaching technique, were patient:

> They took a real interest in the development of the students, and that is one of the major attributes of a good teacher. You think about the student—not only about what they are like in the classroom but how are they getting along in their lives, because a good teacher will look at all the facets of someone. For example, if someone is shy, I will try to open them up, be a little more boisterous, crack jokes. It is a natural thing to open people up to creativity. Also important are patience and diligence.

When Parsons encounters a promising talent, he very consciously sets out to mentor that person. His goal is to "pass on [his] knowledge and help students get a leg up," as "dance is a very difficult business." Although Taylor was not the best of mentors, Parsons considers himself to have been a keen observer: "I watched everything he did, not just in dance, but how he lived his life as an artist, how he dealt with his off time so that he could be calm when he got back into the studio, how he dealt with the business and political aspects, the fundraising, the boards.... So Paul taught me a lot about the reality, the inner workings and mechanisms of the dance company." These insights are among the lessons Parsons passes on to his protégés.

In reaching out to students who never considered attending a modern or classical dance performance, let alone dance as a career possibility, Parsons is extraordinarily creative and effective. Nurturing creativity means getting students to start asking questions and find the answers on their own—"Let the answers blossom into something else—that's creativity."

He welcomes teaching in challenging places, notably programs and clinics for drug-addicted youths and adults, many of whom have been victims of domestic violence and sexual abuse. When he first attempted to teach dance formally in such contexts, he encountered resistance because "they needed a reason to dance." They also wanted to be actively involved in shaping class dynamics. He engaged the students by making short MTV videos, editing the scenes in the camera accompanied by music selected or created by the students, getting them to interact with one another, and "even to dance without knowing it was dance!" For example, he structured lessons in the following way: "OK, Jump! We are going to do stills now. Pull this person across the floor." By teaching them about television and film, media with which they were more than familiar, he eventually led them to dance—"the beauty of dance and being able to create." The edited videos are left with the students—"It's a finished product of them moving and touching, and it's very interesting." He sometimes might offer as many as three such sessions back to back, each one lasting about seventy-five minutes. The ages of the participants range from twelve to sixty!

Jennifer Muller

Muller, like Parsons, focuses on nurturing the creativity of her students. She has developed an impressively coherent philosophy of education. Muller's comprehensive outlook on teaching and dance derives from the seminal experience of spending a summer touring Japan with the Limón Company, while still a student at Juilliard. Eastern influence is evident in her concern for harmonious development of intra- as well as interpersonal skills and dispositions. Within this framework, she has elaborated a training program called "whole body/creative mind." In various workshops, Muller expounds a theory of multiple functioning areas of the human brain that orient us toward the past, present, and future:

We have the analytical part. We have the intellectual part. We have the mind that helps us get through the day and analyzes our past experiences. We have the nagging mind, which is the terrible mind—one that you have to shut off. But the creative mind is unlike other minds. It is filled with imagination, warmth and has a very different, immediate impulse-oriented relationship to the environment and the world around us.

This part of the brain does not manipulate things. Rather, it is the receptacle for ideas and concepts that stimulate the creative work of not only artists, inventors, and scientists but everyone.

Recalling past teaching experiences, Muller noted that what she most enjoyed was working with the imagination of students: "When I went out into the schools, the first thing I wanted to teach people was that they had inside of themselves this phenomenal thing called the 'creative mind' that gave them self-worth."

The connection to dance resides in showing students how to use their imagination in relation to their bodies, "because so much of it is not just a physical exercise.... So much of our growth as dancers depends on the images that we have about our body. How do we work through a visualization concerning how we want our legs or back to be, or how to create a certain shape? It is a circle—listening to your body and directing your body through your mind and creative imagination."

For Muller, many of the "hang-ups" dancers have may be more psychologically than physically based. For example, dancers who are afraid to release into the ground (a false control issue) are unlikely to be able to *plié* effectively. However, if "you convince them that, in some way it's about their perception more than it is about their legs, they will be able to execute the movement."

Dancers, like many musicians, tend to carry a tremendous amount of tension in their bodies. This is evident, for example, in the discussion of what goes into the teaching of technique to instrumentalists. The Muller technique involves replacing tension with energy, a common theme among dance teachers. As dancers lower their tension, they increase the likelihood of achieving desired moves and personal artistry. A certain amount of tension, however, is necessary—otherwise you end up being a "limp rag."

Essentially, Muller's technique "means you have to fill yourself with the polarity of energy and emptiness." This concept is akin to philosophical principles found in Taoism (the *I-Ching* of balancing opposites) and in ancient martial arts forms such as *Chi Gong* (the basis of *Tai Chi*). According to these traditional Chinese beliefs, the human body consists not only of physical systems (nervous, reproductive, among others) but also an energy system with its source located in the abdomen. Although these notions are generally not recognized by Western medicine, Muller believes them to be an accurate guide to achieving elegant movement with the least expenditure of effort.[14]

In more practical terms, she uses the metaphor of "plumbing":

The more the inside of pipes is crusted up, the less water is going to go through. So the more your muscles are bound up, the less energy is going to move through your body, and, therefore, the less flexibility you have. You can't make large movements. You can't really phrase. You can't really use the floor—all these things that, I think, contribute to the excellence of dance.

This pedagogical philosophy is applied to both professional and nonprofessional dancers. She starts her classes with the students closing their eyes and breathing in a relaxed way.[15] The technique helps students "to drop the day, drop old concepts." The purpose of concentrating on breathing is to have students "enter into the interior":

> I believe that excellent dancing is moving from the inside, not from the exterior, not from the positional aspects, but moving from the energy within the body. Even though you're getting your leg up to your ear and you're doing five turns and you're jumping as high as you can, which, are the signs of a great technique, it is coming from the spirit inside you, and it doesn't feel like muscles moving in the end result. It feels like you're dancing.

For Muller, energy and spirit are at one with the movements. Sensation and imagination are the two indispensable attributes (or "strengths") of successful dancing. Here, too, visualization is critical, as dancers must be able to see themselves and their bodies in relation to space.

There is a synergy between the types of pedagogical approaches and methods that work in both outreach classes to the general public and classes for professional dancers and choreographers. In all her classes, there is an emphasis on students finding their own path to self-discovery and creation. Her approach also emphasizes harmonious relationships and peer support for creative endeavor. The dance works she prefers to choreograph and stage reflect her personal transformation: "The work comes from a respect for individual beings and trying to live a compassionate life, which is the philosophical training I've been involved with since I was eighteen."

The titles and substance of two major outreach programs, Faces of Wonder and Imagine That, appropriately reflect everything Muller has been discussing. The first, Faces, is an awareness program. It involves providing dance demonstrations in the schools, followed by bringing students to a real theater to see a performance with full production value. The event includes a question-and-answer session. The program, which is absolutely free for schools, sends materials to teachers to help them discuss what the students have observed. Faces has been in New York City public schools since the end of the 1970s.

The more recent program, Imagine That, brings dance company members directly into classrooms over an extended period. Muller describes what they do as "teaching nonverbal moves and nonverbal communication." This is the program in which "creative mind exercises" are taught, exercises that initially were developed to teach dancers how to act (something not common at the time).

Reminiscent of her childhood theater background, Muller structures intentional exercises to accomplish specific tasks (for example, walking, sitting, and so forth) in order to spark the students' imagination as well as self-awareness: "They teach you how to be emotionally readable, comfortable in your skin and to have intention, focus ... exercises that help students understand body language." In one exercise, "students quickly form groups that communicate to their peers through dance what's happening in a particular place and time of day—there's a lot of theater to the activities."

After the students have engaged in such activities for several weeks, they are then required to assemble scenarios drawn from their own lives. The dance instructors show them how to make dramatic constructions with a beginning, middle, and end. The course ends with students performing their stories for classmates. For students who previously were reluctant to use their imaginations, to be creative, and the subjects of their own life stories, the activities are empowering. As Muller found her own voice as a dancer, so do many of the students in these dance programs.

Student feedback indicates that the dance classes count among their most enjoyable and meaningful school experiences. Even one chance encounter with dance may have a remarkable impact on an impressionable youth. According to Muller, her early dance partner, Louis Falco, was a Lower East Side city kid, involved in a tough existence: "He walked into the Henry Street Settlement and saw one dance concert and it changed his life."

For those already involved in a dance career, Muller's company offers various programs. The Scholarship Apprentice takes place in the company's studio. Classes, which are offered on a work/study basis, provide an opportunity for dancers to take company classes and, on occasion, to learn the company's repertory. The Emerging Choreographers program encourages, mentors, teaches, and gives opportunities for students, company members, and alumni to develop new pieces. More than forty projects have been created, including fourteen that have been staged for the company's regular New York season at the Joyce Theater. A related program, HATCH, enables emerging as well as established choreographers to show their work in a studio environment with supportive feedback from fellow artists and audiences.[16]

Tina Ramirez

Like Parsons and Muller, Ramirez views her role as dance educator as having two major components: outreach for novices and professional training for individuals pursuing a career. She rightly argues that the best teachers should be instructing beginners, something that often does not occur because the most experienced instructors are assigned to advanced classes. To make dancing come alive for young students, Ramirez advises her teachers to use imaging techniques similar to those discussed by Parsons and Muller. For example, teachers might say, "Stretch your spine to the ceiling and let me see how tall you are going to grow two years from today." As Ramirez notes, "Say that to a six-year-old and they'll show you."

Although initially considering it appropriate to wait until age seven to begin formal dance instruction, Ramirez established a "pretechnical program" for children ages three to six. Her ideas changed when she saw how preballet creative dance could be taught well. The children are taught where dancing takes place in the body, different rates of movement, and "pathways" (straight lines, zigzags, and the like). Students learn "to move on the floor like an amoeba, swim like a fish"—all illustrative of the creative imaging of bodies moving in space in seemingly unbounded ways.

Although Ramirez would very much like those serious about dance to have what she calls an "intellectual/creative approach" to performance, time constraints (inherent in an American educational system that does not follow a conservatory model) require that eventually more emphasis be placed on the learning of technique.[17] She regrets that "you usually learn ballet twice a week, which is never enough." Still, for Ramirez, "the wonderful thing about ballet is that you have to do it over and over again—and you get to perfect it."

An important focus of Ramirez's education program is Spanish dance and culture. In the first year of the program, students take two ballet classes and one Spanish dance class. This, Ramirez believes, is the appropriate time to teach the rather difficult tasks of coordinating castanet playing with dance steps—which can be accomplished within a ten-month period—as "they are young enough to do it without even thinking." She stresses the importance of the castanet exercises in enhancing hand-eye coordination, in addition to developing the child's ear for multilayered rhythms in the music. With Spanish dance, as with ballet, expert teachers are required if students are to acquire "the feeling of dance."

For Ramirez, master teachers are "very rounded in their subject matter." The members of her company, similarly, need to be well grounded in ballet as well as in modern movement. Moreover, they must be able to "move in an ethnic way." She believes that if dancers have only one technique, it doesn't fulfill their needs while limiting career options. Dancers also must learn to be dramatic. The requirements for a full-fledged professional career are such that perhaps only one or two out of one hundred students will be able to succeed. Nevertheless, many of Ramirez's students have gone on to successful careers.[18]

Her broader educational mission involves disseminating the belief that "everyone should dance—that's the first thing." The value of dance is that "if you know something kinetically, you remember it for the rest of your life." Dance, furthermore, "teaches discipline and how to work well with others." All sorts of spatial relationships are learned. The earlier children are taught dance, the more likely it is that important lessons will remain with them the rest of their lives.

To teach an appreciation of the cultural roots and changing nature of Latin American arts forms, Ramirez arranges for dance members and students of her school to go on field trips to neighborhood centers and museums such as El Museo Del Barrio in New York City.[19] She also arranges community performances so that parents can invite their extended family and neighbors to see their children dancing. Although the company does outreach to public schools in and outside of New York, Ramirez would like to do more. As she wistfully notes, "That's all you can do; you can't do all things. I wish I had the money."

Sylvia Waters

Waters has the good fortune to be the director of Alvin Ailey II, a well-endowed company that provides a necessary educational experience for dancers transitioning to professional careers. As director, her responsibilities include selecting who will participate in the dance troupe, determining performance programs and schedules, and commissioning new performance pieces. Over the years, she also has arranged and taught master classes.

Alvin Ailey II, as an apprentice program similar to those of American Ballet Theater and the New York City Ballet, works with dancers between the ages of seventeen and twenty-two. The founder, Alvin Ailey, had "the idea of giving young dancers paid professional experience prior to going out into the real world, a bridge between the classroom and the stage." The performing unit of the school consists of twelve dancers who learn the Ailey repertoire as well as works by emerging and established choreographers. The program is designed to provide opportunities for young artists who are "to learn, to grow, to develop, to really stretch themselves, and to hone their performance abilities." Young artists spend one to three years performing with the company.

The members of the troupe do not audition. Waters selects them after observing them in the education program and various workshops. She looks into the eyes of the potential dancers: "You look for an inner light ... for motivation, a willingness to reveal something about yourself." Someone might have the agility of a world-class gymnast like Nadia Comaneci, but without passion, the dancer can be dull.

Waters coaches her protégés to delve deep into themselves to bring something personal to the pieces they are performing: "You have to make your own story with any dance, no matter how abstract the piece." For example, in a Duke Ellington or Count Basie composition, "A train whistle might signify a freight train coming through a town in the South, the route to a better life in the industrial cities in the North." Another example: To get into the mood for performing *Blues Suite*, famed Ailey dancer Judith Jamison told Waters, "Just think of the saddest thing that has ever happened to you." Waters continues the story: "She was absolutely right because when I did the dance, I just concentrated on that and that translated into the right energy and temperament for the movement."[20]

Other important lessons include encouraging the dancers "to be open, to be receptive" to everything they can learn from the teachers and choreographers in the program. As she tells her students, some choreographers know exactly what they want with regard to movement and music; others want to experiment. So the lesson is that "everyone has a process; and as a dancer, you must learn to bend to that process." When the students graduate from the program they are well prepared to perform in diverse dance traditions, from Broadway to neoclassical—"The range of what they know, the range of information that they have in their bodies is much more."

Typically, Waters is a perfectionist with very high expectations for her dancers. Not a screamer, she does have a strong voice and, if frustrated, will let her anger show. But then, as with so many other talented teachers, the negative feelings are gone. Very much in the tradition of Ailey, Waters emphasizes the importance of a generosity of spirit and a humanism about the entire dance enterprise.

Moses Pendleton

Pendleton is unlike the other profiled dancers/choreographers in two respects: he has not established a school associated with his companies, and he does not engage in systematic outreach to public schools. His educational mission and impact reside in pioneering extraordinarily creative staging of human movement in space. One of the most imaginative company directors and choreographers, Pendleton talks about the "poetics of space" and bringing "energy into space." He uses the latest technologies, combined with just the right music, lighting, costuming, and sets to present images and movements that are absolutely dazzling. At the same time, many of his pieces attempt to tap into an "ancient memory" of the earliest origins of our species. To accomplish this aesthetic, Pendleton draws upon the musical traditions and images of indigenous peoples from around the world.

His dancers must be extraordinarily athletic as well as adept in classical technique. Depending on the piece his dancers may have "to run on all fours like antelope" or gradually change from a caterpillar into a butterfly. This all requires what Pendleton calls "full-body training": "I really try to think of the image and then try to typecast the dancers. . . . I just have to find what they can do. Then I try to make it work. There are no rules. We just try to see if we can't make something honest and naturally built around their abilities." Whatever the abilities of company members, they have, according to Pendleton, "a natural energy and a wonderful coordination."

The adaptability of the dancers makes it easier for Pendleton to receive various commissions. Simultaneously, contemporary composers have, in Momix and Pilobolus, an effective outlet for the visual presentation of cutting-edge music.

Pendleton's roles vary from the overall conception of a new piece to "tweaking and fretting over little details." The night he was interviewed, Pendleton was ready "to strangle the technician" for not coordinating to the exact second the last strains of the CD music with the curtain drop—something he admits no one else would have noticed.

His role as an educator largely resides in refining and extending the language of dance to show what the human body is capable of and how our creative imaginations can connect us to the past, to cultures all around the world, and to an environmentally sustainable future. His companies do occasional outreach to publics who normally would not attend his performances. In 2003, his company put on *Baseball,* a show that reached eighteen thousand public school students in Los Angeles. But, because Pilobolus is a for-profit corporation, "it has to make money." However, as Pendleton wryly quipped, "If American Express [one of his corporate sponsors] would put up the money, we would go and do outreach all day. They should, too."

Changing Nature of the Field

Modern dance is a relatively new performance field when compared with classical ballet, which can be traced back to the Royal Music and Dance Academy founded by Louis XIV in 1661. Despite its more recent origins in the United States and England in the late 1920s, modern dance has evolved internationally to the point that there are now well-established dance techniques, a repertoire of what may be considered "classical" pieces, and a continuous flow of new performance works. The boundaries of the field are ever expanding as it draws upon elements of theater and cutting-edge lighting and staging technologies. Consequently, there have been corresponding changes in the skills required for competent, if not peak, performance. Strong athleticism is but one requirement, along with uniquely graceful technique and individual phrasing of movement.

Notions of appropriate body types also have changed. If in classical ballet there was an ideal model for what a dancer should look like, that is no long the case with modern dance companies. In fact, company directors like Jennifer Muller and Tina Ramirez, for example, definitely prefer a variety of body types so that the individuality of dancers is evident.

With a proliferation of new companies over the past two decades, more career opportunities are available to both choreograph and perform, and innovative outreach programs have engaged many students of all ages and backgrounds.[21] The efforts of the artists featured here are creating appreciative audiences for modern dance while arousing an interest in dance as a career for those who normally would have excluded themselves from such a possibility.

School- and community-based dance programs, like those for instrumental music and other special interests such as chess, can be very effective in turning around otherwise unengaged and even failing students. They develop latent potential and lead to academic success and expanded horizons. These are areas in which public funds would be wisely invested instead of being cut, as current national and state educational policies narrowly focus on a narrow range of skills measured by standardized tests. The careers of these modern dance masters provide ample evidence of how exciting programs in the arts can lead to lives of extraordinary creativity and the cultural enrichment of many.

Conclusions

The five featured artists (David Parsons, Tina Ramirez, Jennifer Muller, Sylvia Waters, and Moses Pendleton) have mastered the performance field of modern dance, while going on to establish and/or run studios and schools that have been turning out competent professionals, commissioning new works, and creating their own dance pieces. While drawing on the legacies of classical technique and the pioneers of their own field, they have extended the realm of what is possible in modern dance. At the same time, they have solidified the core of the field's repertoire and the body of techniques and aesthetic sensibilities that distinguish modern dance from other dance idioms. The goal of these artists, however, is to reach out across boundaries in demonstrating the beauty of human movement in space. The language of dance, like that of music, is universal in the sense that it can effectively join people across numerous divides (national, cultural, even linguistic). As educators these artists have nurtured the talent of many who have gone on to make their own mark on the dance world and extend the joys of dancing to future generations of professionals as well as countless publics.

Notes

1. This pattern contrasts, for example, with the classical Indian subcontinent musicians, who form a ritual bonding with a single lifelong guru.

2. See Benjamin S. Bloom, ed., *Developing Talent in Young People* (New York: Ballantine Books, 1985).

3. Notes taken from Thomas F. DeFrantz, "Sylvia Waters: Biographical Essay," *PBS*. http://www.pbs.org/wnet/freetodance/biographies/waters.html.

4. Notes taken from "Steps on Broadway." http://www.stepsnyc.com/faculty/muller/.

5. See program description for "Lunar Sea" at the Paramount Theater, Charlottesville, VA, January 19, 2007. http://www.theparamount.net/calendar_shows_MomixEdu.aspx.

6. Larry Long, a preeminent modern dance teacher who has directed the Ruth Page Foundation School of Dance in Chicago since 1971, similarly was a gymnast in high school. His ability to do tumbling won him an audition and actually led to his being selected by famed ballet teacher Margaret Craske to dance with the Metropolitan Opera Company. See Gretchen Ward Warren, *The Art of Teaching Ballet: Ten Twentieth-Century Masters* (Gainesville: University of Florida Press, 1996), 142, 146.

7. The Hanya Holm Technique is described as a "lyrical modeling of space and technique." Alvin Ailey was but one of her many students who went on to prominent careers. For further discussion of Hanya Holm, see http://www.answers.com/topic/hanya-holm.

8. Her father, with whom she did not live, had an acting degree from Yale.

9. Sylvia Waters later found out that Ms. Maisel was teaching at Lehman College and directing one of its dance programs.

10. Members of the Martha Graham Company included Mary Hinkson, Helen McGhehee, Ethel Winter, and Bertram Ross.

11. Specifically, Casa Galicia, La Nacional, and El Club Obrero Español.

12. The personal interest that Martha Graham took in her students is revealed by anecdotes recalled by Waters concerning the time she attended Graham's summer school. After lessons, young Ms. Waters and some of her peers earned extra money sewing costumes. Graham would visit them late at night. According to Waters, "There was always high drama with the visits." She would tell the female dancers they must always take off their face: "Your face must always reveal who you are, and it is so important for your forehead to be visible—so you don't have bangs." She would pull their hair back so their bangs would stick up. The students would dutifully respond to these and other recommendations, such as always to wear high heels and always to wear makeup: "Yes, Ms. Graham. Yes, Ms. Graham." On one occasion, to illustrate her ideas about makeup, she applied eyeliner under the students' eyes so that, according to Waters, "We looked like football players, and we were trying not to look at each other." She then said, "There!" followed by a dramatic exit!

13. But these very same dancers also have had to battle with their teachers when they wanted to depart from a particular branch of dance—notably, moving from classical ballet to modern dance, or to a national dance tradition, such as that of Spain. Worse yet is the response of company directors to former protégés moving to form their own companies, which happened when Martinez and her dance partner and lifelong companion, Luis Falco, decided to leave the Limón company.

14. Elegance as well as efficiency is achieved when the minimum amount of effort results in maximum effect. I am indebted to (Doctor of Naturopathy) Graham Montague for these insights.

15. Although Muller credits Doris Humphrey's technique of breathing as providing an initial insight into the mechanics of energy flow, she took this technique in new directions based on her research and her own teaching experiences.

16. Among choreographers who have benefited from the experience by forming their own companies are Pascal Rekoert, Leda Meredith, Young Soon Kim, Ronald K. Brown, Michael Jahoda, and Maria Naidu.

17. There are, of course, exceptions at the pre–higher education level with magnet schools for the performing arts.

18. They include Michael DeLorenzo, Rachel Ticotin, Nancy Ticotin, Leelee Sobieski, Priscilla López, Linda Caceres, and Nelida Tirado.

19. An integral component of Ramirez's public mission is "to expand the technique of Latin dance by using Latin music in new ways—both music and contemporary dance are every changing paradigms."

20. Jamison went on to become artistic director of the Alvin Ailey American Dance Theater after initially retiring from the company to work on Broadway and even create her own company.

21. Although career opportunities have definitely expanded for modern dancers, several of the company directors also noted the difficulty of both opening and maintaining a dance studio and school in urban areas like New York City, where rental costs have skyrocketed and public funding cannot keep pace with the demand for support.

Sources

Interviews

Muller, Jennifer. Interview by Anna Strout. New York, 2003.
Parsons, David. Interview by Anna Strout. New York, July 2002.
Pendleton, Moses. Interview by Anna Strout, New York, fall 2003.
Ramirez, Tina. Interview by Anna Strout. New York, January 15, 2003.
Waters, Sylvia. Interview conducted largely by author. New York, September 28, 2002.

CHAPTER 8

A Cross-Cultural and Cross-National Duo

How do talented musicians from greatly differing cultural backgrounds and musical traditions learn from one another and then go on to make creative contributions to world music? The life stories of two musicians, one from America and the other from Ghana, illustrate how talent combined with determination can overcome obstacles rooted in ascriptive factors of gender and ethnicity. The American, Kay Stonefelt, decided, while in high school, to pursue a professional career as a drummer, despite the odds against a woman percussionist, especially in symphonic orchestras. The Ghanaian is Bernard Woma. A diviner had prophesized at Woma's birth that he would be a xylophone player. By age five, he was a prodigy. They joined forces at key stages in their careers and have since formed a unique pair of musicians teaching and learning from each other while performing different genres of world music so captivating that audiences are induced to clap, stamp feet, and, invariably, get up and dance.[1]

In studying the careers of Stonefelt and Woma, we see how sociocultural contexts shape performance fields: who can teach whom and what roles exist as determined by gender, ethnicity, and geography. We also gain insight into what pedagogies are employed and how they differ across national and regional boundaries.

Kay Stonefelt

Stonefelt did not come from a musical family. Her mother expressly preferred, if Kay was going to have a music-related career, that she be a teacher rather than a performer. However, Kay's interest in performing on the snare drum was keen; and at her high school, other girls played the instrument in the band. Although Stonefelt didn't have private lessons until much later, she did have a band director, Robert Kellogg, who took an interest in her and encouraged her drum playing.

Formative Teachers

After graduating from high school, Stonefelt explored several possibilities before settling on studying at Baldwin-Wallace College in Berea, Ohio. The liberal arts college had a strong music program and on its faculty an outstanding percussionist, Cloyd E. Duff, who, since 1942, had been the principal timpanist of the Cleveland Symphony Orchestra. He was widely considered to be one of the finest musicians in the country on this particular instrument and a master teacher as well.[2]

Cloyd E. Duff. Kay's first significant university teacher was more than an expert technician. In an article, "Timpanist—Musician or Technician?," Duff expressed a comprehensive approach to teaching the instrument: "Musician or merely technician? What shall it be? The choice is yours. There is a tendency today for the timpanist to think too much in terms of flashy technique and not enough in terms of musicianship. After thirty years ... the writer feels well qualified to state that missing in the general field of timpani playing is the knowledge of how to play the timpani with quality tone and resonance."[3]

When Stonefelt arrived at Baldwin-Wallace, she admittedly had little knowledge of the classical repertoire: she had been interested in popular band and theater music, and had acquired nothing in the way of technique or theory. So Duff invited her to attend concerts of the Cleveland Symphony. More than that, he worked on interpretation—getting her to play the timpani as if it were a violin:

> He took me back to square one. My first couple of months, I used to wonder if this guy was really good. Then I really began to get a message from him. He was always very patient. He never pushed. He was very supportive and he would say, "Don't worry. You're doing fine." He formed all my musical ideas early on. I didn't know anything about phrasing. He made me play violin solos on the xylophone and he made me sing them. He got me out of the technique of the *tuck-a-tuck-a tuck-a* on the snare drum and got me into the basics of music.

Importantly, he constantly encouraged her ambitions to play one day in a symphony orchestra, despite the many barriers to a woman playing percussion at that time. Opposition also came from her protective mother. When Stonefelt received her first scholarship to spend a summer at the Aspen Music Festival, she had the band director at Wallace-Baldwin write to her mother saying, "We're not training this person for playing in night clubs. We have a greater plan in mind here, and she needs more exposure. And if she can get a scholarship, she should go."

George Gaber. The scholarship was facilitated by Duff's connections with renowned percussionist George Gaber, who spent summers teaching in Aspen. Prior to joining the Indiana University Music School faculty in 1960, Gaber performed and recorded, throughout the 1940s and 1950s, every imaginable genre of music, working with composers ranging from Gian Carlo Menotti and Duke Ellington to Villa Lobos, Darius Milhaud, and Igor Stravinsky.[4]

Over three summers, Kay studied with Gaber, who was a master of technique and had a very different pedagogical style:

> George Gaber was totally the opposite of Cloyd Duff, as a teacher. He was very specific and more demanding and more technical. You had to play faster and you had to play cleaner. We didn't work on phrasing very much. He really wanted the technical facility—that was his strong point. I can remember going back after the first summer [between her sophomore and junior years] and saying to Mr. Duff, "Oh, we worked out of these books this summer and I learned these scales.... Can't we keep doing these?" He just looked at me and said, "For George Gaber you play scales. For me, you play violin solos."

Further Comparisons. For Stonefelt, the lessons learned from the two were invaluable in rounding out her professional preparation: from Gaber she learned basic technique; from Duff, musicianship. Duff, for Stonefelt, was the more open ended of the two. He was willing to give his students leeway, with the understanding that they eventually would end up in the right place. That was very important for Stonefelt, whom he prophetically told, "Look, it's not going to be easy because there are no women with these jobs, but you just go straight ahead. You're going to get a job. Don't worry." Both Duff and Gaber were continually supportive throughout her formative years as a musician; they used their extensive network of contacts to help procure scholarships, teaching opportunities, entrée to other musicians as mentors, and performance opportunities with orchestras.

Testing the Job Market

After graduating from Baldwin-Wallace, Stonefelt began looking for jobs with symphony orchestras. Knowing that she was unlikely to be invited to an audition, she decided to send her first job application to the New Orleans Symphony Orchestra as K. Handelman, her maiden name. She received an invitation—addressed to "Mr. Handelman." She auditioned, but did not get the job.

Whatever the outcome of that audition, it did prepare her, almost immediately, for her next audition. This time it was with the Baltimore Symphony Orchestra. As she recalls, the audition took place, in New York City, on St. Patrick's Day, and she was the last person to perform. The person in charge of the audition was Herbert

Grossman, the associate conductor of the orchestra. According to Stonefelt: "He really liked the way I played.... He would say, 'I want to hear more. I want to hear more.' So at the end, he said, 'As far as I'm concerned you've got the job. I'm sure the conductor isn't going to go for a woman.' But, he said, 'I'm going to really push and do the best I can and I'll let you know in two weeks.' Two weeks went by and they hired some guy."[5]

Not deterred in her ambitions, Stonefelt decided to return to Aspen with its vibrant musical scene. She was there only a short while when she received a telegram from Duff which said that the Ohio State University music program had a graduate student teaching position open—did she want it? Her reaction: "Did I want it? I thought, 'Great! That's it! I'll go there.'"

She attended the university for one year and one quarter with an assistantship. In the middle of the fall term, she received another telegram, this time reading: "The job is open with Baltimore. Are you still interested?" Tired of graduate school and eager to play music, Kay's response was predictable: "I want to tell you I was out of grad school and at that job." It didn't matter if she had to borrow money to get there, which she did.

During her first season with the Baltimore Symphony, she also continued with her graduate studies at the prestigious Peabody Conservatory of Johns Hopkins University.[6] Because the conservatory accepted all of her graduate work at Ohio State University, she was able to complete a master's degree at Peabody in just one semester.

Freelancing and Advanced Studies

Her tenure as a contract member of the Baltimore Symphony Orchestra was brief. After one season, she married a trumpet player, and they moved to New Orleans, where she taught grade school. Tiring of that situation within a year, the couple moved back to Baltimore for another contract season with the Baltimore Symphony and then to New York City, where Stonefelt freelanced and played occasionally with the Baltimore Symphony. During this period, she performed in more than twenty Broadway and Off-Broadway shows and recorded for television and radio commercials.

The drive continually to be improving one's craft, typical of the artists portrayed in this study, characterized Stonefelt's career at this point to a remarkable extent. While performing with the Baltimore Orchestra and different ensembles, she studied sequentially with the following prominent professional musicians in New York City:

- Phil Kraus, a well-known studio person, on xylophone and other mallet instruments that a professional percussionist needs to know;
- Sonny Igoe, at CBS, for drumset lessons pertinent to Broadway shows and commercials as well as progressive jazz;

- Leigh Howard Stevens, for his innovative approach to marimba playing, which involved, among other things, transposing Bach and other classical composers to the pecularities of the keys of the instrument;
- Rolland Kohlof, timpanist with the New York Philharmonic, to brush up on her timpani work;
- Buster Bailey, also with the New York Philharmonic, further to work on the snare drum symphonic repertoire, as she was doing a lot of commercial work.

In 1982, she went to Indiana University to pursue a doctorate of music in percussion performance. She resumed her studies with George Gaber and then, after he retired, with Gerry Carlyss, who had played with the Philadelphia Symphony Orchestra.

In 1992, the year following the receipt of her doctorate, she received a Fulbright Senior Scholar Grant to travel to Ghana. Typical of Stonefelt's endless curiosity and desire constantly to expand her repertoire, she set out to study performance in the context of the popular arts—"whatever the theatrical setting might be, as opposed to traditional settings . . . I really wanted to study how the approach to *gyil* [a traditiional xylophone of the Dagara people] performance was changing."

Studying with Woma

Kay was introduced to Bernard Woma, solo *gyil* player with the Ghanaian Dance Company and a 1990 Musician of the Year in that country. "Right off," he began instructing her—but that would not be completely accurate, because Woma was left-handed and Stonefelt right-handed.[7] This worked to her advantage, as she was able to place herself across from him on the instrument he was playing and watch his hands—otherwise they would have been side by side.

Accurate observation followed by repetition was the style of teaching and learning employed in their interactions, much in accord with traditional Ghanaian and, more generally, African forms of pedagogy. Woma, typically, does not read music. He was taught the xylophone (*gyil* in his culture) within the mode of oral instruction. Explanation is not offered, not even to children, as compared with the didactic approach familiar to Stonefelt by which the teacher says to the pupil: "You put your left hand there and your right hand here. And you play these keys. No, that's not the way at all." To Kay's initial concern and personal challenge, in Ghana, "You observe and you just play."

She surmises that Woma, as a prodigy, probably started "doodling" with the xylophone when he was about two years old: "But, he started with, let's say, basic tunes. That much he knew: that if he started with the most intricate thing, we'd be lost. So he started with the basic outlines of some songs. But he never said, 'You play this one first, then this one.' He'd just play it and I'd play it."

At first, Stonefelt had difficulty with this style of teaching-learning. When, for example, she didn't do something right, "He'd say 'no'—but he wouldn't say what wasn't right." She would be thinking that the rhythm was wrong, when, in fact, "the melody would be mixed up, or vice versa." As she noted: "There were moments of great frustration on both parts, and even an occasional 'You didn't say that the last time!' You know, that kind of thing which is an inner frustration, an inability on my part either to ask the question right or to hear the answer right or to get what he was telling me or showing me—or an inability on my part to communicate somehow."

The communication problem was not related to Woma's command of English, which is very good. Nor could it be attributed solely to different approaches to teaching and learning. In part it was found in the different terms being used for keys on the xylophone. In all disciplines and performance fields, teachers and learners need a common vocabulary. For example, when Woma talked about the "high end" of the instrument, he was referring to the longest and biggest bars that slope up highest from the ground. When Woma referred to the "low end," he referred to the small bars that slope down:

> There was a great deal of confusion there. I was actually taping my lessons, and I'd have to say to him, "Okay, so you're talking about the big bars," because I thought that six months later I'm not going to know which end was up. So, for me, that was a totally different way of learning. I made up my mind that I was not going to write anything down until I got well into the study. I had to remember songs; and, sometimes, just remembering the title and melodic pattern was difficult.

When asked why she didn't jot down notes, Stonefelt responded: "Because I've always done that. I've always relied on the page and the printed music. I wanted to stretch myself in some other ways." After nine to ten months of instruction, with occasional respites, Stonefelt felt that she was "really putting together things that occurred over and over." She was also beginning to understand how he improvised.

Not only were international students coming to study with Woma, but local children were learning from him as well: "The children wouldn't necessarily come to him for lessons. They would watch him play. And then, when no one was around the instrument, they would go pick up the sticks and start to tap." There was nothing unusual about this, as drumming and xylophones are very much a part of Woma's Dagara cultural group—for example, on Sunday afternoons there frequently are musical performances in recreational areas where people gather to watch and dance.

Although xylophones are widely accessible in public spaces, female percussionists are rare. Normally, the xylophone in Dagara culture and mythology is something that is off limits for women. The reasons will be explained as we turn to the following discussion of the amazing career of Bernard Woma as a prodigy and the cultural context in which he grew up and performs.

Bernard Woma

Bernard Woma was the twenty-eighth or twenty-ninth child of his father, who migrated from Burkina Faso to northern Ghana before Bernard was born. One of Bernard's brothers from one of his father's four wives had been born with his hands balled into a fist. Attempts to open the brother's hands had messed them up. Bernard, similarly, was born with his hands clenched the way a xylophonist would play. As Stonefelt notes, "You are born into a xylophone family. However, in Bernard's case, that wasn't true. His hands were born; he was born with his hands in a fist."

Becoming a "Self-Professional"

Woma's father consulted a spiritual leader in the community who recommended the purchase of both male and female xylophones for the child to play on.[8] Almost simultaneously with his walking at age two, Bernard began playing on an adult-size xylophone that had eighteen keys rather than the smaller fourteen-key instrument for beginners. Even though, according to Woma, his hands were not strong at the time, he was still able to play the traditional recreational as well as funeral music that were integral to everyday village life.

When he was around five or six, a xylophone-maker and teacher in the community agreed to teach Bernard. Young Woma was his teacher's first apprentice who was not immediate family. During the day, Bernard would attend school and do various chores around the family farm. At night, when the community was asleep, Tibo (his mentor) would teach him how to play, the traditions of the instrument, and how to construct one. As Woma describes the familiar relationship: "I took him as my xylophone father"—a lifetime relationship that is also common to many non-Western cultures.

Even before he was ten, Woma was gaining a reputation as a prodigy, frequently invited to play at various social events. Incredibly, he also had earned the status of a "self-professional" musician. As he explains: an aspiring musician must perform for pay three times at a funeral ceremony in which all three categories of appropriate music were played, after each performance offering the money to his blood father. The father in turn would use the money to purchase a guinea fowl or chickens in order to make an offering to "the traditional gods to brighten my way of playing the instrument." At the time of the fourth payment, when a portion of it is returned to the aspiring musician, the person is customarily authorized as a self-professional.

Schooling and Performing

By the time Woma had completed eight years of primary school, xylophone playing had nearly cost him the opportunity to continue with his education: "My father said, 'No, because you are a xylophonist and I don't want you away from the house.' My brother said, 'Hey, this guy is clever. I want him to be in school.'"[9] The compromise arrived at involved the brother committing to help fund Bernard's high school education and the father agreeing to limit his work on the family farm during nonschool hours and vacation periods. After a combined ten years of primary and first-cycle secondary education, Woma attended a two-year vocational school and teacher training college just outside the capital of Accra.

He wasn't able to perform while at school, because, as he explains, "I was in the city ... in a different culture and a different tribe of people who did not understand the music; and I didn't even have my instrument there as a student." So, for two or three years, he did not perform in the metropolitan area.

Vacations, however, were a different story: "I could play when it was school vacation. I went back to the village [Hineteng] to weed on people's farms so that they could pay me and I could pay my school fees. There, I could meet my people from our home town who also came there to do the same job. And we always had xylophones in the evening playing."

After graduating from upper secondary vocational college, Woma took a job as the household caretaker for the manager of a housing and construction bank. On Sundays he would attend neighborhood gatherings of Dagara-language people in and around the city, where music would be played communally: "So every Sunday, you'd see tribal groupings playing their own traditional instruments, dancing, enjoying themselves, drinking [a beer called *pito*]. There were always at least two xylophones available to share. Drummers and other instrumentalists also played."

At that time, the Ghana Dance Ensemble, which is affiliated with the School of Performing Arts of the University of Ghana, was looking for a xylophonist.[10] To these Sunday gatherings, a professor was sent to find the right person. He obviously had heard about Woma, who, once he was located, was offered a job at both the university and with the National Dance Company. The year was 1989. In 1990, the Ministry of Culture selected Woma as the musician of the year, the very first time the award was given to a percussionist.

Performance Field

As with any of the musical instruments and sports featured in *Talent Abounds,* there is an established field of practice with specified roles and performance expectations as to who can do what in a particular cultural context. Consequently, the Ghanaian context conditioned what performance roles existed for Woma. This context further explains Woma's approach to teaching Stonefelt.

Like the rest of Africa, Ghana's diverse cultures compose a dazzling national mosaic. Each component of this totality, however, is not commonly known to the other. The company provided a wonderful opportunity for curious and driven musicians like Woma to learn to communicate in as many musical idioms as possible. He immediately began to teach himself how to play within the traditions of specific ethnic groups. As he noted: "I can mention only the tribal people, not the instruments, because each tribe has about four or five different drums." Within five years, he had learned the drumming traditions of such major language communities as the Akan, Moshi-Dagomba, and the Sisala—in addition to those of his own ethnic group, the Dagara.

Although Woma was the youngest member of the company, he immediately won national recognition. He deflected the possibility of jealousy and resentment on the part of the other nine drummers because of his modest nature: "Well, it depends on how you relate to them. If I were bragging about what I got, they wouldn't be happy with the award. But, I was respecting them and doing what they asked me to do for them, and they were happy to teach me."

His award, in a way, was a confirmation of the role his colleagues played in his education. The award also delighted Woma's xylophone father, Tibo, who, unlike his protégés, had not learned to play in anything but the Dagara tradition. Over time, when Woma returned to his village, he would share his knowledge of other cultural groups with his teacher. Furthermore, he consulted him about such issues as whether or not to teach Kay Stonefelt.

Teaching Women?

In recent years, women have begun to play the xylophone in Dagara society; but for the most part, they must learn how to do so on their own. Woma relates a myth surrounding the instrument that has served as a barrier to women playing it:

> There was a hunter who went into the bush to hunt. He heard a fairy play the xylophone. He was so amazed with the sound that he went back to the village, organized some young men who caught the fairy and threatened to kill him if he did not tell them how to make the xylophone and play it. The fairy told them everything, the taboos and traditions of the whole instrument. After that they killed the fairy. They put the blood on the xylophone.... The men told the women don't cross over the xylophone or don't joke with it because you will menstruate, and your menstruation may continue [without end].[11]

The result of this taboo is that women may only dance and sing to the music of the xylophone. However, if you do see a woman playing a xylophone, according to Woma, "she is considered to be 'gifted from God.'"

To receive approval for Stonefelt to become his student, Woma took her to meet his respected mentor. After she played for him, the teacher said: "Since she wants to know the tradition of the instrument, she can learn it and do whatever she wants to do with the instrument."

Teaching Stonefelt

Over the first year Stonefelt was in Ghana, Woma's principal task was to change her approach to Ghanaian music. She arrived concerned with getting the beat to the music. But that was exactly the opposite of his approach, which was to get the melody first before adding the beat, "because we can add any other beat to it." Not only did Stonefelt have to change her approach to playing the instrument, but Woma had to change his approach to teaching: "As a Westerner she sticks to the beat, and I have to change the policy of my teaching. So that each song I teach her, I have to give her the beat. When she has the beat, she is always all right with the music."

Stonefelt was such an avid learner, wishing to absorb everything she could about the music and its context, that she started to learn Dagara. In turn, she provided Woma with background information on Western musical traditions, although, as he lamented, there was a paucity of Western instruments on which to practice.

Teaching Ghanaians

While adapting his teaching approach to Stonefelt's learning style, Woma also was beginning to experiment with teaching a growing number of Ghanaian adults eager to study with him. Tibo had taught him certain skills with regard to coordinating hand movements in playing the xylophone as well as an ethic of not cheating or taking shortcuts in either performing or teaching. Teaching in an urban setting, however, did not permit prolonged apprenticeships or didactic instruction. Woma, therefore, decided to fashion his own technique of teaching: "I let you get the music first, then I add the tempo second, and add the variations of your hands third."

He contrasts his style of teaching with his mentor's approach: "My xylophone teacher was not particularly a teacher who would take somebody and teach him as a beginner. He was a counselor to me. He was somebody who was helping me, trying to show me how to play."[12]

Since he first met Stonefelt, in 1993, Woma's teaching has evolved to the point that it involves a combination of traditional observation, repetition, and correction with more didactic instruction. In the ensuing years he founded a music school outside of Accra, where he teaches African dance, music, arts, and culture. Although the school attracts international students, its main purpose is "to teach young African children, encouraging them to love their music and dance, because we have to keep our tradition.... [N]ow in the city, you have to encourage the young ones. Otherwise, they just end up watching TV."[13]

In his extensive travel abroad, Woma serves as a cultural ambassador for Ghana, willingly sharing his knowledge with fellow musicians, ethnomusicologists, and general audiences. Since 1994, Woma and Stonefelt have collaborated internationally in performing, lecturing, and giving master classes on the drumming of specific African cultural groups and on African music in general.

Stonefelt as Teacher and Performer

Stonefelt's initial and subsequent visits to Ghana also have left an indelible impression on her own trajectory as a performer and teacher. In addition to her tutelage under Woma, she studied indigenous drumming patterns with another master musician, Francis Kofi; and she taught a course at the University of Ghana at Legon on music of the twentieth century.[14]

The same year as her Fulbright Scholarship to Ghana, Stonefelt joined the State University of New York, Fredonia, where she is currently professor of music. Her philosophy of teaching closely reflects her own experiences as a student and performer. Cognizant of the tremendous pressure on students in music schools and the competitive harshness of the performance world, she attempts to prepare her students in a supportive but realistic way—to be both "positive and truthful because it's a cutthroat business out there." Otherwise, "You're going to bomb." She repeats the advice given to her as a student: "If you're not prepared and you want to take that audition, as your teacher, I would say 'You might get that experience.' If it's a recital, I'm not going to let the recital go on because I don't think you are prepared."

When asked whether she thought that it was possible for individuals to be so innately talented that they did not require any systematic instruction, Stonefelt thought that might be possible in a field like jazz—but that even so-called self-taught musicians like Buddy Rich or Earl Garner and Thelonius Monk had role models whom they could observe and emulate. In a field like classical violin, however, there is a given structure with formalized procedures that required someone like a Gingold to teach a budding Joshua Bell.

In her own case, Stonefelt very candidly admitted that she is not a genius: "For me it was definitely learned, acquired skills." She further noted that she had the right teachers who supported her and cultivated the necessary skills.

This exchange was followed by the question: "So what is your philosophy of teaching?" Her answer: "I think there has to be some discipline in the individual. If an individual is totally undisciplined, I don't know what to say. Maybe they'll come around. Maybe they'll find it. But, you know, just thinking that you're going to wave the magic wand. It doesn't happen. You have to work." Although Stonefelt has encountered "extremely gifted individuals who really don't have to work too hard," those students still need to be committed to their craft and put in the necessary hours in order to succeed.

Apart from not believing in a magic wand, Stonefelt doesn't wish to impose instruction on students: "I think with all these teachers that I had, they laid it out and it was there to take—whereas some of them wanted to throw the paint can over your head and say, 'You have to be in red.'"

Her notion of providing substantial leeway and autonomy resonates with what Stonefelt had to say about her seminal teacher Cloyd Duff with regard to "allowing students to find their space, where they are going to be in the music world.... Not everybody's going to get into a symphony orchestra or the Metropolitan Opera ... and not everyone is going to pay their rent by music. And, yet, they may, at heart, be musicians."

Finally, Stonefelt's career, like that of other master teachers and peak performers, has been characterized by relentless drive, intellectual curiosity, and risk-taking to extend the boundaries of her craft. Since the mid-1990s she has gone on to participate in Renaissance and medieval ensembles, playing a diverse array of instruments, including the hammer dulcimer, a newly acquired skill. Her repertoire further includes musical genres of the Middle East as well as Ugandan and West African drumming styles. Her European repertoire, of late, extends to the early music of Finland.

Conclusions

Although Stonefelt and Woma may not be as internationally prominent as several of the previously profiled artists, each has achieved world-class levels of excellence in their performance fields. Moreover, each has overcome barriers placed in their way, based on gender discrimination and the constraints of poverty and geography. Each was able to transcend those obstacles and become a successful performer and educator with the help of key teacher-mentors at critical stages of their lives. Each continues to strive to excel and share his or her knowledge and joy of music making with new and expanding audiences. Together they are truly phenomenal musicians; and through their interactions, they have enriched the musical traditions from which they came.

Notes

1. Kay Stonefelt and Bernard Woma were among the very first performers to be included in this study, almost immediately following my inaugural interview with Josef Gingold in the last year of his life. The magic of their performance is what captured my attention, plus the facts that Stonefelt was completing her doctoral studies at Indiana University at the time and that Woma had just won the Musician of the Year Award in Ghana.

2. While with the Cleveland Symphony, Duff offered classes not only at Baldwin-Wallace but also at the Oberlin College Conservatory of Music, Western Reserve University, the Cleveland Institute of Music, and the school of the Cleveland Orchestra Blossom Festival.

3. The article can be found on the following website for Cloyd E. Duff: http://members.cox.net/datimp/duffart.html.

4. Gaber had studied at the Juilliard School and the Manhattan School of Music as well as being privately coached on various percussion instruments with David Gusikoff and Karl Glassman, and on the keyboard with Joe Castka. After starting professionally with dance bands and touring the United States with the Ballet Russe De Monte Carlo Orchestra (1937–39), he was timpanist with the Pittsburgh Symphony under Fritz Reiner (1939–43). In 1940, he was chosen by Leopold Stokowski to perform with the All American Youth Orchestra on a South American tour. Information found on the following website of the PAS (Percussive Arts Society), Rebecca Kite, "George Gaber." http://www.pas.org/About/HofDetails.cfm?IFile=gaber. Also see Brady Billihan, "Renowned Percussionist, Retired IU Professor George Gaber Dies," *Herald Times* (Bloomington), November 23, 2007, A1, 7.

5. The discriminatory situations Stonefelt experienced as a woman are reminiscent of what David Baker, as a black musician, felt he would face in applying to symphony orchestras in a period some ten years earlier.

6. George Gaber played an important role in facilitating her admission to the elite institution.

7. When inquiring about the acceptability of Bernard Woma's being a left-handed musician in Ghanaian culture—as in many societies, left-handedness is often harshly discouraged—Stonefelt noted that in the Dagara language the term "lefty" denotes someone who is talented.

8. The difference between the female and male xylophones resides in the number of keys.

9. Woma, in fact, had been such a "clever" student that he had skipped a number of primary school grades.

10. The ensemble is a part of the larger official organization, the National Dance Company.

11. Xylophones are still considered to be inhabited by spirits, and in constructing the instrument rituals are followed to purify it.

12. There was, however, one time when Woma was thirteen years old and had to play a festival xylophone with which he was unacquainted. Tibo specifically explained to him the structure and use of the instrument and how not to play what he called the "odd keys." He also taught him a particular song to which Woma knew the melody but not the words.

13. "An Interview with Bernard Woma and Valerie Naranjo," *Mandera Music*. http://www.mandaramusic.com/recordings/ziemwea6WomaInt.html.

14. Prior to this teaching experience, she had been an associate instructor of percussion at Indiana University, while still a doctoral student rounding out her studies in ethnomusicology and jazz history.

Sources

Interviews

Stonefelt, Kay. Interview by author. Bloomington, IN, July 26, 1994.
Stonefelt, Kay, and Bernard Woma. Interview by author. Bloomington, IN, August 16, 2002.
Woma, Bernard. Interview by author. Bloomington, IN, July 26, 1994.

Websites

Kay Stonefelt: "Kay Stonefelt: Percussion." *SUNY Fredonia*. http://www.fredonia.edu/som/facultybios/Stonefelt.asp.
Cloyd Duff: "Cloyd Duff: Principal Timpani-retired-Cleveland Orchestra." http://members.cox.net/datimp/duffart.html.
George Gaber: Kite, Rebecca. "George Gaber." http://www.pas.org/About/HofDetails.cfm?IFile=gaber.
Bernard Woma: "An Interview with Bernard Woma and Valerie Naranjo." *Mandera Music*. http://www.mandaramusic.com/recordings/ziemwea6WomaInt.html.

CHAPTER 9

Prodigious Talents

Although most of the master teachers and peak performers featured in *Talent Abounds* were interviewed during the mid- to late stages in their careers, the individuals profiled here—Jonathan Biss, Corey Cerovsek, and Sara Caswell—were identified at an early stage and followed as they developed into mature artists.[1] What distinguishes their careers are a set of favorable circumstances matched to natural inclinations. They all have enjoyed very supportive families who encouraged the unfolding of their talents while helping to find appropriate teachers. Each has proceeded through a series of teachers who developed essential skills and progressively refined their musicality. Both Cerovsek and Caswell studied with famed teacher Josef Gingold. Caswell, who now solos as a jazz violinist, also studied with David Baker.

Jonathan Biss

I have followed the career of Jonathan Biss with great interest over the past eleven years. At the time of our first interview, he was sixteen. I was impressed not only with his technical ability as a pianist—he already was garnering critical acclaim for his skilled performance of virtuosic compositions—but also with his articulateness concerning influences on his musical career and approaches to music making.[2] He displayed a level of maturity that was extraordinary. Over a hundred interviews later with leading musicians, teachers, and coaches, Jonathan Biss still stands out as one of the most thoughtful and clearly spoken of artists.

Family Background

Jonathan Biss is the youngest son of two prominent musicians: violinists Paul Biss and Miriam Fried.[3] Prior to meeting with Jonathan, I had interviewed them individually with regard to their beloved teacher and mentor, Josef Gingold, as well as their own thoughts on how best to teach music. Both were adamant that teachers should not impose a particular style on their students in order to create musical clones. Both thought that natural talent, hard work, and motivation are essential ingredients to success as a concertizing artist, and that the teacher's principal role is to cultivate and refine inborn qualities, a belief similarly expressed by Jonathan. Moreover, teachers can provide shortcuts. But, according to Fried, "The more I teach the more I realize that we overestimate ourselves. We are facilitators rather than creators in any sense at all."

In 2002, following his graduation from the Curtis School of Music with a bachelor's degree, Jonathan reflected on the role his parents and teachers had played in his musical development:

> I think that there is no question that an incredible amount of my musical personality comes from the fact that I heard good music from a very early age. I was in a house where a certain value set was represented.... I think there's no question that the amount of music I heard from the time I was born, and the value placed on music, shaped my musical personality to an immensurable degree.... If a person is talented, surrounded by music, and encouraged at home to have a healthy attitude toward it, those are already huge advantages. But none of that will help correct physical problems, which is why good teaching is critical right from the beginning.

Biss did not start playing the piano until age six. His older brother Daniel, a brilliant mathematician discussed in the following chapter, had started the piano a couple years before at the age of seven. According to Biss, "I must have said, 'I want to play the piano, too.'" He thinks that he may even have insisted on piano lessons as early as age four, but his parents decided it was unwise to do so. As he admitted in our first interview, there are serious limitations to what someone that age can do. Moreover, his mother, a world-class soloist, did not begin violin lessons until age eight—"considered old age now"—and something increasingly uncommon with parents pushing their children to start lessons at incredibly young ages.

Progression of Teachers

Karen Taylor. At the appropriate time, his parents found an excellent beginning teacher, Karen Taylor, who headed the Young Pianists Program at Indiana University. She provided young Biss with the "necessary knowledge" while allowing him "to develop naturally." This was stated with the proviso that Taylor may have allowed him to "go his own way" almost too much.

When queried about his strong sense of independence as well as his driving determination to play well, Biss mentioned an incident from the time he was seven. As told to him by his family, he was playing a Debussy composition at a student recital. Although it was not a very easy piece, he had learned to play it properly with access to the pedal. During the performance, the bench must have been higher, because he couldn't reach the pedal: "This was a major disaster for me ... and everyone couldn't believe this little seven-year-old—'What does he care if he reaches the pedal or not?' I don't remember any of this, but I must have cared to some degree about things that I guess not all starting musicians really care about."

Evelyne Brancart and Leon Fleisher. After three years with Taylor, Biss found a teacher who would play a significant role in furthering his development. He first met Evelyne Brancart in Israel, where Jonathan's parents were playing in a musical festival. Brancart, who also was performing in the festival, agreed to work with him over a two-week period. He found Brancart's approach to teaching "amazing," unlike any instruction he had encountered until then.

In a subsequent family visit to Houston, he had an opportunity to take another lesson with Brancart, who was teaching at Rice University. Shortly thereafter, Brancart joined the Indiana University Musical School faculty. She then became Jonathan's teacher over the following six formative years of his life. What he had found "amazing" about Brancart's instruction at the time was the "sophistication with which she dealt with technical and musical problems." Unlike the general instruction provided for beginners, Brancart was following a long-term process of developing skills individually tailored to Biss's specific strengths and weaknesses. As he recalls, her instruction involved "examining what one wanted to do musically, what the musical problems were, and then how to go about achieving it—in a way that was orderly but at the same time completely imaginative. I was immediately 'blown away.'"

During what would have been his junior high and high school years, Biss studied once a week with Brancart and attended her master classes with the seventeen or eighteen other university students that were a formal part of her normal teaching load.[4]

Upon graduating from high school, he reached the decision that it was time to move on and find another teacher. The choice was the Curtis Institute of Music, one of the outstanding conservatories in the world, whose mission is "to train exceptionally gifted young musicians in careers as performing artists on the highest professional level." His teacher was the internationally renowned pianist and teacher Leon Fleisher.[5] As Fleisher's main job was at the Peabody Institute, Jonathan traveled to Baltimore to receive his lessons. He was one of a small group of Curtis students to study with Fleisher, who because of his performance schedule, other demands on his time, and advancing age also limited the number of Peabody students with whom he worked.

In a follow-up interview, after he had graduated from Curtis and was already a full-time solo artist, Biss compared the unique contributions of Brancart and Fleisher to his musical education. Biss had a personal relationship with Brancart. He would occasionally visit her at home, and she would attend all his public performances. Brancart worked on specific skills. She showed him "how to sit and how to hold your hands and how to move, and how to practice—which was very important in helping [him] develop a routine of what [he] would work for." Although not always conscious of specific lessons taught by Brancart, Biss believes that "a lot of [his] very basic value system" of what he strives to achieve and the way he goes about doing this is a result of her instruction, much of it internalized.

Brancart, who had studied with Fleisher over a two-year period at a later stage of her development, has a fascinating personal history. Briefly, she was home schooled until age eleven, when she entered the Belgian music conservatory to study piano, followed by a succession of teachers, many of whom focused on only specific physical habits—for example, use of hands as against the arms—often to the exclusion of her overall development.[6] These experiences shaped her philosophy of teaching, best expressed in the opening comments of our interview: "I have a basic very strong concept of what to teach—what I know that I want to convey. But I find that you don't teach the same way to everybody because the person himself is one of the most important things. And everyone is different."

Taking into account specific needs of each student, she also wishes her pupils to become problem solvers: "I'm not the kind of teacher who tells the students you have to do this and this and this. But, look what's in the music and how are you going to communicate what you see, what you hear, and what you feel."

For Brancart, teaching technical skills is the easiest part of instruction for both children and adults. More difficult is to teach students to "hear music," which is absolutely essential for creating and communicating music to others. In order to "hear" correctly, it is necessary to have an ear that is naturally attuned to music. That is very difficult to teach. Biss, according to Brancart, was "an example of somebody that appeared, very specifically, to need help in one area, which was the physical one." Conversely, he had an innate ear for "the poetry of music." This talent, according to Brancart, can not totally be explained by all the music Jonathan heard in his house, "because there are other kids that were in a house where music was played all the time." As she explains, "When you heard Jonathan play a mazurka when he was ten or eleven, he had the soul of playing mazurka.... He had a sense of how to use time in expressing himself in music. It's something that you cannot teach. I cannot even teach myself timing."

Working on the physical problems, however, was something else. There were occasions when Brancart felt that she was butting heads with Biss, times when he was obstinate about changing certain habits. Beyond technical problems, what Brancart was trying to achieve in Biss's professional as well as personal development was an overall "balance" between his intellectuality, which she considered to be very high, and his emotionality—a balance that she attempts to achieve with all her students (and something that may have been missing in her own education). Biss, himself, admits to occasional "growing pains" with Brancart—whatever the reasons, the turbulence of adolescence or the desire for autonomy in self-expression. In hindsight, he also recognizes how difficult it was "to teach the body very basic things and very difficult to learn listening habits."

By contrast, as Biss notes, Fleisher's "whole philosophy of teaching doesn't involve a personal relationship.... He doesn't believe in taking personal responsibility in the development of the student outside of lessons, but while you are with him in the lesson, his focus on the music and your relationship to it is absolute."

For Biss, Fleisher is one of the most eloquent speakers about music that he knows. Although he is not a "how-to" person—because he wants the students to find their own solutions—he is very specific in terms of illustrating his idea of how one should process information and what needs to be processed.

What Fleisher taught Biss "is a respect for the score, respect for the composition, and idea of performance as a re-creative process rather than a creative one, which is a basic hallmark of the ways he works and thinks." Accomplishing this, however, is more complicated than it sounds. It involves "coming to a mature, sophisticated understanding of what is meaningful in the score and what its details are ... and then developing a relationship with the music so that you can use your body, your mind, and your ears in a way to produce what the music demands."

Lessons with Fleisher were both inspirational as well transformational:

> He's the kind of person who, while you're working on something with him, almost makes you forget about everything else. He has such a vision about music. I think it's an idealism about music. To say that it's wonderful wouldn't be enough; it's somehow spellbinding. You hear it in the playing and also when he teaches he makes you feel it. I think we say about the greatest performers that they transport you into a different world when you listen to them; and he's able to transport you into a different world while you have a lesson with him, which is something that very few people are able to do.

For Biss, while "there are many people who are able to deal with the problems of repertoire and the problems of technique, he's someone who makes you able to focus to an almost unbelievable level when you work with him."[7] This is something that Jonathan believed he needed and that he received in working with Fleisher.

The Role of Teachers

At age sixteen, before leaving Evelyne Brancart and going to study at Curtis with Fleisher, Biss remarked that he "absolutely would not be content not to have a teacher" who would be constantly challenging him and contributing to his growth as a musician. Weighing the relative influence of his teachers, as compared with natural talent and family background in his professional as well as personal development, he had this to say:

> I think that certainly a good teacher for someone my age, for the formative years, is extremely important in developing the student, technique, and musical ideas, but I do believe that one's fundamental musical personality is a very individual thing. And I think that there are a number of things that will not be affected by the teacher no matter how strong a personality the teacher has. I would certainly say that teaching cannot produce; it can improve. And I think that there has to be a major basis [of talent and motivation] before teaching can really be productive.

Musical Personality

The "basis"—so critical to years of dedication to a performance field—existed from an early age. There is no question that Jonathan Biss has a great love for music-making, despite the drudgery of hours of practice that frequently involve repetitious work bordering on boredom.[8] But, as he acknowledges, practice also carries challenges, as well as working on new material, perfecting technique, and plumbing the spirit of the compositions he is working on. In his adolescent years, he admitted to frustrations with the limitations of the piano—something a string person might find bizarre, given the enormous size and scope of the piano. But, speaking on behalf of pianists, he noted that "what it means to have a wonderful technique and be a wonderful pianist is that you can transcend the instrument and somehow create an orchestra on the instrument."

What keeps him going is that he has always adored music: "There may be serious work I don't like on a given day, but I always know that the point will come when the greatest pleasure in the world for me will be working on that music and performing that music."

In common with other virtuoso artists, Biss is a perfectionist. Not paying attention to the reviews of media critics—whether positive, if not superlative (which they often are) or negative (seldom, if ever, the case)—he will pay attention to the comments of colleagues and friends he respects, an increasingly wider circle since moving to New York City after Curtis. No one, however, can be as critical as he is of himself:

> But nothing anyone else could say could be as upsetting to me as if I were unhappy with my playing, which has happened before. It's very difficult, because then you have to go back and look at it honestly and think, "Where were the holes? What did I do wrong?" But you have to know that it will happen. And it's only fair that if we musicians are lucky enough to have something we feel so passionately about and which can bring us such exhilaration, then the reality is that we are also opening ourselves up to self-dissatisfaction, at times severe. Really, it's inevitable, because your playing is the

deepest possible form of self-expression: it's you. What other people have told you and what you've worked on is no longer relevant, it's what you go up there and do.

During a performance, when everything goes well, there is a transcendental state. All the hard work to that point is forgotten. Playing before a live audience, "You have to trust your emotions. You have to know that you know the music and be at peace with yourself and with the music. And when you're stimulated by the audience, when the circumstances are stimulating, it's more than exhilarating."

Even at an early stage in his career as a soloist, Biss was well aware how playing before audiences contributed to his development as a musician. By age twenty-five, following graduation from the Curtis Institute, he had become one of the most accomplished young pianists performing internationally with the most prominent musicians and orchestras to great acclaim.

Performance Career

Following high school graduation, in 1997, Biss immediately signed a contract with ICM (International Creative Management, Inc.), a major booking agency.[9] With a busy schedule of classes at the Curtis Institute and solo engagements, Biss no longer felt a need to enter competitions.[10] His talent, however, did not go unrecognized. In 2002, based on national as well as international nominations, he received a prestigious Avery Fisher Career Grant, followed by an equally significant Gilmore Young Artist Award.[11] In 2003, he was the first American chosen to participate in the BBC's New Generation Award Program.

Among a long list of leading orchestras and world-class musicians with whom he has appeared are the following: the New York String Orchestra led by Jaime Laredo at Carnegie Hall; the New York Philharmonic with Kurt Masur, followed by a joint concert with Isaac Stern in Washington, D.C., for his eightieth birthday celebration; the Pittsburgh Symphony Orchestra conducted by Pinchas Zukerman; and the Staatskapelle Berlin conducted by Daniel Barenboim.[12] He has been an artist in residence on the National Public Radio program "Performance Today," which frequently features his playing, including a duo recital with his mother, Miriam Fried, charmingly replayed on Mothers' Day in 2006.[13]

Typical of the critical praise he has received is the *New York Times*'s review of his 2000 debut performance at the New York Philharmonic under the baton of Kurt Masur. It read: Mr. Biss played with "assurance, intelligence, and vitality." *New York Times* music critic Anthony Tommasini, having heard Biss perform in three different musical settings over a three-year period, observed in his review "New Ways to Conquer New York" that, among various accolades, the best compliment he could pay "Mr. Biss is to report that while walking out of the museum [the Metropolitan] I overheard several groups of people animatedly talking about Beethoven"; Jonathan had played three sonatas as well as the popular "Appassionata." Tommasini, then, went on to observe: "My point is not to trumpet Jonathan Biss as the next big thing but to show how, in his own varied ways, he has already proved himself an accomplished and interesting musician."[14] As a Bloomington music reviewer had noted when Jonathan was just fifteen, "With each passing year ... pianist Jonathan Biss moves further away from the label 'amazing child pianist' and closer to being simply an accomplished pianist who happens to be young."[15]

This fact was evident in the December 2007 Kennedy Center Awards ceremony honoring Leon Fleisher. Biss was the only one among all of Fleisher's renowned students to be selected to perform as a tribute to his former teacher and now colleague. His performance of Beethoven's "Choral Fantasy" was perhaps the crowning achievement to that point of an already distinguished career.

The portrait of Jonathan Biss illustrates how natural talent combined with a supportive family background, hard work, and a love of music making are essential components of a successful career as a performing artist. It is also evident that, at critical stages of his development, appropriate teachers provided the skills, work habits, knowledge, and inspiration that greatly enhanced Biss's uncanny abilities to hear music and interpret it with integrity and passion for its meaning and beauty. The lessons his teachers wished to impart were learned well. There appears to be no limit to how far Jonathan Biss can ascend as a concretizing pianist.

Corey Cerovsek

Considered to be one of the most brilliant students to graduate from the Indiana University School of Music, Corey Cerovsek, by age seventeen, had earned master's degrees in both music and mathematics, and by age eighteen, completed all his doctoral course work. Soon thereafter, Corey was a widely sought after violin soloist. Although music has been at the core of his professional life, his intellectual interests range from mathematics to the philosophy and social contexts of science as well as current public policy issues. He represents to an extraordinary extent the close relationship between music and mathematics frequently found in very gifted individuals. This relationship is explained in great part by Cerovsek's family background.

Family Influences

In 1970, two years before Cerovsek was born, his parents decided to move from Austria to Canada. Typical of his family's interest in music, an upright piano was one of the first objects purchased, possibly even before basic furniture. His sister, who was three years older, started lessons right off. Corey, wishing to emulate her, used to climb up on the piano bench and insisted on playing. At age four, he started lessons. Those did not last long, as he did not like his first teacher. He describes it as a "personality thing." He did not like being "put on display as some cute thing" playing a tune emblazoned, to this day, in his memory—"The Little Roguish Clown." His parents then decided to give him a violin as a Christmas present. As his parents recall, five-year-old Corey ran around the house exclaiming, "Santa brought me a violin!" Years later, he couldn't recall whether he had ever asked for the instrument. But a family tape and school drawing on the refrigerator capture his telling everyone a couple of weeks later, "I want to be a violinist when I grow up."

According to Corey, "There was a division of labor in the family." Corey's mother took classical music singing lessons and also sang folk and popular music around the house. She was a major musical influence on the siblings. With his father, on the other hand, Corey would often discuss mathematics and science when they were together. That was especially the case when he drove Corey to take music theory and history lessons forty-five to sixty minutes away in Vancouver. During this time, the father would sometimes explain calculus and engineering to his son.

Progression of Schools and Teachers

When Corey was twelve, he moved with his family to Indiana.[16] By then Corey had excelled in school, frequently skipping grades and being placed in advanced mathematics and science courses, which he found easy.[17] Not yet thirteen, he entered the Indiana University Music School as a specially admitted junior-year student.[18] The music theory and history lessons he received in Vancouver, following the program of the Royal Conservatory of Music based in Toronto, had prepared him so well that he tested out of a number of the undergraduate music courses.[19] In fact, he achieved the distinction of being the youngest student ever admitted to the music school.

Although Cerovsek was expected to study with Josef Gingold the summer before the academic year began, the maestro was away from Bloomington teaching and performing. To keep himself occupied, Corey spent time with his sister in libraries and local bookstores. He also worked through a calculus textbook he had found in a friend's apartment the previous April when he came to audition with Gingold: "It was going to be my puzzle book fun for the summer." In the fall someone suggested to Cerovsek that he visit the math department. The head of the departmental undergraduate program was sufficiently impressed with the conversation to grant him admission as a third-year student.

Lessons with Gadd, Goldner, and Gingold. Cerovsek came to the attention of Josef Gingold through his principal violin teacher, Charmian Gadd, who had been a student of the maestro. Gadd and her husband, Richard Goldner, who also gave Corey lessons, lived a two-hour drive from Vancouver in Bellingham, Washington. A close personal relationship was formed. Cerovsek would occasionally stay overnight at their home. Gadd, Australian by birth, spent half the year in Sydney. Cerovsek was invited to spend two months in Australia during the winter of 1983. That was when Gadd set about to find the best teacher and school for Corey. She at first considered a conservatory such as Juilliard or Curtis, well-known destinations for very talented young musicians, but decided to call her former mentor instead—something she had never done before.

The spring 1984 audition with Gingold was perfunctory, as his teacher's recommendation had been very strong and Cerovsek already had distinguished himself by age twelve with a Gold Medal with top string marks upon his graduation from the University of Toronto Royal Conservatory of Music. Furthermore, Cerovsek recounts that Gingold actually had remembered him from a master class he had taught in Vancouver, when Corey was seven and sat on his lap. At first Cerovsek doubted this was possible, but after spending time with Gingold, he realized that the maestro had "a prodigious memory for students."

Before coming to Gadd and Goldner, Cerovsek had studied with two other violin teachers. The first he describes as extremely stern (a "shouter"). By contrast, the second was a very nice person but undemanding, giving students a "free ride" by not providing fundamental technique. Gadd, who had been a judge at a local competition involving Corey, called his parents aside to express concern that, although talented, he was not being taught properly because his playing was "completely wild and instinctive."

The move to instruction with Gadd and Goldner was beneficial. Right off, they gave him etudes and worked on technique. As with his parents, there was a "charming division of labor." Goldner taught Cerovsek technique in the morning; in the afternoon, Gadd would concentrate on "music matters." Jokingly, Corey noted that there was a "good cop" (Gadd), "bad cop" (Goldner) routine. Overall, Cerovsek describes the relationship among them as "very loving," and the comfortable situation he felt well prepared him for his studies with Gingold, whom Corey described as being famous for being so personable.

What Gingold was able to do was to take Cerovsek from where he was (with a solid grounding in technique) and introduce him to "the expressive and emotional aspects of music." Whereas Gadd was "relatively dispassionate" in her approach to music, Gingold was "heart and soul given to music." The "warmth and tactile approach" of Gingold's playing—"how his personality expressed itself in music"—had a dramatic impact on Cerovsek's views in ways that he could not previously have imagined. Initially, as Cerovsek recounts, expressive tools may have started out as physical matters—for example, how to slide his hand or place a finger on the instrument; but "somehow through the years magically that changes from a physical act to a communicative one filled with meaning—something you feel deeply."

Cerovsek also was grateful to Gingold for not following "a slave-driving tradition." Unlike many teachers and coaches who "strive for the last 1 percent and the importance of spending hours to get everything perfectly in place," for Gingold "the communicative impact was more important than note perfection." Moreover, Gingold supported Cerovsek's interests outside music—even though, as he admits, Gingold may not have really understood what he did. That was greatly appreciated by Cerovsek, who now has "a better sense of putting music in context for [himself] in terms of other interests," rather than seeking "absolute perfectionism and special-ization" as a musician.

Personality

Cerovsek's ability to successfully balance competing demands from different fields of endeavor does not preclude his becoming intensively, if not sometimes compulsively, involved in pursuing specific interests that capture his attention. Reflecting on his childhood, he notes that he frequently got into trouble for not sticking to the task at hand. Teachers would assign him a research project to complete in the library. Instead, as he admits, he "would get lost in an encyclopedia and emerge hours later on a completely different topic."

Despite an active performance career as an adult, he continues to have "the time of his life reading huge amounts and wandering into all sorts of fields that [he's] not supposed to be in with a vague tinge of guilt." He reasons that "respectable people have well-defined research projects—and yet as long as I can get away with it, I might as well. I have a musical career that essentially supports me, and then my passion on the side is to take in anything that intrigues me." At times he has to reassure himself that it's all right "not to eat and breathe music" because he grew up around people who saw making classical music as an "almost divine calling." Experience taught him that not everyone on the planet has the same view of the significance of his musical repertoire, and that playing classical music, far from being a sacrosanct activity, is not an "absolutely superior form of expression." Although humbling, Cerovsek has ultimately found this to be "liberating because somehow it reduces the pressure." A performance career, however, is still what anchors his everyday existence.

Performance Career

Cerovsek started concertizing at an early age, when he was nine or ten. During his teens, he performed approximately a dozen times a year. As he explains, those per-formances were mostly "a not-for-profit thing" and were arranged by a "manager of sorts in Canada." At age nineteen, he was invited to join the roster of a professional management agency in New York. With an appreciable increase in his performance schedule, he progressively saw less of Gingold. However, with Bloomington as his home, Cerovsek would return to consult with Gingold on mostly musical matters until Gingold's death in January 1995. At the time of the signing of Cerovsek's management agreement, for example, Gingold came to dinner at Corey's parents' house to discuss the nature of the contract and a performance career.

Since the late 1980s, Cerovsek has performed around the world with orchestras ranging from the Boston Symphony to the Melbourne and Sydney symphonies. Among the distinguished conductors with whom he has worked are Zubin Mehta, Charles Dutoit, and Michael Tilson Thomas.[20] He has appeared twice on NBC's *Tonight Show* with Johnny Carson and Jay Leno, on the *David Frost Show* in England, on the PBS special *Musical Encounters*, and on CBS's *Sunday Morning*. His recordings on the Delos label include the critically acclaimed "Corey Cerovsek Plays Wieniawski," accompanied on the piano by his sister Katja Cerovsek, and two releases with the Moscow Chamber Orchestra ("Mozart Adagios" and "Russian Soul").[21]

Teaching

Corey Cerovsek offered his first master classes when he was twenty-one. At first shy about doing so, he was able to draw inspiration from the lessons he received from Gingold, whose approach to students was very positive and not overly directive. Cerovsek, for example, recalls how Gingold encouraged him to try new ways of interpreting a composition. Although Cerovsek was sure that Gingold had "seen every permutation of any given piece," the maestro would say, "Oh, that's a great idea—can I use that?" He never said, "This is the way you have to do it." He would say, "Here is a suggestion," and "Try this."[22] Cerovsek describes this approach as a "generally cheerful interactive method" that he attempts to integrate into his own teaching. Another characteristic of Gingold, requiring students to find their own solutions, also appeals to Cerovsek. He believes, along with Gingold, that working pieces to death, in the long run, is not as useful as covering a large repertoire— "It's like casting seeds which take years to germinate"—that can be drawn upon in later years.

Putting the Pieces Together

With regard to seeds planted early in his education, Cerovsek recalls the impact of a fourth grade teacher, Mrs. Nielsen, who believed in giving free rein to the imagination of children. The teacher's warm personal engagement and individualization of instruction, which subsequent teachers and education programs provided for the gifted musician and mathematician, were building blocks of a remarkable career. They are all of a piece with other influences, especially family ones, nurturing his talent and facilitating its expression in unique ways. The same set of fortuitous factors helped shape Jonathan Biss's development as it did Sara Caswell's, who successfully bridges the worlds of classical and jazz virtuoso violin playing.

Sara Caswell

Family Influence

Like Biss, Sara and her sister Rachel come from an extraordinarily musical family. Their mother, Judith Caswell, an adept organist with a Ph.D. in musicology, could have had a career as a university music professor. Instead, she decided to stay at home "to nurture [them] from the cradle."[23] Her father, the late Austin Caswell, was a musicology professor at Indiana University.[24] Although he played the piano, he was primarily a vocalist. From an early age, Judith Caswell would sit next to both Sara and Rachel and play along with them on the piano. Rachel, who initially studied cello, eventually switched to becoming a jazz vocalist. Sara, although dabbling at the piano, inclined more toward the violin. She began lessons on the instrument at age five and a half.

According to Sara, her mother "went to all my lessons to assure me I wasn't alone in learning to play the violin.... She said, 'I'm going to learn right along with my kid.'"[25] She also would make up piano accompaniments to the pieces Sara was playing: "She would write out each piece in decorative colors in order to make them more fun to learn.... As I grew older, she would continue to accompany me on concerti and sonatas while suggesting musical ideas to consider. She was one of my most influential teachers."

Progression of Teachers

Family support was bolstered by a progression of excellent teachers associated with the Indiana University String Academy, Rebecca Henry and Mimi Zweig. She also worked with renowned early music violinist Stanley Ritchie on Baroque violin. Sara then studied with both Josef Gingold (classical violin) and David Baker (jazz improvisation). An outstanding high school music educator, Janis Stockhouse, contributed in significant ways to Sara's development as a performance artist. Another influential instructor was Henryk Kowalski, who was her university-level professor of classical violin in the years following the death of Gingold in early 1995.

Henry and Zweig. For the first two and a half years, Sara studied with Rebecca Henry, who was "known for her excellence in teaching beginners." Henry provided young Caswell with a solid foundation. That included "having a love for music and wanting to learn as much as possible." She instilled in Caswell "the idea that if I wanted to do something with music, I had to set goals for myself and progress forward."

The next logical step was to move onto Mimi Zweig, the principal force in the String Academy and a renowned teacher whose former pupils include Joshua Bell among a host of career musicians. Zweig's approach to violin instruction involves engaging "the physical, the psychological, and the musical abilities of the player." For

Zweig, "the fundamental principles of violin teaching are based on nurturing natural physical motions in a nonjudgmental environment" that "allows the development of a facile and secure technique that gives the performer the freedom to play with musical sensitivity and confidence."[26] According to Caswell, what she received from Zweig was "a solid technical background." Zweig further exposed her to an expanded repertoire while providing her with plentiful performance opportunities to exhibit her skills and be aware of what was involved in a career as a soloist. Sara studied with Zweig for four years, before being referred to Gingold at age twelve.

Gingold. In describing what it was like to study with Gingold, Caswell's list of superlatives attests not only to his incredible musical gifts and teaching ability but also to his qualities as a loving human being who inspired his students in ways no other teacher could. Sara's words merit repeating, even as they echo the memories of his other profiled students: "I'm almost at a loss for words when talking about Mr. Gingold because working with him was such an incredible experience. He was a wonderful man ... a human being who genuinely cared about people. His musical skills were incomparable. Every note he played came directly from the heart ... and that was just so influential in my playing."

Gingold would challenge her technically as well as emotionally. For example, he would encourage her to "look at a piece from another angle, to tell a story through the music."

Baker. At age eight, Caswell began to study improvisation with jazz master David Baker. According to Sara, "My parents wanted me to have a broader musical education. So, although I focused mainly on classical violin, I studied Baroque violin and jazz improvisation as well."

Baker's genius as a teacher was in recognizing how to build on Sara's natural talents and her initial violin instruction based on the Suzuki method of children playing by ear: "Professor Baker opted to build my jazz vocabulary and improvisational approach—on an aural rather than theoretical foundation, given that I had developed strong ears from my classical violin training. This was done through call and response exercises, solo transcriptions, and ear-training etudes." Once Baker was assured that Caswell had a firm, albeit intuitive, grasp of basic jazz principles, he provided her with a more theoretical approach, teaching her specific color scales and substitutions on chord changes.

She studied regularly with Baker for three or four years and then only occasionally, when his busy performance schedule permitted a lesson. Later on, as an undergraduate music school student, she enrolled in various courses with him and performed as a featured soloist with the big jazz ensemble he directed.

When I interviewed her during her junior year, as a double major in violin performance and jazz studies, she was taking a class that consisted of Baker's pointing out attributes of a good arrangement and then assigning students to work on a piece: "Although he teaches a class of twenty people, he knows how to address individual students' needs, mine being no exception."

Stockhouse. Prior to her university studies, Caswell pursued a normal four-year high school degree. During that period, she came under the influence of Janis Stockhouse. For more than two decades, Stockhouse (a former protégé of Dominic Spera) has directed one of the finest high school band and jazz programs in the United States.[27] She incorporated Sara into various "projects" that not only taught her social skills (how to interact with people from diverse backgrounds her own age) but also expanded her repertoire. To stretch Caswell's arranging abilities, Stockhouse would give her oboe and English horn parts to transpose to the violin. Stockhouse further encouraged her to play in the pit orchestra and basketball pep band. These experiences, both personal and professional, may have contributed to Caswell's overcoming her inhibitions about playing jazz: "The idea of standing in front of people to improvise was scary, especially since I was playing an instrument not often associated with jazz. By the time I was a sophomore in high school, however, I began to overcome this fear and approach improvisation with more confidence."

Personality and Performance Field

Whatever qualms Sara Caswell may have had about performing as a jazz violinist, and being female as well, are in the distant past. Aware that the field of jazz has been dominated by men has not deterred her in the least. Prior to graduating from Indiana University and going on to a master's degree at the Manhattan School of Music, she had this response to the challenges before her: "You really can't be shy. You have to go out there and say, 'Look, I know this as much as you do. I can fiddle just as well as you can. So don't push me down because I'm female and because I'm playing an odd instrument.'"

Seven years later, in 2006, her attitude was this: "One shouldn't apologize for what one chooses to do as a performing artist. When I walk on stage, I do so with the belief that I have something to share with the audience that transcends our differences."

Her self-confidence and ability to cope with criticism also was revealed in a comment about her university classical violin teacher, Henryk Kowalski. Although he was very direct in telling her what she did right and wrong, Caswell observed that this was exactly what she needed at the time: "I need to have a teacher who is frank with me, who says what needs to be said in order to help me achieve my goals."

Caswell's willingness constantly to learn and extend the violin's expressive qualities as a jazz instrument are exemplified by the role models she sought to emulate while an undergraduate student. Among them were Baker (first a trombonist, then a cellist) and Pat Harbison (trumpeter). As she confessed, "Professor Baker encouraged me to draw influence from jazz masters on all instruments. I have applied this approach to my search for those with whom I study."

Her openness to crossing the boundaries between musical genres attracted criticism from those who thought her interest in jazz would detract from her development as a classical musical violinist. Faculty members approached violinist Kowalski to ask him: "Why are you letting Sara waste her time playing jazz?" At the same time, jazz performance opportunities were presenting themselves that were too valuable to ignore. Undeterred by the criticism of fellow classical musicians, Caswell was resolute that her career direction was to play both classical and jazz music. Her unique combination of skills and talent has enabled her to achieve critical acclaim in both fields.

Performance Career

By the time she graduated with a master's degree in jazz violin from the Manhattan School of Music, Sara Caswell had won dozens of competitive awards as a classical and jazz violinist, including, while still an undergraduate student, five *Down Beat* awards in the two genres. She had performed with other major artists such as guitarist Charlie Byrd, violinist Claude Williams, and the Turtle Island String Quartet. Her debut CD, "But Beautiful," was featured in the "Encore" section of the April 2005 issue of *Strings Magazine* and received these independent accolades:

- Her instrument's voice takes listeners on a thrilling musical journey that is more than a simple treat; it is a sheer delight (Veronica Timpanelli, *Jazz Review*).[28]
- Caswell, who plays world-class violin, is at home on either side of the classical/jazz fence.... [She] is stellar and subtle with a technique that is formidable without being showy.... What a gift for improvisation (Bill Falconer, *Jazz Review*).[29]

As the Falconer review pointed out, Caswell's gift for improvisation reflected not only her training in jazz but also her background in Baroque music with "its emphasis on improvisation." Sara had prepared well to achieve her ambitious goals.

Comparing and Summing Up

Like Corey Cerovsek, Sara Caswell crosses boundaries and performs successfully in different fields. For Cerovsek, however, those fields are music and mathematics. Like Jonathan Biss, Caswell's identity is firmly rooted in the world of music. Biss, Cerovsek, and Caswell are but three exceptionally gifted individuals who could have been featured in this book. They were chosen for what they exemplify with regard to the beneficial synergy of a set of very favorable natural attributes, environmental influences, and educational interventions. In all three cases, it would be difficult to separate natural talent from the nurturing influences of family and a succession of teachers who progressively built a foundation of requisite technical skills, cultivated a love of music, refined expressive abilities, deepened understanding of the interpretative as well as creative roles of artists, and acquainted prodigious, but novice, talent with the nature of their respective performance fields. The nature of the field of mathematics is examined in the next chapter.

Notes

1. In 2007, Biss and Caswell were in their mid-twenties and Cerovsek in his midthirties.

2. Among the virtuosic compositions was the *Kreisleriana*, Op. 16, by Robert Schumann.

3. They are now members of the New England Conservatory of Music in Boston. It also should be noted that Jonathan's grandmother, Raya Garbousova, was "one of the first well-known female cellists (for whom Samuel Barber composed his Cello Concerto); cited from "Jonathan Biss." http://www.jonathanbiss.com/home/.

4. Biss believes that Brancart, at that time, had a student who was even a couple of years younger than he. But, as he recalls, he never saw her because she lived three hours away from Bloomington. When queried if he felt intimidated by playing before older students, he said that really that was not the case. The master classes were under the control of Brancart with very little interaction among the students. Although he had very little in common with the other students, because of age differences, he recalls his classmates as being friendly toward him.

5. Fleisher was a child prodigy (who had had his first public recital at age eight and made his public debut with the New York Philharmonic at sixteen). In midcareer he suffered a debilitating ailment of the right hand, prompting the development of a musical repertoire for the left hand.

6. The family background and musical career of Brancart is a story in itself, but one that will not be told here.

7. As Biss cautioned in a March 8, 1999, interview, "He's not the right teacher for a person who is at a loss in how they need to develop and who needs to be told exactly what basic problems they have and what they need to be fixing before they move on." This comment recalls a point made in Chapter 1, by his violinist and conductor father Paul Biss, about the difference between Ivan Galamian, who was a "Mr. Fix-It," and Josef Gingold, who inspired musicality and overall personal as well as professional development in his students.

8. At age seventeen, when interviewed by the local newspaper as one of nine Bloomington students to be honored as a National Merit Scholarship semifinalist, Biss provided this self-description: "It's music that makes me who I am." Laura Lane, "Nine Scholars Recognized," *Herald-Tribune*, November 15, 1996, C 1–2.

9. The agency prides itself on representing "exceptional creative ability that sets the standard for excellence in their respective fields." See the ICM website: http://www.icmtalent.com/index.html.

10. While in high school Biss did enter two major local/regional competitions. He won the Indianapolis Symphony and Bloomington Symphony concerto competitions, which involved subsequent performances of the Mendelssohn Piano Concerto in G Minor with both orchestras in the spring of 1994.

11. Other honors have included the Wolf Trap's House Debut Artist Award, the Lincoln Center's Martin E. Segal Award, the Borletti-Buttoni Trust Award, and the Andrew Wolf Memorial Chamber Music Award.

12. Other orchestras have included the Boston, Chicago, Munich, Philadelphia, San Francisco, and Vancouver, as well as the BBC Symphony and BBC Philharmonic with such prominent conductors as Charles Dutoit, James Levine, and Neville Mariner. He gave his New York recital debut in the 92nd Street Y's Tisch Center for the Arts in 2000.

13. He has performed chamber music concerts with Fried in various venues, including the Metropolitan Museum of Art and the 92nd Street Y in New York City, as well as the Kennedy Center in Washington, D.C., and various venues in St. Paul, Boston, La Jolla, and many other cities.

14. Anthony Tommasini, "New Ways to Conquer New York," *New York Times*, November 24, 2002, AR 33.

15. Kathleen Mills, "Young Pianist to Make Liszt for Camerata," *Herald-Tribune*, October 17, 1994, D 8.

16. According to Cerovsek, "Once Indiana was in our sights as the best place for me to continue my studies, my teachers Gadd and Goldner urged my father to seek work in Indianapolis. When he was offered an attractive job there, it certainly made my studying [at IU] more practicable."

17. The British Columbia school system as well as the individual schools he studied in (a Montessori school for kindergarten) were flexible and supportive enough to accommodate his unique combination of talents. For example, he was allowed to complete his high school requirements by correspondence from Indiana.

18. Although he was granted "special admission," Cerovsek followed the same coursework as other students.

19. For further information on the education programs of the Royal Conservatory of Music (Toronto), see its website: http://www.rcmusic.ca/flash/Intro/playintro.html.

20. In recital, he has appeared regularly at the Kennedy Center (Washington, D.C.), the Isabella Stewart Gardner Museum (Boston), Lincoln Center's Walter Reade Theatre and the Frick Collection (in New York), the Place des Arts (Montréal), Wigmore Hall (London), the Cemal Resit Rey Concert Hall (Istanbul), and the Théâtre du Châlet (Paris). As an avid chamber musician, he has appeared at the Spoleto Festivals (United States and Italy), Kuhmo (Finland), and Tanglewood (United States).

21. This description of Cerovsek's performance career has been extracted from the following website: http://www.artsmg.com/cerovsek. The website indicates a very active international performance schedule.

22. It is doubtful, however, that Cerovsek uses the same running joke of Gingold, who would say, "Do you buy that?" with Corey responding, "I buy that—sold!"

23. For a period, she was an associate instructor (AI) in the Theory Department of the Indiana University Music School. The quotation is from the following website: http://www.caswellsisters.com/sara.

24. A popular teacher in both the music school and the university's honors program, Austin Caswell was noted for his ability to capture students' attention and personalize instruction even in large lecture halls of two hundred or more. He taught music history courses, including women's music, popular music, and Baroque improvisation. He was particularly fond of engaging students in intellectually challenging conversations about controversial issues.

25. Information cited from the following website: http://alumni.indiana.edu/magazine/issues/200403/caswells.shtml; and interview with Sara Caswell, in Bloomington, March 10, 1999.

26. Cited from the website http://www.stringpedagogy.com.

27. For further information on Janis Stockhouse, see: http://www.music.indiana.edu/publicity/press/ArticlesPreviews&Reviews/articles/2005–02/2005–02–07-HT-Kauffman.shtml.

28. Cited from the following website: http://www.saracaswell.com/sara/index.html. The website includes other honors accorded the CD.

29. Ibid.

Sources

Interviews

Biss, Jonathan. Interview by author. Bloomington, IN, November 21, 1996.
———. Interview by author. Bloomington, IN, February 24, 2002.
———. E-mail correspondence with author. September 20, 2006.
Brancart, Evelyne. Interview by author. Bloomington, IN, March 12, 1999.
Caswell, Sara. Interview by author. Bloomington, IN, March 10, 1999.
———. E-mail correspondence with author. October 20, 2006.
Cerovsek, Corey. Interview by author. Bloomington, IN, June 27, 1999.
———. E-mail correspondence with author. November 30, 2006.

Selected Websites

Jonathan Biss: "Jonathan Biss." http://www.jonathanbiss.com/home/.
Sara Caswell: "Sara Caswell." http://www.caswellsisters.com/sara.
Corey Cerovsek: "Corey Cerovsek." http://www.artsmg.com/cerovsek/cerovsek.htm.

CHAPTER 10

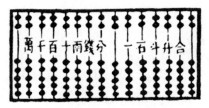

Mathematics

The Nature of Talent and Its Development

Mathematics is one of those fields in which great talent is manifested at an early age. How early promise is nurtured is the subject of the following profiles of a major mathematical talent and a renowned teacher of gifted youth. Daniel Biss, the older brother of pianist Jonathan, is considered to be one of the most promising young mathematicians of his generation. Sylvain Cappell, a prodigy in his own right, heads a program at New York University that is a recommended destination for mathematical talents of all ages. The educational and professional careers of these two individuals illuminate the nature of the field of mathematics:

- How talent is recognized and developed;
- Strengths and weaknesses of preuniversity mathematics education in the United States, compared with that of other countries;
- Advantages and disadvantages of specific, nationally prominent higher education programs; and
- How peer and societal expectations contribute to personal fulfillment or, alternatively, to frustration and departure.

Whether extraordinary mathematical talent is cultivated and achieves mature expression depends on a balance between genetic endowments and environmental nurturing. Not only appropriate instruction by skilled teachers but also societal encouragement and support are involved in fostering self-identity as a mathematician and commitment to a career as a theoretician or practitioner.

Daniel Biss

A Nurturing Environment: Family and Teachers

Daniel Biss grew up in a family of talented musicians (violinists Miriam Fried and Paul Biss). Although he continues to play the piano as a hobby, he never seriously contemplated a career in music like his brother Jonathan. By age fifteen, he realized that mathematics not only came easy to him but also was something he was "very much in love with."

When Daniel was a sophomore in high school, his father found an Indiana University colleague, mathematician Ciprian Foias, to work with him on a one-to-one basis. Prior to that, he had had the good luck of having an excellent eighth-grade calculus teacher, Andy Strawn, who made him "excited about what he was doing." He also sought out a graduate student to deepen his knowledge of calculus.

Foias, a distinguished mathematician from Romania, quickly recognized Biss's natural talent and twice a week during the school year guided him through a problem-based program. According to Biss, Foias demonstrated "how math should be presented and how it should be developed." The summer following his sophomore year, he worked as many as four hours a week with the professor.

Foias recommended that Biss enroll in an upper level university honors course in *real analysis*. Initially daunting, the course was "the first exposure ... [he] had to any kind of so-called real math." By his senior year in high school, he was taking three university math courses the first semester, and six the second semester! In this way, Daniel earned high school and college credits simultaneously.

The summer before his senior year, he participated in the MIT Research Science Institute (RSI). The program connects high school students interested in science with researchers in the Boston area who serve as mentors on individual projects.[1] At first, the experience was disappointing; the faculty member assigned to Daniel seemed more interested in having him copy-edit one of his own research papers than in furthering Biss's own project. Undeterred, Biss received clearance from the program director to switch projects. Based on the recommendation of a fellow student's advisor, he began working on the topic of "cwatsets" (within the general field of combinatorics).

When Biss returned to Bloomington, he received "tons of guidance" from Ciprian Foias and then Kent Orr. Because "cwatsets" was a subfield outside Foias's area of expertise, he recommended Biss to his colleague Orr. As Orr recalls, Daniel stopped by his office to leave a copy of his paper and briefly discuss the nature of his research. Orr, at first, didn't think much about the paper: "It was perfectly clever—very nice for a high school student and nothing of particular depth." Orr noticed, however, that there were several interesting "permutations" in the structure of the problem Biss was studying. He sent Biss away and told him to return when he found something interesting. Two days later he returned with a major insight into how the permutations composed a "transformational group within a very important fundamental mathematical structure." For Orr, Biss's finding was "just an amazingly beautiful thing ... the level of sophistication involved was just astounding!"

Although Biss enrolled in a course with Orr—a set of preparatory sessions for the William Lowell Putnam Mathematical Examination (administered by the Mathematical Association of America)—the lion's share of their work together was on Biss's research project in combinatorics and algebra. He had spent the entire summer before thinking about a specific problem he was unable to resolve until he met Orr:

> Only when I began working with him [Orr] did I begin to find results. I believe that this is true for a combination of reasons. First of all, because of his committed attitude toward students, he approached this almost as he would approach a collaboration. Of course, since the idea was for this to be my work and not his, he did not attempt actually to solve any problems, but developed in his own mind a potential program of how the work could be done. This distinct way of approaching the problem allowed him to make much more penetrating and useful comments when I did any discoveries.... He was careful not to do too much; he felt his role was to ask certain questions that he found relevant, and thus to stimulate progress. In doing so, he provided the most important help I had.[2]

Orr's approach to fostering Biss's natural mathematical talent also characterized Foias's problem-solving strategy. As Foias admitted, Biss's talent was so great in the field of combinatorics—"a field that distinguishes the truly, truly great mathematicians"—that at a certain point, all he could do was serve as a mentor, raising significant questions that could be explored by Daniel. This particular teaching style was what Biss expected in his relationship with subsequent advisors at Harvard (B.A.) and the Massachusetts Institute of Technology (Ph.D.).

Undergraduate and Graduate Studies

When he graduated from high school, Biss had his choice of the most selective mathematics departments in the country: he was one of forty national finalists in the Westinghouse Talent Search; his research project was selected for publication in a major mathematical journal; he had a perfect score on the mathematical section of the SAT; and his recommendation letters referred to him as an extraordinary talent. At Harvard, he was immediately selected for special attention. He was offered an accelerated program.

Although Daniel had good relations with his advisor at Harvard, he did not experience the close mentoring he had received while in Bloomington. But, according to Biss, "Mathematical education is much more than one teacher." More important was the overall level of instruction and the quality of graduate and undergraduate students. When comparing the undergraduate courses taken at Indiana and Harvard, Biss observed that the courses at Harvard were substantially harder in every respect. They were not only paced faster, but the problems posed were generally more difficult. Instructors designed problems with the idea of students developing a theory on their own.[3]

Aware of the positive features of Harvard's undergraduate program in mathematics, Biss also was quick to point out features not to his liking. The competitive and elitist atmosphere of the department, and the entire university, led to the stratification of the student body into those placed in fast tracks and receiving special attention and those left more on their own: "At Harvard a lot of people seem to get lost in the masses and a few people don't." He considers himself lucky in that he became part "of the social fabric of the department" that brought graduate and undergraduate students together into a community of shared values and endeavor.

One downside of the accelerated program was a first-year course for the most select group of mathematics students. The department "essentially turned loose the instructor to do whatever he liked." Taught by a respected mathematician (who was both young and inexperienced as a professor), the course turned out to be a "disaster and definitely decreased the population of math majors that year," among them some of the brightest students.

Observing poor teaching led Biss to realize that he had the potential to be an excellent math educator. The following year, he served as the teaching assistant in the above course and was officially expected to "hold office hours, grade homework, and give an hour of supplementary lessons." By the end of the year, "with the faculty member's lectures not accomplishing anything, I was giving about three hours a week of supplementary lectures." In his words, he "loved the three hours a week of teaching," and the students, in turn, "adored" him—as anyone would have been better than the professor of record (modestly stated).

After graduating from Harvard, Biss continued his graduate work in a doctoral program at the Massachusetts Institute of Technology. A highly sought after graduate with a growing national reputation, he was the recipient of the Morgan Prize for an undergraduate research paper published in two major mathematics journals.[4] He selected MIT over Princeton, Berkeley, and Chicago because his undergraduate thesis advisor, Michael Hopkins, was there.[5] Daniel found Hopkins, one of the world's foremost algebraic topologists, someone with whom he could maintain a friendly, "personal relationship," a mentor who would not tell him what to do but would be a guide and colleague in exploring intriguing problems.[6] They worked well together, even though Biss's dissertation was not within Hopkins's immediate field of expertise.

Biss received his doctorate within three years, and in the process garnered the most prestigious prize awarded young mathematicians, the Clay Long-Term Fellowship. The five-year postdoctoral fellowship led to an appointment in the Mathematics Department of the University of Chicago, where he has been since 2002. The fellowship allows him to pursue his individual research agenda and personal interests, while offering occasional lectures at the university.

Personality and Career

The path to success in the field of mathematics is an extremely difficult one, in which brilliant promise may never lead to major contributions. The pressure on young mathematicians to make major breakthroughs in knowledge creation is extraordinary and not easily borne. Commitment and a belief in one's abilities are essential, but possibly not sufficient, to support persistence in the field of pure mathematics.

Daniel, like many peak performers, was passionately committed to his field at an early age. When I first interviewed him at age seventeen about his ability to get totally absorbed in thinking about mathematics, he observed: "I've found that when I'm unhappy about some normal thing, it's possible to imagine myself in math so much that I can fade out temporarily. When I'm unhappy about something mathematical, no matter how everything else is going, I can't fade out." As a teenager, in 1996, he often would spend a whole day thinking about a mathematical problem. He occasionally would "feel overwhelmed by the volume of work there was to do." But he seldom felt that he "want[ed] to get away from math as a collection of things to think about." As he noted, "When on vacation and not doing math for a couple of days, or half a week, I start to miss it a lot."

By 2002, Daniel had seriously begun to question the nature of a career in mathematics and how fulfilling that would be. Among the frequently mentioned frustrations experienced by other young mathematicians was this particular one: "Being a mathematician you have to be a creator—that's what the job is. There are other walks of life where one is asked to be the creator, but one doesn't start creating at the age of twenty-four—doesn't take twenty years of classes and then get told—make something."

If research in mathematics is a creative process of finding proofs to long unresolved problems, Daniel noted that "nobody knows how to teach you to be a researcher. No one that I've found does. It's something that has to happen inside of you. It happens in an inexplicable way—you were thinking of something and there wasn't anything particular you could point out that you were thinking about, but it sparked something else."

Is it a matter of gestalt? *Wham-oh,* suddenly you have a great insight? What role do teachers play in the discovery process? Biss's mentor at MIT, Hopkins, told Daniel how he treated his mentor "as a Zen master who would send him off every week to do some sort of menial task.... Every task seemed absurd and unenlightened, but he knew there was some sort of grand plan being laid in front of him, and all of a sudden, [while] making cider, he would get hit in the head with a frying pan and ... he would be a researcher with original ideas—and, of course, it didn't happen."

Biss's assessment of the situation described by Hopkins is that the "advisor was probably giving daily menial tasks because he had no idea what to do." That may not be an accurate assessment of how Hopkins's mentor or any teacher responds to gifted individuals. Biss's mentors at Indiana University worked with him on a one-to-one basis, giving him problems to work on, hoping that this would develop mathematical knowledge and skills and nurture his talent. Both Foias and Orr, among others, had simply recognized extraordinary giftedness and responded to Biss's initiatives by asking the right questions and guiding him in the right direction.

Teachers also can inspire. Reflecting on his doctoral studies, Biss observed: "No greater thing has ever happened to me than getting hooked up with my resident advisor [Hopkins]." Rather than in any specific body of knowledge bestowed by Hopkins, Daniel found inspiration in his mentor's vision of mathematics and the way in which it was expressed.[7]

Engaging with challenging peers may be one essential condition for Biss continuing as a research mathematician. A principal reason for selecting the University of Chicago for his postdoctoral work was the mix of outstanding mathematicians: "I decided that what has worked for me in the past is to be surrounded by a lot of interesting ideas.... In Chicago there are five to seven different people who do all of the things that interest me."[8]

Another attraction is the lively seminars at the University of Chicago. The presence of a large group of Russian émigré mathematicians in the department has made for a more participatory and emotional exchange of ideas than in the normal U.S.-style seminar, which Daniel describes as "more of a performance."

Topology, Biss's specialization, is one of the most exciting research frontiers in mathematics at this time. He described it this way: "It's about shapes and structures and how to manipulate objects—how to push things and pull things and understand the nature of form."

His current research is a long-term project, on the border between topology and combinatorics, that grew out of his thesis. This is how he describes his general field of inquiry: "I guess the prime direction of twentieth-century mathematics is headed to where you no longer think of a mathematical object, you think of a pair of mathematical objects in the way of transforming from one to the next ... and what are the different ways you can embed one sphere into another."

Thomas Goodwillie, a Brown University leading researcher in topology and geometry, has had great success in studying problems along the lines mentioned above. But, as Biss acknowledges, "There are so many problems that you can never completely resolve them [all]."

With regard to difficult and open problems in mathematics, a recent breakthrough in topology by a reclusive Russian, Grigory Perelman, caused an international sensation on several accounts: he solved what was considered to be an impossible problem, the Poincaré conjecture, concerning the deep structure of three-dimensional objects; and, even more implausible, he showed no interest in the worldwide acclaim, refusing to accept the Fields Medal, the highest honor in mathematics, and possibly spurning a $1 million prize from the Clay Mathematics Institute in Cambridge, Massachusetts. Perelman's self-effacing reaction to all the attention is striking: "I do not think that [whatever] I say can be of the slightest public interest."[9]

This is a point similar to one Biss made: "Mathematics is almost always fairly esoteric, and people spend a tremendous amount of energy learning about a very specific subfield that almost no one else in the world really understands. Unfortunately, human nature has it that if you spend enough hours doing it you will need to convince yourself that it is the only interesting thing in the world."

Balance is achieved in Biss's life by other pursuits and passions, not all mathematical. Biss has contributed to a website: "SoapBlox: A Progressive Blog on Chicago and the Midwest." As a youth he juggled and played piano. He continues to play piano as often as he can, enjoys photography, and is seriously involved not only in grassroots but statewide politics.[10]

Since moving to Chicago, he also has become much more involved in teaching. In addition to lecturing to Research Science Institute students in China in the summer of 2006, and teaching elementary school children in a special Maryland summer program in 2007, he has been very much involved with a charter school in an impoverished neighborhood on the West Side of Chicago that aims to get all students into some form of postsecondary education.[11] He describes his involvement as "a mix of garden-variety homework help/teaching assisting and running of my own enrichment courses." He enjoys the experience because "it's a chance for students who've long stopped paying attention to their math teachers to plug back in and learn some material that is quite approachable but nonetheless completely new to them."

The idea of writing a general-interest book on the beauty of mathematics and how everyone has the capacity to enjoy it intrigues him. He has toyed with the title "The Music of the Spheres." The relationship between music and mathematics explored in the previous chapter is apparent to Biss, who sees the ability to learn the complexity of a musical score rapidly as akin to studying the intricacies of a mathematical problem and articulating an elegant solution. He is not sure, however, that what attracts him to mathematics is the same as what attracts others to music: "I'm very attracted to abstract ways of thinking, and mathematics really is in the end a way of taking fundamental everyday pieces of the human experience and transforming them into a very abstract language."

Teaching Mathematics

Writing a book that reached and engaged a larger audience in thinking about mathematics in these terms would possibly be the most professionally satisfying experience Biss could imagine. For now, he leads occasional seminars at the University of Chicago and gives five to ten lectures a year at different institutions.

For Biss, as for most mathematics educators, undergraduate mathematics instruction faces enormous and conflicting challenges. One challenge is to remediate largely inadequate preuniversity instruction. As widely acknowledged by educators and substantiated by international tests of educational achievement, U.S. mathematics curricula tend to be highly repetitive and do not allow the specialization that takes place in countries excelling on these tests. An interesting anecdote concerns an Eastern European Indiana University graduate student who tutored Biss in calculus. Despite Daniel's mathematical giftedness, the student found his level of knowledge to be abysmal.

The major conflict faced by university mathematics instructors involves introductory courses serving two purposes: (1) contributing to a solid foundation in mathematics that enables individuals to use mathematical knowledge and skills in various pursuits throughout their adult lives; and (2) screening out students wishing to pursue careers in medicine, the sciences, and related fields.

For Biss, "The first purpose is to give students bad grades so that they can be weeded out of different departments like the business program and secondly to mesh well with the first year physics and chemistry course." With regard to the second purpose, Biss maintains that the mathematics teachers are "told that by a certain week you must teach this and by that week you must teach that." The result is that "teachers aren't allowed to design interesting courses—so none of the teachers want to teach those courses and it's a horrendous cycle."

Ciprian Foias, who has taught in Romania, France, and the United States, similarly observed the difficulty of teaching undergraduate mathematics: "Half the class hates me—this happens everywhere.... I was never able to teach for the lower levels."

Large-scale efforts over the past twenty years to improve the quality of mathematics education have been fraught with controversy.[12] On one side, there are the initiatives of the National Council of Teachers of Mathematics (NCTM) to make mathematics more accessible to all students by involving them directly in raising issues related to the application of mathematics in everyday life.[13] Research in developmental and cognitive psychology and in anthropology examines the daily use of mathematics by largely unschooled populations (such as carpenters in South Africa, street vendors in Brazil and Ghana, and fishermen in northeastern Brazil), and the relationship between informal and formal systems of mathematical notation and symbol manipulation. Innovative curricula and pedagogies resulting from this research have a strong affinity with learner-centered, problem-solving "constructivist pedagogies."[14] Such pedagogies are strongly associated with the philosophical writings of John Dewey and L. S. Vygotsky, who placed emphasis on individuals' direct encounters with their material and social surroundings and how they go about constructing meaningful understandings from such experiences.[15]

In opposition to the tenets of what is considered "progressive education," there are those who advocate a "return to basics," to teacher-centered, textbook-driven courses, and the rote memorization of formulas and algebraic expressions. This group believes, among other things, that the "new math" has gone too far in turning classroom control over to students. They argue that liberal reforms have led to a decline in student performance on standardized tests of mathematical achievement compared with other countries and a corresponding loss of national economic competitiveness.[16] Parallel tensions exist between university faculties of education (which are inclined to favor preparing mathematics teachers who are equipped with learner-centered pedagogies) and mathematics departments (which tend to be more involved with turning out teachers who follow more traditional teaching methods). There are, of course, university mathematics teachers who bridge the divide in the academy between those who are oriented toward turning out world-class theoretical mathematicians and those who are inclined to make mathematics available to everyone. One such educator is profiled below.

Sylvain Cappell

One of the leading university mathematics educators in the country, Sylvain Cappell, in 1963, at the age of sixteen, was the top national winner in the Westinghouse Science Competition.[17] As a senior scholar his honors have included being a Guggenheim and Sloan foundations fellow.[18]

Many of his views on the field of mathematics mirror those of Daniel Biss. His biography, however, differs in several distinctive ways: one being his thirty years of experience as an educator, and the other his childhood as an immigrant kid living in Brooklyn and attending one of New York City's special schools for gifted students in the sciences and math.

Different Childhood

By the time Cappell was midway through elementary school, it was clear to him that he wanted to be a research scientist. Socially, he considered himself to be "out of it." First, he was a Jewish immigrant from Belgium. But, even going to Jewish school, his interests "were very different" from those of his peers. He was almost totally absorbed in reading "college level books about mathematics, science, and history."[19]

In high school, Sylvain found peers who shared his interests. Since the late 1930s, New York City has had a number of special-interest schools for talented youth in the sciences, mathematics, and arts.[20] At the Bronx High School of Science, Cappell met "lots of smart kids." In fact, there were numerous "smart kids in the neighborhood in the Bronx where he grew up who became very good scientists." This was evident when he attended Princeton for his graduate studies. At the time, Princeton had what many considered the world's best graduate program in mathematics. "Astonishingly," according to Cappell, "three of his student cohort came from one block in the Bronx. So we used to kid that where we came from, it was tough being the 'best mathematician on the block.'"

As an undergraduate, Cappell attended Columbia to study with Professor Sammy Eilenberg, whom he met at age fifteen or sixteen. Eilenberg, one of the leading mathematicians internationally and a legendary collector of South Asian art, told Cappell, who had solved some difficult problems posed in a National Science Foundation course, "You're going to go to Columbia." According to Cappell, "Eilenberg was the first really great mathematician that [he] had met." Although tough, Eilenberg provided the right mix of stimulation and support that advanced Cappell's career as a research scientist.

Although Cappell is acclaimed as a researcher, he also has made major contributions as a mathematics educator. Recognizing the advantages that he was given throughout his academic career, beginning with the opportunities provided by the Bronx High School of Science, he has felt a "sense of obligation to give back to another generation." And, as he adds, "I enjoy kids."

Teaching and Learning Styles

Very much in the mode of master teachers, Cappell attempts to individualize his instruction, especially given the wide age range he teaches and the different levels of mathematical knowledge and aptitude found among even a very select group of gifted students. Research problems, for example, are assigned to match the particular learning style and talents of each student: "With students who are too formal in their approach, you try to make them more comfortable with their intuitions. The reverse also happens. With someone who is overly dependent on intuition and doesn't think about how you formalize and organize [an answer], you try to modify the style."

Much of Cappell's teaching involves advising graduate students' doctoral research. He often has more than one conversation with a student before deciding to be a mentor: "I try and get some feel for where they are coming from, what their background is, what their strengths are. I don't have a formula."

Cappell is concerned not only with the mathematical aptitude of the students but also their overall emotional balance—an important factor in determining their persisting in a demanding line of work: "My impression is that the academic success of many students, in the long run, is affected by a lot of personal issues that are not immediately connected to mathematics.... I think one needs to be very responsive to individual development." But, as Cappell recognizes, there are a "million things" affecting development—among them, appropriate family support, academically stimulating programs and interactions with like-minded peers, and the guidance of knowledgeable instructors.

Nature or Nurture?

When asked if mathematical giftedness is something inborn, Cappell responded, "I support the general egalitarian thrust of our society and, in many ways, find it very agreeable. But there are large innate differences in mathematical ability." He also was quick to point out that mathematical ability may not be a unique gift, and there are many different forms of it.

When asked if it were possible for someone with exceptional innate ability to become a world-class mathematician without the intervention of some form of teaching and coaching by knowledgeable individuals, he said that the trouble with the word "intervention" is that it "covers a lot of territory." What kinds of intervention, by whom, when? He went on to say, "There is very little development of great research scientists on desert islands. Obviously nothing happens in a vacuum.... Nobody becomes what they are without being influenced by and benefiting from the interventions of lots of people."

To illustrate the point about unusual mathematical talent manifested at an early age and the importance of recognizing and nurturing it, he told "the most unusual story" he had experienced. It involved a four-year-old, which in itself is not so unusual, as Cappell's colleagues are constantly referring students of all ages to him. In this case, the mother contacted Cappell to tell him that her son was interested in mathematics: "He comes to my office and we talk. He literally starts jumping up and down on my desk—you know the way four-year-olds are. What he wants to discuss with me is the density of prime numbers: how dense they are. In other words, what percentage of numbers are prime as a percentage of numbers up to a given number, and how that goes down as you go up."

As Cappell noted, this was not a naive question: "It's well known to mathematicians that, in fact, a full understanding of the density of primes is to be among the deepest and hardest problems in mathematics." He then asked the child, "Do you think there are an infinite number of primes?" The child responded that he didn't know, but he had thought about it, and he thought there are. This, according to Cappell, is a "classical fact in mathematics." The child then said something remarkably intuitive: "He said that he 'had noticed the number of prime numbers as a percentage of numbers goes down, but it goes down kind of slowly,' so he 'doesn't think it's ever going to get to the point where there are practically no more primes coming.' Therefore, he 'expected there to be an infinite number of primes.'" This, for Cappell, "was an intuitively correct statement to justify the answer."

Blown away by the sophistication and subtlety of the child's response to the question, Cappell decided to call his sister, a private practitioner specializing in children's learning development. After telling the story about his encounter with the four-year-old, he asked her: "Is there any literature on children this exceptional?" Her response: "Not really, this is just beyond the literature. But my professional advice to you is to telepath to the other Martians that we surrender!"

Rather than surrender, Cappell worked with the prodigy over a period of twelve or thirteen years. The interactions depended on the child's taking the initiative to visit him—"some years fairly often." There were years when the person was less engaged mathematically, and, for Cappell, "that was all right." In our 1999 interview, Cappell indicated that the individual was an undergraduate at Harvard, several years ahead of course work, and "doing brilliantly." For Cappell, "There are many things besides that initial ability that go into making a mathematician's life." This student had "many other things that made it work for him: energy level, enthusiasm, good temperament."[21]

With regard to the inheritance of mathematical giftedness, Ciprian Foias provided this insight: "In the history of mathematics there are very few families, which had several generations of mathematicians." Personality, willingness to persist at mastering a set of challenging tasks, may be as important as a supportive family environment and natural inclinations. Foias cites the case of his own daughter, who, doing well in math in high school, initially decided that she wanted to major in it. Her first year in college she did very well in a chemistry honors class, reinforcing her belief that she was capable of succeeding in math. The following summer, Foias administered a two-and-a-half-hour mathematics aptitude test and recommended that she take an honors class in mathematics her sophomore year. He also counseled her to seek the advice of the professor of the course to see if she had a talent for mathematics and if he could suggest a long-term path to a career in the field, one she could follow. According to Foias, "One month later she called back and said, 'Yes, you are right: mathematics is not for me.'"

According to Foias, as well as Cappell, "You cannot teach mathematics to someone who is not willing to spend the time and to put in the hard work. It's like sports in the sense that there is a very great difference between being a fan and being a performer. If you don't do the work and if you are not concerned about the answers to the problems ... or why this proof was done in this way and not another way, then you cannot become a mathematician."

"Burn Out," "Breakdown," and Leaving the Field

During the 1999 interview Cappell consistently came back to the point about personal development and how a number of favorable factors had to coalesce for talented individuals to stay in mathematics and eventually distinguish themselves. The teenage years were a period when a number of initially gifted youth lost interest. The factors could be many—inadequate instruction in school, lack of a supportive peer culture, and, conversely, too much family pressure on the child. But, as he admits, he cannot get involved in all aspects of his students' lives. His overriding concern is not to do anything that would damage his students in any way. Providing opportunities for the students to pursue their interests—so that they don't feel frustrated—is important, but so is restraining the impulse to push students too hard. These pressures, however, are there and increase as one moves up the educational ladder.

At the graduate and especially the postgraduate levels, as Biss noted, the emphasis is on achieving creative breakthroughs in your specialization. That is becoming ever more difficult as knowledge increases rapidly in mathematics overall and leading-edge research often involves interactions across specialized branches requiring up-and-coming mathematicians to master more than one subfield. According to Cappell, "It certainly can be a problem for good, but not brilliant, students to manage several paradigms."

The pressure is even greater on someone like Biss, who is extraordinarily talented and does work in several related fields, to succeed before age thirty. Foias, prognosticating the future for Danny in 1999, thought it "extremely important for a young fellow like him to move as fast as he could," to be well established in the field in his early twenties.

Why this emphasis on youth? According to Cappell, although young people may not be as knowledgeable, they are generating ideas at a faster rate. One reason suggested by him is that "their neurons are putting out more of them and they are in better shape." Other research suggests that around age thirty individuals begin to take on family responsibilities and acquire other commitments that may lessen total absorption in mathematics.

Cappell also believes that the field of mathematics is highly supportive of young scholars contributing significantly to knowledge creation: "Mathematicians are eager to invite in new talent. It's more true than in other professions." This positive view of the field contrasts with those who criticize the tendency of many theoretical mathematicians to be arrogant and defensive about their narrow specializations.

Whether the field is inviting or not, within a brief time (probably no more than five years) after completing a Ph.D., young mathematicians reach a crossroads. If they have not achieved a substantial record of scholarly production, they are unlikely to remain in the academy as pure mathematicians: "Within mathematics itself, the standards are very high and exacting. So, before you are considered to be a first-rate theoretical mathematician, your level of accomplishment has to be, by common general human standards, remarkable."

According to Cappell, "For better or worse, academic careers tend to have a fairly straightforward pattern of development. A lot of people leave academic life. Relatively few return once they have left. There's an old mathematician's proverb: 'There's no telling how far a good man will go once he quits mathematics.' I believe what it reflects is that mathematical talents and abilities are in vast need by society."[22]

Given the intense pressures on theoreticians, Cappell reasons that many young mathematicians are willing to trade off a life in the academy for useful contributions in applied fields. He maintains that the contributions of applied mathematicians, in both direct and indirect ways, "to the success of American society are much larger than is commonly realized."

For Biss, there are other choices. Theoretically inclined mathematicians can choose to leave the rarefied atmosphere of the most elite university programs and teach in any number of higher education institutions—a continuum of opportunities exists. However, for a musician aspiring to a performance career—especially as a soloist—there may be a zero-sum situation at play: either you make it or you leave the performance arena and teach.

For those who remain in the academy, however, there is the challenge of teaching undergraduates who may be ill equipped and not interested in taking required mathematics courses. In addition, as noted before, the introductory courses serve conflicting aims of screening out students for advanced work in other fields while attempting to provide a solid foundation in mathematical reasoning that can serve individuals throughout their lives.

Mathematics Education

Sylvain Cappell shares many of the ideas expressed by Biss and Foias about the shortcomings of mathematics education. With regard to primary and secondary education, Cappell underscores the failure to create and support special programs for gifted individuals as well as the inadequate mathematical content of many U.S. school programs. Generally, society is not investing the effort and resources needed to achieve an excellent mathematics education.

At the university level, many students arrive with skill defects and a general fear of mathematics. For Cappell, "What they are most phobic about is dealing with symbolic manipulation and the idea content behind formalisms. They haven't learned to relax and see mathematics as formalization of ideas that they could have." Instead, too many prefer "a cookbook or undemanding course because that frightens them less.... It's what they have experienced in elementary school and high school. I think that's a sign of an unsuccessful educational system." The challenge for education is to communicate "an understanding of mathematics as a rich web of ideas that translates naive intuitions into more formal contexts and computations."

There are reforms underway in mathematics education for students of all ability levels. These initiatives involve curricula and pedagogies that engage students in working like mathematicians and that provide teachers with insights into the level of knowledge and the reasoning processes of their students. Instruction can then be more attuned to what is needed to guide students to requisite levels of mastery. Group learning activities, whereby teams of students work on common problems, have proven to be successful, especially in courses like calculus, which otherwise have high failure rates.

An initiative of the National Science Foundation encourages mathematically inclined undergraduate students to undertake original research projects. Cappell, however, has misgivings about what would seem to be a well-intentioned effort. His reluctance is based on the relatively lower level of mathematical knowledge of beginning U.S. graduate students compared with their European or Asian peers: "It's not altogether clear to me that taking them away from knowledge acquisition toward premature research experience is going to work. On top of that, I'm not sure that there is one paradigm that works for all students."[23] Certainly, such innovations should not be mandated.

Equity vs. Quality?

A number of the issues raised in this chapter refer to public policy: commitment of adequate public resources to the identification and nurturing of talent; development of rigorous mathematics curricula and effective pedagogies that engage all students in the acquisition of useful knowledge and skills; and recruitment and retention of talented mathematics teachers at all levels of education.

The extent and nature of ability grouping and tracking are closely related to how educational systems address these issues. In a comparative study of seven countries (Canada, China, France, Germany, Japan, South Korea, and the United States), Zimmerman and I pointed out the promises and pitfalls of ability grouping for achieving both educational equity and quality.[24] At its worst, sorting out students and placing them in ironclad categories on the basis of limited definitions of ability substantially narrows the horizons for most students. Not surprisingly, the losers in this sorting-out game tend to be the children of low income and minority backgrounds as well as female students—as their gifts are less likely to be recognized by dominant groups. Conversely, when there are multiple measures of talents and flexible curricula that permit students to develop along multiple paths at their own pace, both individuals and society benefit.

The Biss and Cappell profiles reveal that exceptional talent can be guided to achieve its potential under favorable circumstances. They benefited from the availability of teachers who recognized their innate gifts and employed appropriate educational strategies. Such strategies involve attention not only to the specific skills of the individual but also to overall personal development. At the school-system level, a number of precollegiate programs and opportunities benefit mathematically gifted students:

- Within-school accelerated and advanced placement programs;
- Special schools, such as New York's Bronx High School of Science, Stuyvesant High School, and Brooklyn Technical High School;
- Credit for enrollment in university courses;
- Opportunities to work on an individual basis with expert teachers;
- Summer camp programs;[25]
- Opportunities to teach classmates and younger schoolmates; and
- On-line software and Internet connections to special courses and networks of peers.

Notes

1. Recently, MIT has taken initial steps to expand its Research Science Institute (RSI) to China. In the summer of 2006, Biss lectured in Shanghai to thirty-five RSI youths who were considered to be among the most advanced science students in the area.

2. The quotation is from a letter of June 7, 1996, written by Daniel Biss to the Mathematics Department of Indiana University on behalf of the promotion case of Kent Orr to the rank of full professor.

3. An example of the stimulating instruction that Biss particularly liked, interestingly enough, was that of the Indiana University algebraic geometry course taught by Ciprian Foias, who wrote down the definition of a mathematical object, a Lebesgue integral (a concept Biss had heard mentioned but knew nothing about), and said, "I want you to do as much as you can with that definition." This was right before the summer break at the end of Daniel's sophomore year. Over the following month, he worked on developing an understanding of the concept— "and that's really making you into a researcher.... That's the best kind of problem."

4. The *American Mathematical Monthly,* and *Topology and Its Applications.*

5. Biss's Harvard advisor, Raoul Bott, was only half-time at Harvard and not generally available when Daniel was writing it.

6. Hopkins, as of July 1, 2005, left MIT to join the Harvard University Mathematics Department.

7. One is reminded of Daniel's brother Jonathan and his discussion of how inspirational his lessons with Leon Fleisher were for the same reasons.

8. Many of the mathematics faculty that have been hired in recent years at the University of Chicago are immigrant Russians, recalling the role that Russian émigrés have played in advancing chess instruction and playing in the United States.

9. See George Johnson, "IDEAS AND TRENDS: The Math Was Complex, the Intentions, Strikingly Simple," *New York Times*, Sunday, November 19, 2006; and "Grigori Perelman." http://en.wikipedia.org/wiki/Grigori_Perelman, Wikipedia.

10. In the spring of 2007, he officially announced his candidacy as a Democrat for the 17th District seat of the Illinois State Legislature. If he is elected, he will serve in the legislature in Springfield half the year, and teach the other half of the year at the University of Chicago.

11. North Lawndale College Preparatory High School.

12. See Stanic and Kilpatrick, *A History of School Mathematics* (2003), for in-depth discussions of the nature of the reforms that have been attempted for the past fifty years.

13. NCTM, *Principles and Standards for School Mathematics* (Reston, VA: 2000).

14. See work of D'Ambrosio (2001), and Kloosterman and Lester (2004 and 2007), in bibliography.

15. On Vygotsky and Dewey, see bibliography.

16. See Tamar Lewis, "As National Math Scores Lag, a New Push for the Basics," *New York Times*, November 14, 2006, A1, 22. But there is reason to believe that this claim is unfounded; there has never been a time in our nation's history that U.S. students have fared well in comparison with other industrialized countries in mathematics performance (see http://www.mathematicallysane.com/analysis/goodolddays.asp#top).

17. The Westinghouse Science Competition is now the Intel National Science Talent Search.

18. Other distinctions include chairing the main prize committee of the American Mathematical Society (AMS), as well as being elected to its council and executive committee, and delivering invited addresses to the International Congress of Mathematicians and to national meetings of the AMS.

19. As an immigrant child, Cappell was not interested in key areas of U.S. popular culture, such as baseball—certainly of interest to New Yorkers of all ages when one of the local teams was in the World Series. To the dismay of one of his protégés, Shmuel Weinberger, who has since gone on to prominence as a scholar at the University of Chicago, Cappell did not know what teams were playing in the World Series when the topic came up in casual conversation. Weinberger, then a graduate student at New York University, quipped: "You know, Professor Cappell, living in the free world is wasted on you." It should be noted, however, that Cappell's interests are not confined to mathematics. He reads widely and deeply in psychology and neuroscience as well as history, especially Jewish history—"hundreds of books"—and the history of China and Ancient Greece. As he noted: "I could go on forever." He also is an avid chess observer, who was one of the top two high school chess players in New York City as a teenager. He still does a lot of math in cafés with friends.

20. These schools are now labeled "magnet schools" because of their foci, which attract students from all over the metropolitan area.

21. As of the fall of 2006, this very gifted individual had completed a B.A. at Harvard, a Ph.D. at the University of California at Berkeley, and was the recipient of the prestigious American Institute of Mathematics national postdoctoral fellowship, involving five years of support with no teaching.

22. In citing this proverb, Cappell was quick to express this proviso: "Let's forgive that it's masculine, because it's old." Another proverb worth quoting here is this: "Mathematical

research is a difficult enterprise engaged in to gain the grudging acknowledgment of a few choice colleagues."

23. Carl Wieman, Noble Laureate in Physics, has interesting thoughts on how to teach physics courses in such a way that students are encouraged to work and think the way physicists do when conducting research. See his article with Perkins in *Physics Today,* November 2005.

24. See Robert F. Arnove and Enid Zimmerman, "Dynamic Tensions in Ability Grouping: A Comparative Perspective and Critical Analysis," *Educational Horizons,* spring 1999, 120–27.

25. Residential summer camp programs are especially important for students who may not have access to expert teachers and university courses or whose schools do not offer advanced placement courses. See, for example, Michael Winerip, "Bring on the Problems? It Must Be Math Camp," *New York Times,* July 20, 2003, A15.

Sources

Interviews

Biss, Daniel. Interview by author. Bloomington, IN, December 30, 1996.
———. Interview by author. Bloomington, IN, February 24, 2002.
———. Interview by author. New York, November 10, 2006.
Cappell, Sylvain. Interview by author. New York, April 27, 1999.
Foias, Ciprian. Interview by author. Bloomington, IN, spring 1999.
Lester, Frank. Interview by author. Bloomington, IN, November 28, 2006.
Orr, Kent. Interview by author. Bloomington, IN, spring 1999.

E-mail Correspondence

Biss, Daniel. E-mail correspondence with author. November 20–22, 2006.
Orr, Kent. E-mail correspondence with author. November 22–27, 2006.
Foias, Ciprian. E-mail correspondence with author. November 27, 2006.

Letters

Biss, Daniel. Letter to Indiana University Department of Mathematics in support of promotion to rank of full professor. June 7, 1996.
Orr, Kent. Letter to Tulane University recommending Daniel Biss to its Undergraduate Research Program. February 1996.

Bibliography

Cole, M., et al., eds. *L. S. Vygotsky: Mind in Society.* Cambridge, MA: Harvard University Press, 1978.

D'Ambrosio, U. *Etnomatemática: Elo entre as Tradições e a Modernidade* [*The Link between the Traditional and the Modern*]. Belo Horizonte, Minas Gerais: Autêntica, 2001.

Dewey, J. *Interest and Effort in Education.* Boston, MA: Houghton Mifflin, 1900.

———. *Democracy and Education.* New York: Free Press, 1912.

Kloosterman, P., and F. K. Lester, eds. *The 1990 through 2000 Mathematics Assessment of the National Assessment of Educational Progress: Results and Interpretations.* Reston, VA: National Council of Teachers of Mathematics, 2004.

———. *Results and Interpretations of the 2003 Mathematics Assessment of the National Assessment of Educational Progress.* Reston, VA: National Council of Teachers of Mathematics, 2003.

National Council of Teachers of Mathematics. *Principles and Standards for School Mathematics.* Reston, VA: Author, 2000.

Stanic, G. M. A., and J. Kilpatrick, eds. *A History of School Mathematics.* Reston, VA: National Council of Teachers of Mathematics, 2003.

Vygtosky, L. S. "Interaction between Learning and Development." In *Mind in Society: The Development of Higher Psychological Processes,* ed. M. Cole, V. John-Steiner, S. Scribner, and E. Souberman. Cambridge: Harvard University Press, 1978, 79–91; original work published in 1935.

———. *Educational Psychology.* Translated by R. Silverman. Boca Raton, FL: CRC Press, 1997; original work published 1926.

Chess Masters

Chess has been described as the "game of kings." Often viewed as a game of war or "mortal combat," its practitioners and aficionados also reverentially and lovingly refer to chess as a science as well as an art. Chess is a highly regulated field in which mastery of the sport (a term often used to describe it) is systematically assessed, with increasingly higher levels of performance accorded coveted titles. The progression of titles proceeds from junior championships, to the advanced status of National and International Master, to Grandmaster, and, ultimately, world champion. For many the sport becomes an obsession involving, very much like mastery of a musical instrument, years of concentrated practice in a continuous quest for ever greater accomplishment. As in music and mathematics, prodigies appear. They display a talent so unusual that it appears to be a divine gift beyond explanation. This talent is nourished by a supportive family environment. Teachers and mentors provide needed skills and serve as inspiring role models. They provide the knowledge and strategies, the regimen of practice, and the vision that may lead to world-class accomplishment. In the absence of appropriate instruction and disciplined practice, manifestations of early genius may not result in adult success or professional careers. For those who do not give their lives to chess, but learn key elements of the game—the cognitive skills and behavioral traits associated with accomplished performance—the benefits are many. Chess-in-the-curriculum enrichment programs, as in New York City, have contributed to the academic success of students who otherwise are likely to experience failure or disenchantment. Indeed, some of the most apathetic and alienated students have been turned around by such programs.

This chapter includes portraits of (a) Bruce Pandolfini, who has the distinction of possibly having taught more students chess than any other American; (b) Maurice Ashley, a very successful chess instructor in the New York City education program established by Pandolfini and the first African American International Grandmaster; and (c) Lev Alburt, one of the first and most significant of the Russian émigré chess instructors in the United States. The narrative includes a brief discussion of the Polgar sisters, who are among the greatest female chess players in history, and several other significant chess players and instructors who form part of the American and European chess landscapes. National culture comes into play as does state policy and organized philanthropy in supporting the development of talent.

Bruce Pandolfini

The film *Searching for Bobby Fischer* has an unforgettable scene: actor Ben Kingsley (playing the role of Bruce Pandolfini) brutally scores a teaching point with prodigy Josh Waitzkin (the protagonist of the movie). With a dramatic sweep of his hand, Kingsley knocks all the pieces from the chessboard. Was this Hollywood invention or a portrayal of exactly what happened?[1] Pandolfini, not denying that something similar occurred, remarked that he was a pragmatist: "In teaching if you want to get students' attention, what better way than to knock over the pieces? They will surely pay attention after that. It's a teaching technique. It's not a hurtful thing. It works ... and I'll do whatever I think works."

What follows is a discussion of how Pandolfini came to identify successful, if controversial, teaching techniques for both one-on-one as well as large group instruction. It is a story of preparation meeting opportunity.

Formative Period

As a competitive chess player, Pandolfini started later than many of his peers. Although he had developed an intense interest in the game by age nine, it was not until four years later that he became obsessed with chess. This occurred when he fortuitously came across chess books while wandering the stacks of the Brooklyn Public Library: "I just fell in love with the pictures and diagrams, the personalities. I think there was something like thirty-two books, and you were allowed to take out maybe six or so at a time. I took them all out that day. I cleaned them out. I didn't go to school for a month."

When Pandolfini returned to school, he successfully combined an interest in mathematics and science with chess. At the university he majored in physical chemistry. His coursework consisted of a heavy dose of quantum mechanics and differential equations. While a graduate student, he played chess competitively. At the time, he was considered to be among the top ten juniors in the country.

His passion for chess eventually led him to a career choice to leave graduate school. Students quickly followed, especially after he worked as a commentator for the Public Broadcasting System coverage of the 1972 world championship Fischer-Spassky games in Reykjavik, Iceland.

Before that event, large-scale, systematic chess instruction was uncommon in the United States. According to Pandolfini, there were chess teachers, but instruction was usually limited to the teacher sitting down with the student, playing some games, and maybe making a few comments. Following the 1972 championship games, that all changed. After the match, PBS gave Pandolfini a list of three hundred potential students: "I quickly took fifteen or twenty of them for my own clientele, and divvied out the rest among the other potential chess teachers in the New York area. That's really how chess teaching started in New York City. I probably have given more chess lessons than anyone in America."

Chess in the Schools

Pandolfini started the first large-scale scholastic chess program at the Hunter College elementary school in 1975. Immediately, he had as many as one hundred students and no assistants. The program, offered as an enrichment class for academic credit to students in grades four to six, was later taken over by two other coaches.

Pandolfini was particularly intent upon extending the program to the inner city to prove the value of chess for students who were not being challenged intellectually. One of his first assistants was Maurice Ashley, whose program was so successful that a number of his teams went on to national championships. Remarkably, the students who participated in the programs were generally considered by their teachers incapable of accomplishing cognitively demanding tasks.

Arguments made for introducing chess into the school curriculum usually center on how learning game strategy improves analytical thinking. According to Pandolfini, "That's how I sold it to the Board of Education. They would never have allowed the Chess in the Schools program if I hadn't been able to show them that there was significant carry-over. Many of the chess problems we typically solve rely on techniques that are helpful in solving problems in other disciplines." For example, "One thing you learn from solving a chess problem is that sometimes we get the right elements, but we get them in the wrong order." To reverse the order of problem-solving steps, chess players have to examine, if not imagine, a range of options, often drawing on analogies to figure out the winning strategy.

Initially, it was not thought that teaching chess also would improve reading skills. But that actually turned out to be an unexpected outcome, as students fascinated with the game eagerly read chess books. A more recent outcome is the development of computer skills as chess instruction increasingly uses software programs to analyze typical games. Pandolfini, for example, will play with a student in tandem against the computer, discussing the game in progress. Doing so enables him to "get immediately into the student's head." Because, in Pandolfini's words, "the computer is deaf and doesn't 'hear' or react to our commentary, I'll suggest a plan and the student will see it implemented. It can be powerful instruction."

Improved self-esteem is another selling point for chess in the schools: "If you do well in one endeavor, it helps you in everything else. It gives you a better self-opinion, and you can use that as a springboard. You just need to do well in one thing in life, and then you've got it made."

The synergy between self-esteem and chess playing is revealed in the example of a third grader who had a terrible stammer. According to Pandolfini, that was the chief problem in the student's life. Pandolfini decided to focus on the stammer rather than on the individual's chess playing, even though he was fairly talented at chess:

> I think he got virtually nothing from the chess end of it. I would engage him in the military conversations he was interested in, various puzzles, just to try to get him to talk. But then he moved away to another part of the country. I got this call one day, and it was from the same kid, who was in the twelfth grade at the time. He said: "Bruce, I don't know if you remember me. I just won the twelfth grade nationals. I want to thank you so much for everything you did." He spoke in perfect English.

Perhaps the most interesting twist in the story is that Pandolfini "always felt that ... [he] had cheated the student by not teaching him chess."

Chess playing, however, involves having to suffer the pangs of defeat. As Pandolfini notes, "Ego gratification is the number one reason kids do anything. If they don't have lots of winning and success, they will tend to give up. They want to start beating their opponents immediately."

How teachers respond to the success and failure of their students, how they balance praise and criticism, can have long-term consequences. Like other sports coaches, he would rather have his students lay out a plan and execute it properly than achieve a win that had nothing to do with it. He is particularly hard on students who come back from winning a tournament 4 to 0, because "he can afford to be critical if they've just had a success." When they come back with a failure, it's not advisable to be very critical: "I'm trying to find ways to show them that they actually played well."

Pandolfini admitted that he often makes up stories about how he lost in similar situations so that the students don't take losses as a personal failure but as the result of a common strategic or tactical error. His job is to help the students "get through defeat, so they can then go on with life.... Coaching is all about making individuals feel that they can achieve whatever they set out to do." But "how you do that may not be so simple." One challenge is when best to start chess instruction.

Developmental Stages

A review of various performance fields suggests that the most effective instruction accords with general developmental stages of human growth, both with regard to the physical ability and emotional maturity of children, and to their level of cognitive skills. One consideration is their ability to think abstractly.[2] For Pandolfini there are certain points in child development when systematic instruction in chess makes sense:

> I think several ages are ideal. The first is around four or four and a half. At that age you also can begin to deal with some abstract concepts in math and music. But of course, most children don't turn to chess at that point. There are many rules that you have to learn that have no immediate interest for them. So it's difficult to get involved in chess at that point. But if you can, it's a great advantage. Then, when you come to age six, that's a great learning period. The second phase I would focus on is twelve or thirteen. It also seems to be a period where one can develop significantly, especially in chess. I guess that was the age I came in.

Teaching adolescents is preferable because they are likely to retain more instruction, and "by age twelve or thirteen, they can deal with defeat better." Furthermore, "If students start too early, and don't have good teaching, they can pick up very bad habits, and those habits will stay with them forever."

Personality and Physical Traits

In addition to traditional areas of chess intelligence—spatial relationships and logical mathematical operations—that need to be honed, Pandolfini considers "personal intelligences" to be important. These traits include not only the ability to analyze oneself but also skill in figuring out an opponent's psyche and playing style: "They tell you to play the board and not the man. That's a bunch of baloney. If you know something about the man, why shouldn't you take advantage of it? It's just that usually you don't. It's a very intimate game. You are sitting across from someone for five hours. You never talk or touch. You know a lot about that person at the end of the game, though. You know if you like the person or not."[3] Most chess instructors, however, "don't get into those areas," and consequently shortchange students.

Other traits associated with success are a "sense of combative and tactical play and having really good concentration skills." Persistence and patience are extremely important: "You learn not to give up ... to be resourceful, to fight to the end."

Major chess tournaments often require days of emotionally and mentally exhausting work. Physical stamina, especially in championship games, is a must. It is not uncommon for those preparing for world championship matches to undergo a rigorous physical exercise regimen.[4]

Gender

Gender differences in playing styles appear early on. According to Pandolfini: "A talented six-year-old boy will say something like: 'What can I attack now?' A talented six-year-old girl will say something like: 'What can I defend now?' It's a profound difference."

The Polgar sisters are an example of an extraordinary regimen of systematic preparation to overcome such gender differences and shatter stereotypes. Determined that his children would be geniuses in some field, even before they were born, Lazlo Polgar decided to keep his three daughters at home. He established an exceptionally demanding regimen of study eight to ten hours a day focused on chess. Judit, the youngest of the three sisters (also including Zsuzsa and Zspofi), by age five was beating her father at the game; at fifteen years of age she was the youngest ever Grandmaster, achieving that status one month earlier than even Bobby Fischer.[5]

Natural Talent and/or Tuition?

The Polgar sisters raise the question of what accounts for prodigious performance. Is early genius a manifestation of genetic inheritance or personal drive with unending hours of practice to perfect innate skills, or is it the consequence of a set of environmental factors, including a supportive home environment and abundant resources favoring talent development?

Pandolfini's response suggests a combination of natural talent, concentrated practice, and appropriate instruction at key stages of development: "I think you need to work incredibly hard. And you need to be very gifted. You need a natural flair for the game." Years of dedicated practice are required as students must work on improvement within their own level and then acquire the knowledge and skills to move to the next level:

> Let's say, crudely, that you have to learn a thousand things before you get to the next conceptual level. As you are going along, obviously you are getting better. But you don't really see many practical results yet, if any, until you put the thousandth thing into place. So you can even be in the 990s as far as acquiring information for ideas. But it doesn't show itself in a practical way yet. Suddenly you experience a quantum leap.

Here is where coaches and more advanced teachers come into play. Even a world champion like Kasparov benefits from instruction by lesser-skilled trainers: "How are they helping him? They have objectivity. They can look at his game critically in a way that perhaps he can't. That's their contribution. That's very valuable."

Sometimes it's just the little things coaches do that cumulatively lead to world championships: for example, the impact of coach Doc Counsilman on the record-breaking accomplishment of Mark Spitz. For Pandolfini: "If you accumulate little advantages, you will have an overwhelming advantage. [Normally,] we dispense with these little things. We don't pay much attention. We think they are not that important. But they are the key things. At the top, everyone is virtually equal. It's just these little things that separate them and distinguish them." He drives home this point by referring to the film *Chariots of Fire*: "There is a famous scene where one of the runners is trying to engage a famous running coach. Eventually, the running coach sees him run, and he comes to him and says, 'I can get you two yards. That's all I can do for you, but that's all you need.' Two yards to win the 100-yard dash!"

To get that two yards, however, close attention usually needs to be given to the individual characteristics of the performer: "You must first analyze the student, and make an assessment of what you think that student needs to do." That is possible with one-on-one coaching. The most difficult problem for public school chess instruction is that "you follow formulaic teaching and a given curriculum." One way certain societies approach this challenge is to single out and provide systematic, intensive instruction to those with great promise in the arts and athletics.

National Differences

Pandolfini, as well as Maurice Ashley and Lev Alburt, noted how the former Soviet Union established special programs and schools to cultivate talented youth. The state played a key role in fostering competitive play throughout the far-flung empire. By contrast, chess programs in the United States have been heavily dependent on private sector funding. Another significant distinctive feature of the United States is that "we have to teach everyone in an egalitarian way—the talented, the untalented. I think it's a much harder task."[6]

In cities like New York, public funds do become available for tournament play for those enrolled in the Chess in the Schools program. Pandolfini, however, argues that competitions aren't the only way students improve: "In fact, it's not even the best way. You need lots of casual practice in leisure time—and you need a long period of time to do that, too."[7]

One route for mobilizing more financial support for chess—instructors, tuition in chess clubs, travel to tournaments—is corporate sponsorship. Yet it is unlikely that there ever will be enough funding from that source: "You have to increase the base of support. The way you do that is by working with the young. My goal is to achieve a day when everyone in America will know the rules of chess. They don't necessarily have to play well, but if they have the ability to get into the game, observe it, then we as promoters of the sport have somewhere to go with it."

Like Harvey Phillips with tuba playing, and other master teachers, Pandolfini's ultimate goal is to expand his performance field. He has relentlessly pursued that goal through starting Chess in the Schools programs, teaching hundreds of students one-on-one, and writing more than thirty books. However, all fields draw boundaries around themselves. They establish barriers to entry on various discriminatory grounds, most commonly those of race, ethnicity, social class, and gender. Although, historically, world-class competitive chess has been similarly exclusive, the game has changed in significant ways in recent years.

Maurice Ashley

One of those individuals who opened the door to African Americans in competitive chess is Jamaican-born Maurice Ashley. Like Pandolfini, Ashley was only casually interested in the game until he opened his first chess book and became totally engaged; he taught in the Chess in the Schools program started by Pandolfini; he has had phenomenal success teaching marginalized students; he uses computer software programs to constantly challenge his skills; and he thrives on defeat. As a world-class competitor and a role model who has popularized what might be considered an elite sport, Ashley has been appropriately called the "Tiger Woods of chess."

Early Years

Ashley describes his early interest in chess the way someone with a competitive streak might play checkers, dominoes, cards, or monopoly. When he was growing up in Jamaica, his family, like many others, was "very much into games, because there wasn't much else to do."

In his early adolescence, Ashley followed his father to the United States, where he attended Brooklyn Technical High School. At age fourteen he saw a friend playing chess. Naturally, he thought he could beat him because he was a "big game player." The result: "He crushed me." Shortly thereafter, he went to the library and found his first chess book: "I opened it up, and it was like love at first sight. Immediately I was entranced by the game."

Over the following three years, Ashley and his friends started reading chess magazines and identifying with the careers of famous chess players. They also followed the games of older African American players in nearby Prospect Park and, when weather was inclement, in their homes. The best teenage players were from the Black Bear School. Even the youngest, according to Ashley, would "kick his butt most of the time." Rather than be deterred by defeat, he was motivated to "read books, play in tournaments, come back again, lose again, until [he] was better." In fact, one of his memorable quotations in our interview was this: "The best games that ever happened to me were my losses."

He didn't have what might be loosely considered a "teacher" until he was seventeen. Willie Johnson, eighteen years his senior, was more a mentor than an expert player, as young Ashley almost immediately was his equal in skill. As Ashley's father wasn't home much, Johnson "was just a very good older man to have around." He would provide advice and share Maurice's interest in sports and chess. At this point in the interview, Ashley admitted, "I never learned the game formally."

As with jazz players who have not formally studied their instruments, Ashley learned by observing the performances of masterful practitioners, sometimes directly but more frequently by studying chess games in magazines, newspapers, and, in later years, on computer software and the Internet. At key points in his career, however, he benefited from the direct intervention of talented coaches who helped him overcome problems blocking his path to the highest levels of competitive chess. Today, however, more affluent players—as young as eight or nine—may have trainers who, according to Ashley, "teach them all the nuances of playing as well as about the problems they are having."

The Road to International Grandmaster

Maurice Ashley's career is testimony to an extraordinary commitment to excel in chess. While studying full time at City College, he also served as president of its chess team and taught in the New York City Chess in the Schools program. The balancing act, at times, had its costs in negatively affecting his tournament play.[8]

The progression to the top of the chess world requires years of concentrated study and testing in increasingly brutal competitions. Ashley began playing in tournaments when he was fifteen or sixteen. By the time he was eighteen or nineteen, he had chosen chess as his lifetime career. He modestly describes himself as starting at "rock bottom." His commitment to improving his game led him to gain 600 points in three years, a remarkable achievement rarely found among older players. He moved from the 1800-point Class A level to the 2400-point Senior Master level in the United States. According to Ashley, those 600 points are usually the most difficult ones to obtain. As he explains, "Between the ages of nineteen and twenty-one, I became an Expert Master and Senior Master just boom, boom, boom, right on top of each other. During that period, I was studying chess all the time. I was playing chess all the time in tournaments. I was devouring the game. Everything about me was chess."

He recalls arriving at Prospect Park during the summertime around noon and often playing until after dark. It was not unusual for him to spend up to six hours a day playing or studying the game, something that he does to this day.

Dramatically breaking the ceiling of 2400, Ashley suddenly found himself "totally stuck." To that point, he had not received any formal coaching; the cost had been prohibitive. The faculty advisor to the City College chess team used his connections to the American Chess Foundation (ACF) to obtain a coach for Ashley on the grounds that he was a very promising player. Ashley's first coach was Ukrainian chess master Vitaly Zaltsman, who helped Ashley attain the level of International Master.

The next barrier (2500 points) was International Grandmaster. Once again, Ashley reached a plateau (around 2470 points) beyond which he was unable to ascend because of teaching and coaching commitments and lack of funds for further training. Although it might be assumed that coaching would have honed his skills on the chess board, that was not the case. He was primarily teaching beginning players: "I wasn't talking to strong chess players who were on my level."

To obtain the services of another trainer, the ACF, once again, came to his rescue. They helped Ashley obtain the services of Gregory Kaidanov, who "took [him] over the hump to International Grandmaster."

Between 1997 and 1999, when he was preparing to achieve the status of International Grandmaster, Ashley withdrew from teaching and coaching completely. To prepare for the tournaments, he analyzed the latest games played by the Grandmasters in the top tournaments. First thing every day, he downloaded the games off the Internet. By 1999 he had developed a software database on his laptop computer with "a million chess games that have been recorded throughout history." As early as 1996 he had created a software tutorial, an award-winning CD-ROM, "Maurice Ashley Teaches Chess."[9]

In addition to studying games, Ashley practiced weekly with a fellow chess player, the International Master Josh Waitzkin, the protagonist of the movie *Searching for Bobby Fischer.* Once every two months he worked with his trainer, Gregory Kaidanov, whom Ashley describes as one of the top five players in the United States, and one of the top fifty players in the world. Kaidanov would spend three or four days going over Ashley's latest games, suggesting what he needed to do over the subsequent months.

Teaching Winning Traits

Because of the demands incumbent upon an International Grandmaster, Ashley retired from classroom teaching in 1999, but he continued to direct the New York City chess program in the schools. In September 1999, he opened the Harlem Chess Center.

As an educator, Ashley has attempted to inculcate in his students the same attributes, behaviors, skills, and knowledge that led him to become an International Grandmaster. Much in accord with other outstanding coaches and teachers, his primary interest has resided in the students' personal development. The traits that make for successful performance in a specific field are also those that contribute to a well-lived life:

> For me it's how you handle yourself. It's how you develop skills and attitudes from playing the game, whether it's intellectual growth or problem-solving ability, having determination, being willing to defer gratification ... learning how to be graceful when

you lose and equally gracious when you win. These are the kinds of things I really want to instill more. Because I think chess is more like life. Very much like life despite the fact that it's this war game to win pieces.

His approach to teaching "as a matter of fact is to talk about chess like life. Like sports, like a battle, like a war, like self-analysis." Ashley captures his students' attention and imagination by talking about the chess pieces as if they were heroic figures in a romantic novel: "They see the king, the queen, the rook, the knights, and suddenly the medieval quality to it.... I talk about the pieces as if they were alive. I see the bishop going out, and I know it's thinking about sacrificing itself so that a queen can checkmate. So I infuse all of my lessons with connections to life. The students are excited right away. They like the heroism of the game."

Such stories captivate even the youngest of students. Although four would seem, for both Ashley and Pandolfini, not the best age to start teaching chess, it was precisely at that point that Ashley's daughter asked him to teach her the game. Actually, he had been planning to wait just another year. But since she insisted, he decided that he would not only teach her but also play the game well. When she lost, she was "incredibly upset." What he then did is illustrative of his pedagogical values: "I explained to her that I lose chess games too, even though [I'm] a Grandmaster, I lose. You have to learn to take losses gracefully and shake hands when you lose. And the next time we played, it was incredible. The game ended and she shook my hand.... You can teach a four-year-old these kinds of attributes. It was wonderful."[10]

In teaching "every chess game as a story" with its protagonists, victories, and defeats, Ashley sets out to stimulate the creativity of his students: "One of the great exercises we do with the kids is to have them write the story of the game anyway they want to. Some kids have written it as a rap; others, as science fiction. It's beautiful to see the creativity that the kids come up with when you give them this kind of liberty to do this."[11]

Furthermore, Ashley had his students articulate their strengths and weaknesses in writing. The exercise strengthened individual performance and enabled the players to know one another better, thereby contributing to a more competitive team. The personal assessments also proved to be a valuable tool in individualizing instruction.

Over the years, Ashley has worked with teachers as well. When he was coordinating the Chess in the Schools program, he had teachers brainstorm how chess could be used more effectively in the classroom. A mutually beneficial relationship developed. They showed Ashley and program colleagues innovative ways to express the relevance of chess to different curricular areas. The teachers, in turn, discovered new ways to teach higher-order cognitive skills. The results were demonstrably positive. Teams initially coached by Ashley and subsequently by others have achieved national prominence: the "Raging Rooks" from Harlem's Junior High School 43 won the National Junior High School Championship in 1991; and Harlem's Mott

Hall School "Dark Knights" have won eight national championships in the Junior Varsity Division since 1994.

Lev Alburt

The third prominent player-educator profiled is Ukrainian-born Grandmaster Lev Alburt. In 1979 he defected from the Soviet Union to the United States, where he resides in New York City. He is a three-time U.S. champion, and a two-time European Cup and U.S. Open Champion. Alburt is one of the select players to whom Bruce Pandolfini sends his more promising students for further instruction.[12] Alburt, however, does not confine his teaching only to advanced students. He is willing to teach even the most unaccomplished player. He has published a number of very popular chess books, among them the best-selling coauthored *Comprehensive Chess Course*.

There are several striking differences between Alburt's development as a player and that of Pandolfini and Ashley. Differences arise out of family background as well as national contexts. Striking similarities also appear.

Formative Years

Unlike Pandolfini or Ashley, Alburt enjoyed an early edge in his chess playing. His aunt started him on chess at age five. His father (a 1600-level player) then taught him to age seven, by which point the young Albert was already a stronger player. A coworker of his father was then enlisted to work with Lev several hours a week. Playing skills were honed by playing in a big public park near his house and entering local tournaments. By age eight or nine he was at a level comparable to a 1700-point player.

Another advantage enjoyed by Alburt was being singled out for early, systematic instruction in a select chess program or "mini-school." In the Soviet Union, as in other socialist societies, special schools or enrichment centers were established to nurture talented youth in the arts and athletics. Alburt continued in his regular primary school while attending chess classes for several hours a week.

Chess wasn't an all-consuming commitment. His mother, an engineer by training, also gave piano lessons.[13] For a while Alburt studied the instrument with his mother, and then he studied in a special school. Music, however, was not his forte. Whatever his varied talents, and especially his early promise in chess, his parents did not push him to excel in one thing or another. Here, Alburt compared the "unhealthy" competitive pressure put on many of the students he teaches in the States with his own family background. According to Alburt, they simply wanted him to be happy and successful in whatever he chose to do.

By age eleven or twelve Alburt was a remarkably strong player, but not a chess prodigy. He improved his skills working with stronger players and studying with a master teacher in a public chess program. The teacher, Roman Peltz, followed the same course of instruction with younger players that he did with topnotch ones. At that point, Alburt became one of the best players of his age in his home city of Odessa.

As a member of the Ukrainian chess team, he competed mainly with other youth at the regional level. He was considered to be a Category 1 player. To become a Master, he had to accumulate approximately 2400 points.

Becoming a Master

Until age eighteen Alburt had not won a major tournament. During his college years, something remarkable happened. Like Ashley, he made a quantum leap in chess standings, becoming both an Expert and Master.[14] He came close to qualifying for the Soviet Championship, ranking twenty out of tens of thousands of applicants at various playing levels; only eight, however, were chosen for the tournament. He was among the fifty best players in the Soviet Union, which, at that time, had only about two hundred masters.

He explains the dramatic improvement that occurred at age nineteen as the result of accumulated knowledge and experience, "extra hard work," and tournament play. The more he competed and lost, the more he studied, which was seven or eight hours a week (excluding tournament time). Compared with Ashley, that was minimal. But Alburt had had the benefit of years of formal instruction.

Lessons learned from tournament play were critical to his success. He especially recalls playing in the Odessa championship games. As many as eight masters and thirty "A" players reached the tournament finals. The lower-ranked "experts" qualified for the semifinals. (Alburt, age sixteen or seventeen, considered himself to be a very strong "A" player.) In order to beat the experts, he tried to avoid their strong games, while working on vulnerabilities in his repertoire of strategies and skills.

A question arises here whether a world-class chess player should be strong all around. A prominent example is that of the Estonian-born Mikhail Tal, 1960–61 World Champion, who was considered an attack genius but whose end game was less than stellar. In our June 2006 interview, Alburt mused whether for certain very talented individuals like Tal, it might be best to let them play in their idiosyncratic way rather than attempt to fit them into some mold of an ideal chess champion.

Alburt followed the traditional, steady path of achieving general excellence. He did not reach the level of Grandmaster until a relatively late age, thirty-two. The reason, he explains, is that travel to international competitions was absolutely essential. The Soviet state, however, granted permission to only a very small number of the top players each year.

Becoming a Teacher

As the state was not supporting his career as a professional chess player, Alburt turned to teaching. His pupils ranged from beginners to intermediate players. At the same time he worked on his own chess game and went to tournaments with the support of the Odessa Chess Federation.

For a brief period, he was a doctoral student (all but dissertation) and an assistant professor of physics in Odessa. That changed when a generous sponsor from the federation provided the financial means for Alburt to devote himself full time to chess as both a player and a coach of the university's top players. When he became a Grandmaster he was able to make so much money—even more than his distinguished mentor professor—that he left the academy. At that point, his professor jokingly asked Alburt if he would not care to become his chess instructor, as that certainly might lead to an even more lucrative career for himself.

Teaching in the United States

Alburt defected from the Soviet Union during the European Cup in 1979. Ensconced in New York, he has established a definite niche for himself in the American chess landscape. He is a prominent teacher, author, and Grandmaster. His teaching resembles in some ways that of Pandolfini, whom he considers to be one of America's outstanding coaches, as well as that of Ashley. In other ways, Alburt is remarkably different.

One similarity is that Alburt teaches students at all levels and by all means: "I take all kinds of students. Some of my students come to me and they don't know how the pieces move. I take more advanced students that come from the Chess Federation. I give advice over the telephone and mail. I write my books."

Although he would prefer committed students, Alburt, by his own admission, is willing to teach even the most rudimentary beginner or less-than-motivated children—so long as they are willing to pay $100 an hour. Not only that, he believes that with reasonable innate talent, systematic study, and good coaching, just about anyone can ascend in the World Federation of Chess rankings: "If someone who is very talented works on his own and plays in tournaments and analyzes his game, he could become a Grandmaster. Of course, he would get a coach on some occasions. He would work with others close to him and exchange ideas, which is what I did in Russia with a number of players."

Moreover, he believes that under the right conditions, "even an average person, every second person" has the potential to become a Master if "he would work with me for five years, five hours a week, twenty hours of tournament per month."[15] One reason for his confidence is the instructional system he learned in Russia. In comparing the U.S. and Russian chess contexts: "It's easy to become a better player in

Russia, because you are taught a certain system from your childhood. It's also easy to pick up a very good coach in Russia ... [and] good materials."

In the former Soviet Union, master chess players also were national heroes and could enjoy a high standard of living. Since the collapse of the Soviet Union and the move toward a more market-based economy, however, conditions are no longer as favorable for chess professionals. With the relaxation of emigration controls there has been a large exodus of quality chess professionals.[16] Compared with what he considered a repressive life, Alburt enjoys a general sense of freedom living in the United States.

He believes that living in the United States has tempered his teaching style. Having the advantage of studying U.S. and Russian pedagogies has provided him with a greater range of teaching strategies. Although he may be considered relatively "harsh" in his style, a reflection of the Russian system, he also makes every effort to individualize instruction according to the capacity and level of each student, more typical of American pedagogy. When Alburt teaches amateur adults, who are simply interested in perfecting their chess skills, he makes every effort to make learning a pleasant experience.

Identifying Qualities of a Good Player

All three chess educators have taught pupils at all levels of competence. Like master teachers in the arts, the three claim they can almost immediately identify the qualities of promising players. For Pandolfini, a good chess player, among other traits, needs to be able to control emotionality and expressiveness. For Ashley, a certain intensity and drive are necessary. For Alburt, "If you're not a fighter, you will not become a strong player." More important for Alburt, however, is a student's ability to learn principles in one context and apply them to another: "If a person takes twenty minutes to learn a combination and then I show him something very similar and if he has a problem, then maybe it could be miraculous, but probably he will not become a good player. I can find out very often in the first lesson."[17]

Chess and Computers

As the profiles of Pandolfini and Ashley suggest, computers play an increasingly important role in chess instruction. Computers can supplement, but not substitute for, years of systematic practice abetted by the intervention of expert teachers and coaches. Educators play the critical role of pointing out shortcomings and providing the immediate steps and long-term strategies required to advance to the highest performance levels. Master teachers are able to provide shortcuts based on their knowledge of a field.

A frequently asked question is this: are the very best chess players a match for the most sophisticated computer programs? The difference between computers and humans reveals the types of mental processes involved in being a world-class player. A major factor in determining who has an advantage is the speed of a game. According to chess coach Hearst:

> In terms of very fast chess, when games are played within five or ten minutes or half an hour, computers have already achieved Grandmaster status. If you look at it in terms of playing more slowly, which might well be forty moves in two or three and a half hours, which world championship players have played at, there's some question of how good the computer really is. The British Grandmaster John Nunn, who has a Ph.D. in mathematics, recently did an extensive survey. His view is that no computer would be able to beat a Grandmaster in a match that was of reasonably slow speed. So, at a high speed, computers can compete with the best in the world. They don't make any mistakes.[18]

The differences are attributed to the ability of a computer to analyze all possible moves immediately, which places a human at a disadvantage in a fast-paced game. However, as Eliot notes: "Chess players, contrary to usual beliefs, do not look at a lot of possibilities in a position. They only look at three or four moves usually. And that's true even of weaker players, too. The computer looks at all kinds of moves, but it's not thinking the same way a human being is. A human being is really narrowing down the possibilities very quickly."

A Grandmaster has the advantage of thinking strategically, so that a set of limited moves ultimately leads to victory. Paradoxically, for Ashley, the strength of the computer is also its greatest weakness: "With insufficient crunching power, the computer is unable to see truly far-reaching consequences of its decisions because it is looking at all of a singular decision ... when it would be best served if it could just look at two and just use all of its computing power analyzing those two."

Conclusions

Learning chess well involves acquiring the analytical skills required to envision possible consequences of actions and to think hypothetically and critically. These higher-order cognitive skills are similar to those essential to success in rigorous academic programs and the most challenging jobs in an information-age economy.[19] Although genetic factors may be important, genes alone do not tell the story. Profiles of world-class chess players strongly indicate that environmental factors are critical. They include supportive families, the quality of education programs, and the availability of expert teachers with effective pedagogies and learning materials.

The teaching approaches employed by Bruce Pandolfini, Maurice Ashley, and Lev Alburt involve:

- individualizing instruction;
- enabling students to evaluate their own performance, learn from mistakes, and build on strengths;
- providing a progression of specific steps for improvement and long-range strategies for long-term success in a highly competitive field;
- teaching collaborative behavior to strengthen team efforts;
- acquainting students with an abundance of learning resources to enhance performance; and
- preparing students for adulthood and being able to live a fuller life.[20]

Among significant environmental factors is the degree of development of a field and its openness to individuals from differing backgrounds. Public support for chess significantly expands opportunities for thousands, if not millions, who otherwise would not have the resources to develop their talent fully.[21] Until recently, special programs and publicly funded coaches were uncommon in the United States. Few individuals could make a living playing or teaching chess full time. Thanks to the pioneering efforts of educators like Bruce Pandolfini and Maurice Ashley, public school systems are more aware that chess can teach significant cognitive skills as well as successful behavioral and attitudinal traits. This realization has led to a growth in enrichment courses and programs with academic credit. Master teachers and world-class performers as role models and innovators can and do make a difference in the expansion and development of a field of endeavor, just as they do in enhancing the lives of countless individuals.

Notes

1. In the filming, the real-life people were often present on the set next to the actors, commenting on the accuracy of the characterizations.

2. The work of Swiss psychologist-educator Jean Piaget is particularly relevant here.

3. With regard to the ability to size up one's opponent, Pandolfini had this interesting observation: "If we're looking at a chess board, I'll look at their eyes. Their eyes tell me everything. Of course the game is spatial relations. And your thoughts are reflected in eye movement. You can't hide that. As you get more sophisticated, you attempt to disguise that. Because you know the other person will read your thoughts."

4. See, for example, Fred Waitzkin's book *Mortal Games*.

5. Lindsey Baker, "Sports Hero: Judit Polgar." http://myhero.com/myhero/hero. asp?hero=j_polgar.

6. In China and other socialist societies, such as Cuba, there are specialized schools in sports and music. In addition, after-school programs at Cultural Palaces that offer instruction in instrumental music, dance, song, and hobbies (such as model plane building) provide enrichment for those who already have a certain inclination or family support for honing skills and talent. Despite the egalitarian motivation behind such programs, they also tend to be segregated by gender, not by design but by previous societal norms and stereotyping. Also, despite the more egalitarian thrust of these societies, social class background also stratifies children according to their interests and pursuits.

7. That is the central argument of the many publications by K. A. Ericsson on the underpinnings of world-class performances in different fields.

8. Tournaments are the means by which rankings are determined by the World Chess Federation.

9. He immediately began using the software package with the Chess in the Schools program, as it suited his style of teaching by problem solving.

10. When I was in Caracas, Venezuela, in April 2006, visiting the Gran Colombia school complex that contains educational programs from preschool through the university, one of the first things to catch my attention was that two-year-olds were being taught chess. At that stage, they were simply learning the names of the pieces. At all school levels, chess was integrated into the curriculum in order to teach various cognitive skills, and, I assume, desirable attitudes and behaviors.

11. Although he first majored in electrical engineering at City College, and he would gladly have majored in chess if such a possibility had existed, Ashley settled on pursuing a degree in creative writing: "I fell in love with writing. I was inspired to do that because of a professor I had in school in a basic writing class." It may be surmised that this teacher was more influential in shaping Ashley's literary approach to teaching than any chess coach.

12. Although Pandolfini has worked with individuals like Max Kluge, who went on to become a chess Master, he usually works with students for no more than three to five years. He starts them off with "a firm grounding" and then refers them to other more advanced players like Grandmaster Lev Alburt, because, as he admits, "I've said everything I have to say. I'm not a guru." Given the strong personal bond that often forms between students and their chess coaches, it is not that easy to then tell students that they must now find another mentor. The difficulty for both teacher and student is explained by Pandolfini: You've been intimately involved in a family.... Suddenly, for whatever reason, you are supposed to terminate the lessons. You can suddenly feel as if you've lost a part of your family. That's very hard.

He finds as pleasant a way as possible to do this. He will refer his students to their next coach while still leaving the door open for students to return to consult with him: "I'll be a mentor, so I'm not left out. I'm factored in. And I feel better about that."

13. Alburt describes his father as a locally prominent head of the economics department in a major Odessa factory.

14. Alburt studied physics and had completed all but his dissertation for a doctorate in the subject. He was an associate professor of physics before giving up the academy for a career as a professional chess player and teacher.

15. This opinion reflects that of chess great Emanual Lasker (World Champion, 1894–1927).

16. Many of the émigrés are Jews, who left because of anti-Semitism.

17. Alburt will still teach a student with such problems. With his more promising students, he tells them, "You can become great if you practice twenty hours a week. You have a chance." For a beginner with average talent, he will say: "Look, you have a chance to become a Master, but don't think too hard. When I was seven years old, I wasn't thinking about how to become a Master. I was thinking about how to reach the next level."

18. Eliot Hearst is a retired psychology professor, writer on the subject of chess, and a past coach of the U.S. Olympic team that included Bobby Fischer.

19. Robert F. Reich, *The Work of Nations: Preparing Ourselves for 21st-Century Capitalism* (New York: Vintage Books, 1992).

20. For example, Pandolfini claims that "his ultimate goal as an educator is to provide lifelong lessons, enabling students to become more mature, self-reflective, and responsible adults."

21. To introduce a comparative perspective: on a 2006 trip to Caracas, Venezuela, I had an opportunity to visit a preschool center in the Gran Colombia educational complex. The center was teaching two- and three-year-olds about the game of chess. Bulletin board announcements in various schools in the complex indicated that chess instruction and tournament play were woven into the curriculum at all grade levels.

Sources

Interviews

Alburt, Lev. Interview by author. New York, April 26, 1999.
Ashley, Maurice. Interview by author. Brooklyn, NY, April 22, 1999.
———. Interview by author. New York, June 2, 2006.
Hearst, Eliot. Interview by author. Bloomington, IN, August 2, 1994.
Pandolfini, Bruce. Interview by author. New York, April 23, 1999.
———. Interview by author. New York, June 2, 2006.

Books

Alburt, Lev, and Al Lawrence. *Three Days with Bobby Fischer & Other Chess Essays.* New York: Chess Information and Research Center, 2003.
Ericsson, K. A., ed. *The Road to Excellence: The Acquisition of Expert Performance in the Arts, Sciences, Sports, and Games.* Mahwah, NJ: Lawrence Erlbaum Associates, 1996.
Ericsson, K. A., and I. A. Faivre. "What's Exceptional about Exceptional Abilities?" In *The Exceptional Brain: Neuropsychology of Talent and Special Abilities.* Edited by L. K. Obler and D. Fein, 436–73. New York: Guildford Press, 1988.
Pandolfini, Bruce. *Every Move Must Have a Purpose: Strategies from Chess for Business and Life.* New York: Hyperion, 2003.
Piaget, Jean. *Language, Literacy, and Cognitive Development: The Development and Consequences of Symbolic Communication.* Mahwah, NJ: Lawrence Erlbaum Associates, 2002.
———. *Play, Dreams and Imitation in Childhood.* London: Routledge, 1999.

————. *The Child's Conception of Physical Causality.* London: Routledge, 1999.

Reich, Robert. *The Work of Nations: Preparing Ourselves for 21st-Century Capitalism.* New York: Vintage Books, 1992.

Waitzkin, Fred. *Mortal Games: The Turbulent Genius of Garry Kasparov.* New York: G. F. Putnam's Sons, 1993.

Websites

Maurice Ashley: "Maurice Ashley." http://www.mauriceashley.com/; "Maurice Ashley Teaches Chess." http://www.thechessdrum.net/MAshleyCD.html.

Lev Alburt: "The Chess Games of Lev Alburt." http://www.chessgames.com/player/lev_alburt.html.

Judit Polgar: Baker, Lindsey. "Sports Hero: Judit Polgar." http://myhero.com/myhero/hero.asp?hero=j_polgar.

Gregory Kaidanov: "Grandmaster Gregory Kaidanov." http://chess.lexchess.com/index.html.

CHAPTER 12

Chicago's Master Chefs

Is there a secret to the great artistry of master chefs? According to *Kitchen Confidential* antic chef Anthony Bourdain, "What most people don't get about professional-level cooking is that it is not all about the most innovative presentation, the most creative marriage of flavors and textures; that, presumably, was all arranged before you got to dinner.... The real business of preparing the food you eat ... is more about consistency, about mindless, unvarying repetition." Conversely, internationally renowned Swiss chef Fredy Girardet, a role model for Charlie Trotter, "never repeated a menu and seldom repeated a dish at his restaurant in Crissier." According to *Wine Spectator*, which selected Trotter as the best chef in the world in 1997, "[He] regards recipes the way musicians see musical scores—as frameworks for improvisation. The results follow a discipline, but they spring from the moment, not from a carefully plotted script."[1]

Is it possible to reconcile these opposing approaches to the art and practice of cooking: routine high-quality performance with extemporaneous creativity, disciplined practice with spontaneous leaps into the unfamiliar? If as 1997 Australian chef of the year Philip Johnson observed, "You are only as good as your last meal"; or, for that matter, as many world-class artists, such as pianist André Watts, will tell you, "as successful as your last performance," then extraordinary risk-taking can be potentially career destroying. Yet master chefs, like acclaimed artists in other fields, are typically characterized by a continual striving for new heights of performance and extending the boundaries of knowledge in their field of endeavor.

The chefs in this chapter are among Chicago's and the nation's finest. They operate four-star restaurants, as rated by *Chicago Magazine,* and have garnered an impressive list of the most prestigious national and international awards in dining.

The list includes, in alphabetical order, Rick Bayless, Jean Joho, Roland Liccioni, Tony Mantuano, and Charlie Trotter. In addition, I have included in this discussion 2000 Indianapolis chef of the year Steven Oakley, who apprenticed at both Charlie Trotter's and Printers Row; Philip Johnson, Remy Martin–award winning chef of E'cco in Brisbane, Australia; Philippe Graeme, highly rated chef/owner of Battery Point Brasserie in Hobart (Tasmania), Australia; Jacques Thorel of L'Auberge Bretonne La Roche Bernard, France (listed in *Les Grandes Tables du Monde*); and Antonella Scardoni of La Locanda Solarola, Castel Geulfo, Italy (with past ratings of one and two Michelin stars).[2]

These chefs represent two fundamentally distinct methods of induction into the culinary arts: (1) a formal process that includes an extended period of apprenticeship in a traditional, hierarchical system of teaching and learning by which the novice chef increasingly acquires more responsibility and learns the most sophisticated cooking skills; and (2) an informal process by which a self-taught individual learns first by reading and then seeks out opportunities to serve in the kitchens of outstanding chefs. Although there are instances of supposedly self-taught world-class performers in music (such as Andrés Segovia) and chess (Bobby Fischer), their achievement of mastery, as with jazz musicians, occurred through listening or observing and being coached, albeit less systematically, by more experienced players. Of the Chicago area chefs highlighted in this article, Joho and Liccioni represent the traditional apprenticeship system, while Trotter, Bayless, and Mantuano were primarily self-reliant learners. Whether self-taught or highly schooled, one characteristic essential to being a first-rate chef, according to Philippe Graeme, is a high degree of intelligence and a capacity to be analytical and self-critical.

Early Fascination with Cooking

With few exceptions, Charlie Trotter being one, these master chefs marked out their careers before age ten. Jean Joho, perhaps the earliest, recalls photographs of himself at age three in a chef's uniform. At age five or six he was baking Christmas cookies with his sister, which led to preparing Sunday breakfasts, and eventually one of his specialties—Kougelhopf, a breakfast bread.[3]

From the time he was eight or nine, Rick Bayless, who comes from an extended family of restaurateurs (his parents owned a barbeque restaurant), would plan and prepare three or four dinner parties over the summer vacations around specialty themes, such as Hawaiian cooking. For his tenth birthday, he requested the gift of Julia Child's newly published *Mastering the Art of French Cooking*, the basis of the series aired on public TV in his hometown of Oklahoma City. He then proceeded to work his way through the book. Although his extended family probably would have preferred athletic prowess in the young Rick to his penchant for the unusual, "doing new projects, learning new things, and tackling new endeavors always," Bayless particularly remembers with great fondness his grandmother as a constant source of support and inspiration.

Joho's family background also was formative of his interest in cooking. His father was constantly bringing clients from his construction business home for dinner.[4] His first truly gastronomic and mind-opening culinary experience was at age nine, when he was taken to the 3-star Auberge de L'ill, where he ordered foie gras, black truffles, and lobster, delicacies that still seem to be his favorites. Several years later, his father arranged for him to work in the restaurant kitchen.

Roland Liccioni's family migrated from Vietnam to Biarritz, France, where they ran a restaurant that drew upon both culinary traditions. (His father was French and his mother Vietnamese.) With this background, it is not surprising that he began his professional career early—at age ten he began working in the restaurant—and that his signature culinary style would reflect a fusion of European and Asian influences.

Although Tony Mantuano did not begin his culinary career until after entering college, he was raised in an Italian family where "every event was centered on food," and his grandparents owned a grocery store. Both grandmothers were great cooks, and one of his grandfathers had "great big gardens, from which he would take seeds from the biggest tomatoes and save those for the next year ... [and] every year the vegetables became stronger and bigger and the best of the best. So that there was an appreciation for that [the quality of ingredients] long before I became involved professionally."[5]

Charlie Trotter, who did not begin his full-time, headlong plunge into cooking until after he completed his undergraduate degree in political science at the University of Wisconsin, Madison, identifies among his childhood influences—besides listening to jazz greats like Miles Davis—a key lesson imparted by his father.[6] He told Charlie, "Whatever it is you want to do—I don't care if you want to deliver mail, pick up garbage, add up figures all day—whatever it is you do, you choose it because that's the only way you're ever going to be happy." And happiness in life is what Charlie Trotter discovered as he became one of the most highly respected chefs on the international culinary scene.

Apprenticeships, Mentors, and Role Models

Charlie Trotter

Trotter's odyssey, if not meteoric rise to stardom, began at the lowest level, typical of all the other chefs with the possible exception of Bayless. In fact, it did not even begin in the kitchen peeling and scrubbing vegetables or serving on the line. After finishing college, in 1982, "he decided he wanted to become a cook or a chef or wherever that route would take, and began looking around for a restaurant opportunity." Not deterred by being turned down at about forty restaurants, he applied to the newly opened suburban branch of Gordon's in Lake Forest, where he met chef Norman Van Aken. Trotter was initially assigned to wait on tables, which he had done during his college years.

Both Van Aken and restaurateur Gordon Sinclair were early-stage guides in several but different respects. In my interview with him, Trotter, whose role models include novelists Henry Miller and Fyodor Dostoyevsky as well as conservative writer and ideologue Ayn Rand, expressed his appreciation of Van Aken, "more from the standpoint of who he was as an artist, as a person, as a lover of literature, than necessarily with respect to cuisine." However, in a later interview with *Wine Spectator,* Trotter also credited Van Aken, a well-known and frequently cited chef/author, "with teaching him not to compromise on quality," and restaurateur Sinclair with "demonstrating how to create a gracious dining room"—both important elements of Trotter's vision for the restaurant he was to open five years later, in 1987.

But to get to that point, his journey would first take him out to California the year following his apprenticeship in Lake Forest. He moved "on a whim" after reading in *Time* magazine that "the whole food movement was overtaking the country and that the epicenter of this culinary revolution was really the Bay Area up to the Napa Valley." In San Francisco he worked at the Café Bedford, which featured modern American cuisine, and then at the Compton Place Hotel with Bradley Ogden, "who was one of the most important chefs on the West Coast at that time." On only his second day in the Bay Area, he went on one of chef/author Barbara Tropp's tours of Chinatown, which was a mere couple of blocks from where he lived. Over the next eighteen months he became "fairly intimate with where to shop for this dried produce, for this fish, this duck, and where to eat." Such experiences, along with reading nonstop literally every cookbook he could get his hands on, were shaping his ideas on cuisine.

Meeting Alice Waters and working in Chez Panisse, the mecca of nouvelle cuisine in the 1980s, was a must for Trotter. The attempt was less than successful on first try. In 1983, after taking his bicycle up to Seattle and riding it down coastal Highway One to San Francisco in fourteen days, Trotter showed up on the doorstep of the Berkeley restaurant, saying, "Would you please give me a job? I'll do anything. I'll work for free, I'll wash dishes, I'll peel onions...." The response? "They promptly shooed me away. I wanted to, in a sort of Khrushchev-like gesture [at the United Nations], remove my shoe and pound my heel against the front menu box and declare that I'd be back to bury them." Bury them he didn't, but over time he became a friend of Alice Waters, as he would of some of the great European chefs he admired.

Setting out to learn as much as he could about cooking, Trotter took a summer off in 1985, purchased a Eurail pass, packed a "sort of half backpack/half suitcase" in which he "folded up a sport coat, his one shirt and a tie, a nice pair of pants." When he arrived in a town he would check into a very inexpensive hotel, maybe just a grade above a youth hostel, steam out his shirt, get ready, and go to dinner in world-class restaurants. From Paris, where his eventual wife-to-be lived, he would plot out his visits, including one to La Pyramide, outside Lyon, and Le Crissier, in Switzerland, which he describes as "epiphany-like experiences." Both restaurants and the visionary styles of their founding chefs, Fernand Point and Fredy Girardet, were to be great inspirations for Trotter. Dining alone in these grand restaurants, Trotter observed everything he could. What impressed him was that "things would just happen before you even decided you needed them or wanted them, whether it was a glass of wine or a piece of bread. And there seemed to be an equal devotion to the ambiance, the cuisine, the wine program, and the service. Not one of those things would be more salient than another."

Over the next two years, Trotter would apprentice in a series of restaurants, staying just as long as he felt he needed in order to learn something new—or what not to do. At age twenty-seven, and with no previous experience as an executive chef/restaurateur, Trotter opened the famed dining establishment that bears his name.

Rick Bayless

Bayless, even more an autodidact then Trotter, achieved a level of culinary sophistication at an amazingly early age. His family dinner parties and various research projects were just the beginning. By the time he entered the University of Oklahoma as an undergraduate, he ran a catering business and taught cooking—not ordinary fare but "high-end French" meals. He continued his graduate work at the University of Michigan. There he completed all of the requirements for a doctorate in linguistics except for the dissertation. Disillusioned with job prospects in that field, he followed the calling of his childhood in deciding to open a restaurant, but not before exploring Mexico in depth.

Bayless claims that he never had a mentor or teacher who coached him. Although he "always looked for a mentor," the attempts he made to apprentice with someone did not turn out well. For many years he believed that with a mentor to help him along, he might have been able "to do so much more." But, then, he "realized that probably I wouldn't be as far along if I had someone guiding me ... because I would have been less self-reliant." He admittedly admires Julia Child and Alice Waters as role models, but not mentors. In fact, he would prefer not to be close personal friends but rather "put them out there" and then "judge myself against them all the time."

From childhood on, Bayless has been indefatigable in taking on new projects and undertaking the necessary background research. At age fourteen, he planned a family trip to Mexico. That was the beginning of his involvement with Mexico and its rich culinary traditions. With his wife, Deann, who manages the business end of Frontera Grill and Topolobampo, he has traveled the main highways and back roads of Mexico, visiting local markets (much like Charlie Trotter) and sampling regional cuisines in the most popular local restaurants as well as from street vendors and in Mexican homes. Mexican culture and its foods constituted the formative experiences that led to his twin restaurants Frontera Grill-Topolobampo being considered the finest Mexican cuisine north of the border.[7] His artistry was recognized in 1995 by the James Beard Foundation, which named him the "Best Chef of the Year." In 2007, the James Beard Awards selected Frontera Grill as the very best restaurant in the United States.

Jean Joho

Joho reached the heights of the culinary world by the mid-1980s, in the appropriately named restaurant, Everest, atop One Financial Place, the headquarters of the Chicago Stock Exchange. That memorable meal at Auberge de L'ill, at age nine, may have been the starting point of a brilliant career that has all the characteristics of a traditional apprenticeship in classical French cuisine. While still a high school student, Joho worked two summers at the Auberge, which was a short ride from his home, doing the basic grunt jobs expected of those starting at the bottom. After completing his academic secondary education (the *baccaulaureate*), he entered a culinary institute and upon completion of that stage with specialties in pastries (his *Certificat Professionael*), cheese-making, and wines, attended the Hotel School, in Strasbourg, where he learned the business end of being a restaurateur. After serving as chef at a Michelin 2-star restaurant in Basel (beginning at the amazing age of twenty-three), he returned to Auberge de L'ill, now a 3-star restaurant. There he was mentored by Paul Haeberlin, a master chef who was a protégé of the legendary Fernando Point, founder of La Pyramide.

For Joho, who moved into his own apartment at age thirteen to begin his career as a novice chef while still studying in the Lyceé Hôtelier, Haeberlin was almost a father figure in "everything concerned with business." An enduring lesson taught by Haeberlin was that "you treat every customer the same. Every customer is important." He also learned to be modest, a striking characteristic in Joho, and to be his own person.

In 1984, he came to Chicago to open Maxim's. According to his résumé, shortly thereafter he met Richard Melman of Lettuce Entertain You Enterprises, Inc. One year later, Joho inaugurated Everest with a *Chicago Magazine* 4-star rating. Other top honors and rave reviews were to follow immediately, including being selected as one of the "Top 10 New Chefs in America" by *Food & Wine;* and, in 1997, along with Charlie Trotter, one of the ten best chefs in the country by *USA Today.*[8] Very much an entrepreneur with a vision to share good food, Joho was cofounder of the popular Corner Bakeries that dot the Chicago downtown landscape and, in 1995, opened Brasserie Jo, named one of the top ten restaurants that year by the *Chicago Sun-Times.*

Roland Liccioni

Liccioni's career path from France to Chicago follows along an essentially similar path of formal training in his teens, systematic apprenticeships, and major responsibilities at a relatively young age as a sous chef in highly rated restaurants. Both Joho and Liccioni stress the necessity of learning the basics, respect for tradition, discipline in one's work, and note that without such a solid foundation it is rare to achieve mastery as a chef. At age thirteen, after completing the first cycle of secondary education, he entered a culinary school. At age seventeen he went to work at the oldest brasserie in Paris, where he worked on the grill and prepared fish, sauces, and meat. At age twenty he went to England, where he worked at the then 2-star River Café, which, according to the *New York Times*, "has turned into a kind of finishing school for chefs from Australia [for example, Philip Johnson] to New York"—even though chef Rose Gray has never spent a single day in a culinary institute.[9] Liccioni soon became a sous chef, a remarkable achievement for a person that young.

In 1981, at age twenty-three, he visited the United States on vacation, came to the "Windy City," and "dined at several restaurants, which he liked very much." More important, he met his future wife, decided to stay, and served as chef at the highly rated Carlos' in Highland Park over the next seven and a half years. In 1989 he replaced Jean Banchet, Chicago's first internationally renowned chef, at the famed Le Français, in Wheeling. Banchet had established Le Français as perhaps the most respected French restaurant in the United States in the 1970s and 1980s.[10]

Over the next decade, according to the *Chicago Tribune*, Roland and Mary Beth Liccioni "ran Le Français with distinction," and "the 4-star restaurant's reputation did nothing but improve."[11] When the restaurant closed in July of 1999, the Liccionis moved to Les Nomades, a former private club in downtown Chicago, where they are chef/owners. Very quickly, Les Nomades received top ratings as a "Streetville oasis for supremely civilized dining."[12]

Tony Mantuano

Mantuano, whose pan-Mediterranean cuisine first captured national attention in 1996, while he was chef at Tuttaposto,[13] did not decide to go into the restaurant business until completing several years of college as a music major. His father, who was in the meat-packing business, helped him land a job at the upscale Nantucket Shores in Milwaukee. He started peeling fifty-pound bags of potatoes—and onions, "which was even worse"—in the back room. He "never even saw the kitchen before the first six months." He worked his way up the ladder, first getting to assist the day-time chef, then taking responsibility for specialty lunches. The turning point came when he started working with the professionally trained dinner chef who ignited Mantuano's interest in serious cooking because "he brought the knowledge of how

European chefs do things in the industry." From Tom Manthei, who had studied in France and Switzerland, he learned the correct classical techniques and precise vocabulary. "Moreover, he had the air of professionalism."

Self-instruction followed. Like Trotter and Bayless, he "would read anything and everything. Anything I could get my hands on about food and about culture." Among his favorite chef authors were James Beard and Guliano Bugialli. *Gourmet Magazine*, with its discussion of food trends in San Francisco, Los Angeles, and New York, was a source of ideas, such as serving pasta made from scratch. His purchasing the necessary equipment and making fresh pasta daily in the early 1980s was considered bizarre, if not resisted, by the line staff in the Chicago restaurant where he soon became chef.

His major break came when Larry and Mark Levy, owners of the Chestnut Street Grill, were persuaded by Mantuano's wife, Cathy, a waitress at that restaurant, to meet with him. At the time, the brothers were building One Magnificent Mile, which they envisioned housing a world-class Italian restaurant. They hired Mantuano on the condition that he work for a year in Italy before becoming chef at Spiaggia. As part of the bargain, Cathy would run the restaurant.

Mantuano considers himself lucky to be one of the first U.S. chefs to apprentice in topnotch Italian restaurants back in the early 1980s. The Italian chefs readily welcomed Tony, providing entrée to the restaurants of their colleagues. The chefs "would take you on the side and say, 'This is what you got to do, and it takes [this long].' ... They wanted you to represent their cuisine correctly."

While serving as chef at Spiaggia between 1984 and 1990, Tony and Cathy also would spend time working in Paris kitchens to learn bistro food. As part of "a central think tank" with the owners of Spiaggia, Mantuano developed new restaurants, such as Bistro 110 and Eurasia, before opening his own restaurants, Tuttaposto and Mantuano's Mediterranean Table. In 1999, he became executive chef at Spiaggia, considered by critics to be one of America's finest Italian restaurants.

Curiosity and Creativity, Passion and Devotion—If Not Obsession

Like the world-class musicians and other artists and performers I interviewed, these outstanding chefs read deeply not only in their own domain but often also in seemingly unrelated fields; and they have an interest in and appreciation of the accomplishments of exceptional individuals.

Jean Joho

For young Joho, the dictionary was "the most important book." He would spend hours reading it and "everything, not only about food." Eager to learn about the cuisines of other countries, he studied German, Italian, and English, in addition to French and Latin. Long passionate about art, he attends exhibits at the Art Institute and seeks out museums in any city he visits.

Charlie Trotter

Trotter, who reads widely on topics related to creativity and extraordinary individuals, decries the increasingly vocational orientation of college education. He considers his undergraduate years at the University of Wisconsin, Madison, as a "chance not to think about what I was going to do with a career, [but] a chance to read the great books, a chance to fill out my education."

Once he had decided on his career and moved out to San Francisco, he describes his life this way: "I slept on the floor in a studio apartment. I spent every penny I earned either buying new cookbooks or dining out or buying some kind of kitchen utensil or kitchen equipment.... I'm talking about a level of fanaticism that crushed the typical [cult] religious zealotry that we're familiar with.... I mean it was night and day incessant, thinking, sleeping, breathing cuisine, having nothing to do with anyone who wasn't interested."

Rick Bayless

Like Trotter, Bayless is acquainted with Mihaly Csikszentmihalyi's concept of "The Flow."[14] The "flow" refers to experiences characterized by total involvement of individuals with ideas, discovery, and invention to the point that they lose track of time and place. Bayless, with his need to be constantly involved with new challenges and undertakings, best illustrates the "flow" experience. This was evident in my first visit to Topolobampo in the late 1990s, when Bayless, carefully editing the proof pages of his first book at a table across from the open kitchen with all the bustle of waiters, was oblivious to everything occurring around him. As he describes it, "Total pleasure to me is to be absorbed in a project." But completion of a project may be less important than the process of involvement: "It's really critical. I can't finish a project without having the next thing lined up.... Usually, right at the most highly pressured point of a project, when you're just wrapping it up ... I'll stop working on it and get really involved working on another project."

Despite "driving his wife crazy" when he does this, Bayless describes his wife, Deann, "as being the same way. We get absorbed in slightly different things, so it's kind of interesting that we can both be like that where we're totally in our own little worlds." While working out ideas to complete or start a project, Bayless has to get out and walk the streets. If you pass him in this mode, don't bother to talk to him, because he won't recognize you, for, at these moments, "he loves having the opportunity to block the rest of the world out."

Impact of Career on Family Life

For those who work with their spouses—Liccioni, Mantuano, and Bayless—there may be greater understanding of time lost in the worlds of work and ideas. Trotter's case may be more typical of chefs whose spouses have their own careers: "Much to the dismay of my wife, I'm obsessed with what I do and with cuisine and with what it's all about." Phillippe Graeme, responding with some irony to my question, quipped, "Ask my previous two wives." That evening, however, his third wife was hosting the restaurant and graciously attending to the wants of the diners.

Striving for Perfection

In their constant striving for excellence, these chefs, typical of master artists and peak performers, are frequently their own severest critics. Perfection is hard to achieve and maintain. They expect it not only in themselves but in those who work with them, and they expect it, according to Bayless, "not only in the food but also in the workplace."

When asked what attributes they looked for in the people they hire, the most common answers tend to be attitudes, personality traits, and individual drive rather than experience: "kids who are eager to learn" (Mantuano); "honesty, and the ability to enjoy both cooking and eating" (Joho). For Trotter, "I love it when they say, 'I can't live without it. . . . ' And that's kind of the way I look at what we do here. You have to want this so bad that you're going to live it and breathe it, and this is all you're ever going to want to do." For those who aspire to be chefs, Liccioni's advice is: "Don't worry about the hours first. Work hard. And have good discipline for the other people and the chef you're working with. That's the main thing. And don't try to think you're going to be a chef tomorrow, or next year, whatever. It takes time."

Bayless, who runs a less hierarchical kitchen than Trotter, Liccioni, and Joho—in fact, compared with most outstanding restaurants, the organization with a staff of sixty is rather flat, if not egalitarian, with Bayless frequently working the line—says, "There's no such thing as management vs. workers here. All the management also has to do all the work." All of this makes for the sustainability of consistently high-quality performance and reaching the almost impossible heights of day-to-day perfection.

Vision and Signature

In their chapter on "What's Next? The Chef as Alchemist" (*Becoming a Chef*), Dornenburg and Page aptly capture the ability of culinary masters to transform the most common ingredients into extraordinary objects and experiences. The artistry—science?—involved requires an understanding of the basic nature and potential of the materials with which they are working. The ability to see the world, elemental things, anew has often been compared to the way a child sees the world afresh. In his writings on "Extraordinary Individuals" who shaped the twentieth century, Howard Gardner often describes major breakthroughs in science (for example, Einstein and the Theory of Relativity) and psychology (Freud), art (Picasso), music (Stravinsky), and dance (Graham) in just that way. Analogies to the pristine vision of children are, of course, deceptive, for they necessarily omit the years of relentless study, hard work, and disciplined concentration on understanding and extending knowledge and practice in any human field of endeavor.

Charlie Trotter

The playful brilliance associated with breakthrough artists and peak performers is the result of preparation. Trotter, whom *USA Today* restaurant critic Jerry Shriver described as "having the most personalized style of cooking I've ever experienced," takes as his role models Michael Jordan and Fredy Girardet: "Michael Jordan knows technique; he knows how to guard somebody, he knows how to crossover dribble, how to pass the ball behind his back, how to dunk the basketball, how to shoot it from twenty feet and make a swish, how to make free throws. Within his fundamental understanding of the game and being able to play basic basketball at very high levels, he's also an artist in that he can improvise in any situation.... And he's able to do that at that level when he's competing against the best of the best." (Interestingly enough, *Wine Spectator*'s 1997 review of the Chicago culinary scene fittingly dubbed Trotter "the Michael Jordan of American cooking. He has moves no one else has.")[15] The late Girardet, whom Trotter considers to be the greatest chef of the twentieth century, had these qualities: "Vision: He had a greater vision than just about anyone else. He was able to do things that very few chefs can do. He was able to cook spontaneously with a high, awesomely high, level of consistency and refinement. A lot of people can cook spontaneously, but it isn't always very refined."

One of the signature characteristics of Charlie Trotter's vision is that he thinks not just about creatively putting together the finest ingredients for each dish but rather of "a menu in and of itself and how a course must exist vis-à-vis the following or preceding courses."

Rick Bayless

A January 9, 1997, *Indianapolis Star* feature article on Bayless entitled "Chicago Chef Chases Authentic Flavors in Pursuit of Perfection" may as well have served as a description of all the other chefs in this study. Authenticity is an essential component of the vision of these chefs. An insight into what inspires Bayless's love of Mexican cuisine and culture is his personal credo: "I'm basically a fighter by nature, I guess. And I would never, I can't imagine myself being a French-style chef because they're the top dogs, and I'm the kind that always gravitates toward the underlings. I want to prove in some way that there is integrity to all things. And that's the fire that fuels my mission.... I don't cook Mexican food just because I like to do it. I cook it because I feel that it deserves a tremendous amount of respect and it's got its own integrity."

Jean Joho

A traditional French chef, Joho is eager to demonstrate that even the most common foods that are part of everyday culture are to be savored—and, in many respects, may, with deft touches, be transformed into extraordinary culinary experiences. Moreover, like Bayless, he wants to communicate his message to a larger audience. According to Joho: "With fine dining, I want to prove that you can also make it with casual food, using much less expensive ingredients.... This is what I wanted to see as possible in Chicago, because you can't have a great audience with a restaurant you can't go to many times in a week." There is, however, a distinction between his two restaurants: "Everest is for dining; Brasserie is for eating."

For Joho, Everest is "something much more close to my heart than anything else" because "it's more personalized." When asked about his personal vision for Everest, as well as Brasserie Jo: "The number one thing: I cook what I like to eat."

Rolland Liccioni

When asked about his personal style and vision, Liccioni responded, "I know one thing, one fact, for sure: anything I do or create comes from me. So there's nothing copied from the book." And that style is changing, evolving: "I find new techniques. I find new ways to prepare dishes." When interviewed at Le Français, he gave the example of preparing an eggless béarnaise sauce—a mystery he is reluctant to share.

Tony Mantuano

Mantuano "will look at a certain dish and just have an idea of how to improve upon it—for instance, simple hummus, you know. We slice some smoked tomatoes and garnish it with that or some pickled chili peppers. We try to add more layers of flavor and try to make it a little more interesting. And we just try to make it our style. I'm always looking at food like that." Returning from Calabria, he described with excitement a dish he thought so simple yet ingenious: "It was a whole fish roasted for a group of six people. The fish was taken out of the juices (olive oil and tomato—fresh tomato—and basil and garlic). Linguine was tossed into those cooking juices, served first, and after that followed by the fish. It was such a great dish."[16]

Commonalities in the Makings of Top-Notch Cuisine

Although extremely complicated dishes are frequently described in the reviews of award-winning restaurants and chefs, the essence of excellence may be briefly summarized as simplicity combined with elegance. The alchemy resides in the knowledge of basic elements, combining the very best of ingredients that go into the chemistry, and a disciplined imagination that works the magic.

Master chefs obtain their boutique vegetables and fruits, fresh dairy, fish, and specialty meats and poultry products both locally and globally.[17] Bayless relies on a network of small farmers extending to Mexico, for the exact ingredients he needs. Joho, who looks for freshness—"I just want food that tastes like something"—purchases leeks and green asparagus from Michigan, even though that might seem strange, because "I think there are good farmers over there." Noteworthy is Charlie Trotter's initiative to involve youths living in nearby public housing in growing specialty produce for his kitchen.

Ongoing experimentation and adding a personal signature to well-known dishes also typifies our first-rate chefs. As Steven Oakley of Indianapolis noted: "You know, you aren't going to re-create the wheel. You are going to spin off of that ... and everyone's always coming up with their own little flair and twist."

Communicating and Teaching—Directly and Indirectly

As with the other profiled peak performers and their mentors, these chefs have a desire to share widely their love of cooking and their knowledge of the culinary arts. All, in one way or another, are involved in mentoring apprentices, writing books, starring in television series, or, simply, through the example of what they are doing on a day-to-day basis, attempting to reach a larger audience with an appreciation of fine food. They are trying to change perceptions and habits of the public, while, themselves, attempting to adjust to the changing societal notions of eating and dining. For example, Joho, in deference to a strong aversion to certain foods among local patrons, would never think of placing brains and innards on his menu; but, in response to their preferences, he has grown accustomed to serving rolls and bread warm, contrary to the French classical tradition.

What I found surprising in my study of world-class musicians is that many view their most important role to be that of educators rather than performers—for in their students there is a certain kind of immortality or, at least, the promise of continuing and improving upon cherished traditions that enhance the quality of life for countless others. The most interesting discussion, actually disagreement, I had on the subject of chef as educator was with Charlie Trotter, who was reluctant to see himself as a teacher, despite his cookbooks and television series. Citing Henry David Thoreau as an example, Trotter noted: "I think we should try to be the best that we can be. And people can take from that what they will."

Steven Oakley, who worked summer stints at Charlie Trotter's, affirms that the instruction going on in the kitchen was more or less indirect: "It wasn't a learning experience as far as someone taking you by the hand and saying, 'This is what we are going to do.' You are kind of expected to know what's going on." What did impress him was that Charlie Trotter was "really demanding and really particular.... He's just a perfectionist and really pushes you and demands a lot and it shows in his product and his restaurant and what he has done."

Trotter, whether or not he sees himself as an educator, certainly has reached out to large and diversified audiences with his vision of what good food is all about. Prior to taking leave of daily management of the restaurant in 2003, he regularly brought low-income children into his neighboring teaching and studio kitchen where they sampled the inspirational foods enjoyed by nighttime customers.

Similarly, Bayless works with "Kids Up Front, a program of the antihunger organization Share Our Strength, to educate disadvantaged children about healthful food and nutrition." He has been actively engaged with Chefs Collaborative 2000, a nationwide "group of chefs [including Alice Waters] concerned with sustaining the natural resources of the planet and the health of its inhabitants." Bayless's educational work also includes teaching the network of farmers providing the produce for his kitchen "how to cultivate a particular species of lamb's quarters, purple *tomatillos,* or black *sapote,* a tropical fruit."[18]

Bayless very consciously perceives what he is doing as educating both the public at large and his own staff, which he regularly takes to Mexico each summer. His mission is to bring the "simple, delicious real flavors of Mexico into North America in the most authentic way possible."[19] In doing so, he also is systematically sharing Mexican culture. (Similarly, world-class musicians express an abiding commitment to respecting the integrity of the works they perform and the traditions and context that produced a particular composition.) As a student of both anthropology and descriptive linguistics, Bayless views food, not unlike music, as a form of language and a way in which people communicate with one another.

Sisyphus Revisited—Persistence

Given the level of intensity in many kitchens, one would expect early burnout.[20] In many respects, the daily demands and grinding efforts resemble those of the mythical Sisyphus, ever doomed to push a massive rock up a hill, only to have it roll down again, and then start over.... And yet, the master artists I studied these past thirteen years often continue performing at a peak level well into their seventies—even their eighties! Unlike the futility of Sisyphus's efforts, these chefs do achieve success, recognition, and often the status of rock stars, quite frequently at an early age.[21]

What keeps them going—overcoming Sisyphean fatigue—is a love of what they are doing as well as the excitement, if not the adrenaline rush, that comes from their passionate involvement with their craft. Compensating for the tedious hours of preparation is the joy that comes from performing before a live audience, whether in a concert hall, an athletic stadium, or a restaurant dining room.

Legacies

When these chefs appeared on the Chicago restaurant scene in the early 1980s, they began to transform the city's culinary landscape for the better. They were by no means the only ones.[22] Over the ensuing decade, the transformations they wrought were so remarkable that *USA Today*, in 1996, named three Chicago restaurants among the ten best in the country. As restaurant critic Jerry Shriver noted, "This list is heavily weighted toward Chicago simply because I had more great meals there than anywhere else."[23] The following year, *Wine Spectator*, in its feature story "Now Arriving: Chicago Has Finally Made It," summed up the city's culinary scene this way: "What dazzled us most was the number of top-notch chefs with discipline and imagination."[24]

Charlie Trotter views the legacy of his restaurant in more than just aesthetic culinary terms. With regard to cultural and social contributions:

> I want Charlie Trotter's restaurant to benefit the city of Chicago and the community, the neighborhood ... and the whole Midwest from the same standpoint that the Art Institute is a cultural asset.... What makes a city, a community, worth living in are some of the great cultural assets. Wrigley Field, the Museum of Science and Industry, a great hotel.... It would mean something to me if, after a period of time—and it usually takes many, many years. But it would be great if Charlie Trotter's made Chicago a better city because of its presence.

Final Food for Thought

When I first wrote this chapter, in 2005, Lance Armstrong had just won the *Tour de France* for the seventh consecutive year. This feat placed Armstrong among the most remarkable athletes of the past one hundred years. Reflecting on the traits that characterize peak performance, I find striking parallels between Armstrong's career and the master teachers/coaches/chefs and world-class talents profiled in *Talent Abounds*. Those traits include a vast and intimate knowledge of the general contours, as well as minute details, of the terrain to be mastered, finely honed skills, persistence, consistency, passion, preparation, and clarity of vision—with the ability to work systematically and intelligently toward well-defined goals. A life of striving to achieve mastery of a performance field invariably involves not only respecting tradition and those who went before but also extending the boundaries of a field.

With regard to the nature versus nurture debate: innate talent certainly is a necessary but not sufficient condition to achieve peak performance in athletics and the arts, including those culinary. The personal qualities of motivation, hard work, and devotion to continually learn, improve, and contribute are also critical to achieving major breakthroughs in a particular domain. Along the way, inspirational teachers, either directly or indirectly, invariably become involved in guiding novice talents to world-class performance levels.

The chapter began with a question: "Are routine high-quality performance and exceptional creativity systematically possible in the world of food as well as in other fields?" The early twentieth-century artist and wit Max Beerbohm, who once quipped, "Only mediocrity can be trusted to be always at its best," would have answered "no." Based on my past decade and more of research, I most definitely would say "yes."

Notes

1. "Now Arriving," *Wine Spectator*, October 15, 1997, 68.
2. After writing an initial draft of this chapter in 2003, I interviewed Thomas Keller (French Laundry and Per Se, 3-star Michelin chef), Mark Miller (Santa Fe Café, who popularized Southwestern cuisine), Carme Ruscalleda (the first female Spanish Michelin 2-star chef, restaurant Sant Pau in Santa Pol de Mer), and Edouard Loubet (a 2-star Michelin chef, restaurant La Bastide de Capelongue, Bonnieux en Provence, France). They confirmed the general career path of outstanding chefs who had largely acquired their culinary skills through apprenticeships in a progression of topnotch restaurants with master chefs and, in the case of Ruscadella, growing up in a family in the food business.
3. The bread is featured in Andrew Dornenburg's and Karen Page's *Becoming a Chef.*
4. At that time, Alsatian families, according to Joho, tended not to entertain friends or clients in restaurants.
5. As a child, Antonella Scardoni, executive chef of Laconda Solarola, worked in her family kitchen and had a passion for the produce of the rural area where her father worked as an agriculturist. Rose Gray, who along with Ruth Rogers, runs the River Café on the Thames outside London, considered by many to be the finest Italian restaurant in Europe, much to the displeasure of Italian friends, may attribute her keen interest in gardening and the fruit trees that surround her restaurant to a grandmother who was president of the Royal Horticulture Society.
6. His father was a successful entrepreneur who established his own companies, rather than enter the family business.
7. The two restaurants are joined by a common kitchen but with different emphases.

8. Jerry Shriver, "Here's the Dish on the Year's Best Dining," *USA Today*, December 30, 1996, D6.

9. R. W. Apple, Jr., "The Heart of Italy, by the Thames," *New York Times*, June 12, 2004, D1.

10. Like so many of the outstanding chefs of the twentieth century, Banchet can trace his lineage back to Fernand Point of Le Pyramide through his mentor, master chef Paul Bocose.

11. "Tru-ly Inspired," *Chicago Tribune*, July 23, 1999, Section 7, 45.

12. *Chicago Magazine*, July 2005.

13. Dennis Ray Wheaton, "If the Democrats Arrive Hungry in Chicago," *New York Times*, August 11, 1996, Section 5, 6.

14. Csikszentmihalyi is a University of Chicago psychology professor who has coauthored books with Harvard University professor Howard Gardner. He is best known for his works on "multiple intelligences" and creativity.

15. "Now Arriving," *Wine Spectator*, October 15, 1997, 68.

16. Mantuano is one of the "Wine Bar Superchefs" featured in the March 2008 issue of *Food and Wine*. The issue has his recipe for "Crepelle with Ricotta and Marinara" on page 192.

17. Chef-owners Rose Gray and Ruth Rogers (authors of *Italian Easy*) may acquire early-season *girolles* overnight from Scotland or large live male crabs from Italy. At the same time, seasonal fruits and vegetables come from their restaurant garden/orchard.

18. Steven Pratt, "Chicago Chef Chases Authentic Flavors in Pursuit of Perfection," *Indianapolis Star*, January 9, 1997, C2.

19. Ibid.

20. For a description of the antic intensity in some restaurant kitchens, see Bourdain's *Kitchen Confidential*.

21. None of the chefs was older than fifty-three when first interviewed in 1996–97, and most were in their forties. Ten years later they are all going strong.

22. At the time, a more inclusive list would assuredly have included Sarah Stegner of the Ritz-Carlton Dining Room, Mark Bakers of Seasons, Keith Luce of Spruce, Arun Sampanthawvivat of Arun, and Gabino Sotelino of Ambria.

23. Shriver, "Here's the Dish ... " *USA Today*, December 30, 1996, 6D.

24. "Now Arriving," *Wine Spectator*, October 15, 1997, 6. The full title of the article includes this final clause: "Diners can choose from a fleet of restaurants that succeed by inspired invention and Midwestern friendliness."

Sources

Interviews (in order of appearance)

Trotter, Charlie. Interview by author. Chicago, November 30, 1996.
Johnson, Philip. Interview by author. Brisbane, Queensland, Australia, November 26, 2001.

Bayless, Rick. Interview by author. Chicago, November 7, 1996.
Graeme, Philippe. Interview by author. Hobart, Tasmania, Australia, January 2, 1998.
Joho, Jean. Interview by author. Chicago, January 8, 1997.
Liccioni, Rolland. Interview by author. Chicago, January 9, 1997.
Mantuano, Tony. Interview by author. Chicago, September 28, 1996.
———. Interview by author. Chicago, November 7, 1996.
Oakley, Steven. Interview by author. Indianapolis, IN, March 12, 1999.
Scardoni, Antonella. Interview by author. Castel Guelfo, Italy, June 5, 2002.

Books

Bourdain, A. *Kitchen Confidential: Adventures in the Culinary Underbelly.* New York: Ecco Press, 2000.
Child, J., and L. Bertholle, S. Beck, and S. Coryn. *Mastering the Art of French Cooking.* Vol. 1. New York: Knopf, 1961.
Csikszentmihalyi, M. *Flow: The Psychology of Human Experience.* New York: Harper and Row, 1990.
———. "Society, Culture and Person: A Systems View of Creativity." In *The Nature of Creativity; Contemporary Psychological Perspectives,* ed. R. Sternberg, 325–39. New York: Cambridge University Press, 1988.
Csikszentmihalyi, M., M. K. Rathunde, and S. Whalen. *Talented Teenagers: The Roots of Success and Failure.* New York: Cambridge University Press, 1993.
Dornenburg, A., and K. Page. *Becoming a Chef.* Hoboken, NJ: John Wiley and Sons, 2003.
Gardner, H. *Reframing Intelligence.* New York: Basic Books, 1999.
———. *Creating Minds.* New York: Basic Books, 1993a.
———. *Frames of Mind: The Theory of Multiple Intelligences.* New York: Basic Books, 1993b. (Originally published in 1983.)
Rogers, Ruth, and Rose Gray. *Italian Easy: Recipes from the London River Café.* New York: Random House, 2004.

CHAPTER 13

Bringing It All Together
Lessons Learned

I began this book with a set of questions: What is the nature of talent, and how is it identified and nurtured? Is exceptional talent an innate quality? Even so, does its fulfillment depend on the intervention of expert teachers? How do social class, gender, and ethnicity influence access to instructional and performance opportunities? Can lessons learned in one particular national and cultural context or in one performance field be extended to other societies and fields? How does public policy shape the recognition and development of talent? These are among the central questions driving *Talent Abounds*.

Nature or Nurture?

With regard to the genetic basis of talent, there is no question that certain physical attributes facilitate extraordinary performance in sports and dance, as do family histories in musical prodigies and to a lesser extent in gifted mathematicians. However, innate potential has to be realized. This is best summed up by the legendary Dorothy DeLay at the Juilliard School, who taught such renowned violinists as Itzhak Perlman, Shlomo Mintz, Cho-Liang Lin, and Midori. When I asked her if these former students needed the intervention of a teacher to arrive at their present level of peak performance, she responded, "I think everyone needs it. I would not make any exceptions." She continued:

> Three types of teaching are necessary in a young person's life.... The first one would
> be from age whatever to about age twelve. That should be someone who supports the

family, who helps the parents with their dealings with the child, and who feeds the material to them in an orderly way.... And then, I think when they start to be teenagers, children need a teacher who can really give them good discipline and see to it that everything is well organized. And then, as they get older and are ready to go professionally, they need somebody who can help them toward really first-class performance and who can help them go into the professional world.[1]

This three-stage progression of teachers echoes the same pattern observed by Bloom and colleagues in their study of *Developing Talent in Young People*, as well in many of the profiled gifted individuals.[2]

Sylvain Cappell, who specializes in teaching gifted mathematicians of all ages, has further noted the need for a wide network of support for the development of talent: "There is very little development of great research scientists on desert islands. Obviously nothing happens in a vacuum.... Nobody becomes what they are without being influenced by and benefiting from the interventions of lots of people."

A more reserved view of what teachers can accomplish was expressed by accomplished pianist Jonathan Biss, who, when only sixteen, observed, "I would certainly say that teaching cannot produce [talent].... Teaching is not about creating as much as it is about helping students become aware of what they can do." That is no insignificant matter.

Characteristics of Master Teachers

Helping students realize what they can do is certainly a key characteristic of master teachers and coaches. They motivate their students, unlock previously unrealized skills, and assist them to achieve world-class levels in athletics and the arts. A coach, as attested by Mark Spitz, can help shave vital seconds off the performance of a swimmer that results in Olympic Gold Medals or the setting of world records. Although not equivalent to athletic coaching, one-on-one mentoring has been documented as playing a significant role in advancing the careers of outstanding talents in the sciences, in the types of problems that talented students studied, and, ultimately, in scientific breakthroughs.[3] In music and dance, master teachers similarly empower their protégés to become contributing members of their performance fields and extend the boundaries of what is possible to accomplish with a musical instrument, the human voice, or the body in motion.

Without exception, master teachers and coaches are exceptionally knowledgeable about the various dimensions and essence of a particular field—whether it be refined performance and musicality in the arts or elegant approaches to the study of key problems and puzzles in mathematics and chess. In many cases, master teachers themselves have had distinguished careers as performers before becoming educators.

Outstanding artists, however, may not necessarily be the very best teachers. Jascha Heifetz, for example, was an incomparable musician who nonetheless had difficulty explaining the magic of his playing to students. By contrast, the master teachers and coaches featured in this book stand out as effective communicators.

The metaphors that explain attributes of these individuals are framed in such terms as "X-ray vision," "tailoring instruction," and providing "shortcuts." Based on years of experience, master teachers and coaches have an ability to detect immediately what technical or conceptual problems students have, what students are capable of, and the precise challenge or set of tasks that will enable them to reach the next level of performance.[4] They also have an ability to break down complex problems into specific steps and provide the tools essential to accomplish those specific tasks, eventually leading to peak performance. No matter how innately talented or practiced the student may be, the master teacher refines and polishes initial capabilities.

In some, but few, cases they may shout, scream, and do outrageous things. But mostly, they are gentle, kind, and loving mentors who are likely to care as much about the student as a human being as they do about technical virtuosity and the qualities of performance and work.[5]

Violinist Josef Gingold best exemplifies an exceptional teacher whose humanity is invariably recalled by his students. In turn, when asked what qualities he looked for in his students, Gingold responded: "To me, a human comes first. And then if he happens to play well, that's nice. But this is not what I look for in the young kids that I teach. I want to feel that any influence I have is backed by someone who has good qualities as a human."

Gingold's willingness to embrace and help every single one of his students is evident in this comment: "Someone asked me once, 'Who is your favorite student?' I said, 'The one I'm teaching at the moment.'" In attending to that student, Gingold, as recalled by violinist Jean Piguet, "taught every student individually. He knew what to say to such and such student, and what not to say. He would give completely different fingering and bowing [instructions] according to the idiosyncrasies of pupils he had. And he sort of nurtured the students as you would nurture a plant."[6]

Similarly, Coach James ("Doc") Counsilman had an uncanny ability to know exactly what his swimmers were capable of achieving. Sportswriter Bob Hammel recalls interviewing Counsilman any number of times at poolside with swimmers frequently bobbing out of the water. They would ask Counsilman where they were in their regimen, and Doc would instinctively tell them what their speed was and what they needed to do next.

Attending to individual differences is inherent in Spanish diva Teresa Berganza's approach to teaching: "I like to discover each voice, human being, and personality, color of voice, and spirit, because the voice has a spirit. Each voice has a body, a resonance.... Within each person there is something more, but they may not be capable of drawing it out." This is the challenge to her as an educator following her career as a performer.

In drawing out and leading students, master teachers and coaches are more likely to guide rather than impose. In addition to role modeling, they pose questions, provide cues, and set the students on the path to discovering answers on their own. This approach to teaching has a lasting impact on the students who develop a built-in capacity to be self-learners, problem solvers, and reflective practitioners.

Commitment to meeting the personal needs of their students is another distinguishing trait. Various stories reveal how teachers often were willing to travel great distances to teach their students, spending days at a time with their families as circumstances dictated. In other cases, the teachers served almost as surrogate parents, taking in a young talent to live with them for extended periods. Others offered their homes and free lessons when aspiring musicians could not afford instruction (as when aspiring jazz trumpeter Dominic Spera was befriended by Don Jacoby). As recalled by Spera:

> [Jacoby would] come home from the studios and want to play duets and talk music and trumpet. He did that for about three, four months and never charged me another nickel. I said, "Jake, what can I do to repay you for all this?" And he said, "You can make me a promise that you will do this for somebody else when you get to be my age." So he gave me an insight into what teaching was all about.

Master educators also are dream givers and shapers—offering a vision of what is possible, if only the students commit themselves to excelling in their art form, sport, or discipline. At one time, they too were students inspired by exceptional teachers, many of whom contributed to the advancement of a field. In turn, they wish their protégés to build on the best of what has come before them and to make their own unique contributions to the well-being and enjoyment of others or to the advancement of knowledge and skilled practice in a particular field.

Perceiving themselves as part of a continuum of practitioners and educators may be the key to understanding why, despite brilliant careers as performers, they view themselves first and foremost as teachers. According to Janos Starker, one of the most celebrated cellists of the last half of the twentieth century: "Now, more and more, I feel that what I've done and what I'm doing as a teacher is much more important. I set standards with my recordings and performances, but as a teacher I transmit the messages I've learned from those people I was exposed to since childhood, so it may last way beyond my earthly existence."

It is important to note a proviso here: no single teacher, no matter how exceptionally inspirational and competent, is always the best or appropriate one for every student. There is a question of "fit." Students may choose to leave one teacher for another, or may even be recommended by one teacher to another. Gingold, for example, had no qualms about recommending prized students Miriam Fried and Paul Biss to study with Ivan Galamian, "Mr. Fix-It," in New York City. Opera star and teacher Giorgio Tozzi, with his emphasis on teaching as tailoring and students finding their own voice, similarly, throughout his career, supported students by helping them find the most appropriate teachers and career paths for themselves. This tendency to refer pupils to other master teachers, however, is also culturally patterned and more typical of the European and North American teachers studied than of the Asian and African artists, who form a lifelong, ritualistic, personal bond with their "guru" or mentor.

What these master teachers do not want are students to be carbon copies of themselves.[7] Harvey Phillips, described as the Paganini of the tuba, had this to say: "I'm one of those people who feel that it's not good teaching if all your students sound like you.... I want them to be free to pursue their interests, not just my interests." Famed tenor James McCracken would modestly tell his students: "Don't do what I do, because what I do worked for me, and just barely." His advice must have seemed incredible to his students, who would have been more than delighted to sing like McCracken. And woe to anyone who wanted to sound like Starker: "I want every student to play the cello as well as I do, but God forbid that they sound like I do or that they play music the way I do! Because then it would be simply a cloning."

Master teachers, like their prized pupils, are perfectionists, their own most severe critics. Phillips, for example, tells his students: "They have only one musician to compete with the rest of their days—themselves."

Characteristics of Peak Performers

As the featured master teachers and coaches, themselves, were peak performers, it is not surprising that their most prized protégés share many of the same features. Among them are the following:

- They usually start early, often as a result of family influences;
- They have a passionate love of their vocation—the instrument or the sport they play, the body of knowledge with which they are engaged—often to the point of being obsessively involved;
- They are curious people, exploring in depth not only their own field but also other often seemingly unrelated domains;
- Over time each develops a personal vision and a distinctive signature or individual voice that is highly valued by others;
- They are high-energy people, performing and teaching well into their seventies in fields outside sports.

The following sections focus on what I consider to be the most salient traits of the peak performers—their early involvement with a performance field, a manifestation of a lifelong commitment to mastering an art form or sport, and a striving for perfection, admittedly an elusive goal.

Starting Early

Stories concerning precocity are not uncommon in music and mathematics. An early fascination with music making and solving puzzles characterizes peak performers. Profiles of Josef Gingold, György Sebok, and Janos Starker, in the first chapter, reveal that before the age of ten, those artists had embarked on their careers, performing publicly and, in the case of Janos Starker, teaching others. The 1990 Ghanaian musician of the year, percussionist Bernard Woma, began playing the xylophone at the age of three, based on the divination of a spiritual leader in his village; at age five he was giving public performances. Indian sitar player Kartik Seshadri began lessons at age five and gave solo concerts at age six.[8]

In other fields precocity is less common. For a number of opera stars, modern dance masters, and world-class chefs, commitment to their art began later. Diva Sylvia McNair, for example, first studied violin before her vocal talent was discovered.

Passionate Commitment and Persistence

Whether starting early or late, once they realized their destiny was tied to a particular field, these talented individuals became passionately devoted to it. This is best illustrated by master chef Charlie Trotter. Following his graduation in political science from the University of Wisconsin, he moved to San Francisco to study the burgeoning culinary scene inspired by Alice Waters at Chez Panisse:

> I slept on the floor in a studio apartment. I spent every penny I earned either buying new cookbooks or dining out or buying some kind of kitchen utensil or kitchen equipment.... I'm talking about a level of fanaticism that crushed the typical [cult] religious zealotry that we're familiar with.... I mean it was night and day incessant, thinking, sleeping, breathing cuisine, having nothing to do with anyone who wasn't interested.

By contrast, 1995 James Beard chef of the year Rick Bayless grew up in an extended family of restaurateurs. By age eight or nine, he planned and prepared three or four dinner parties over summer vacations around specialty themes, such as Hawaiian cooking. For his tenth birthday, he requested the gift of Julia Child's newly published *Mastering the Art of French Cooking* and proceeded to work his way through the book.

To reach their high levels of achievement, world-class talents have to be extremely dedicated, often spending tedious hours of practice over numerous years.[9] In some cases they would travel hours to reach their teachers and have complex, demanding schedules involving school work, practice of their sport or craft, and other commitments. One extraordinary example (from Chapter 4) is that of oboist Bob Mayer's amazing odyssey to study with Louis Doucet of the Minneapolis Symphony. Every Friday afternoon he left his home in Grand Forks for a full thirteen-hour train trip to Minneapolis, where he had a long lesson with Doucet, and a short stay in the city, and then take the return trip to have Sunday breakfast with his family in North Dakota.

Persistence in highly competitive artistic and athletic fields requires strong personalities, a confidence in oneself in the face of inevitable setbacks and distant rewards. The pressures to succeed early in certain fields, such as mathematics, at an early age are extraordinary, often leading to burnout and departure among promising talents. In tragic cases, student may take their lives.[10]

The pressure on individuals to succeed, as noted above, commonly comes from themselves. By inclination, they tend to be perfectionists. For instrumental musicians, singers, and dancers, the effusive praise of prominent national critics may have little sway if they are dissatisfied with aspects of their performance; the mistakes of which only they are aware will gnaw at them. The striving for perfection is never ending— as, for example, when Pablo Casals was asked by clarinetist John Banman why he continued to practice the cello four or five hours a day when he was in his mid-eighties. Casals replied: "Because I have a notion that I am making some progress."[11]

An ability to learn from defeats and failures is an important asset. One of the few peak performers actually to thrive on setbacks is chess International Grandmaster Maurice Ashley. Rather than be deterred by defeat, he was motivated to "read books, play in tournaments, come back again, lose again, until [he] was better in chess." According to Ashley, "The best games that ever happened to me were my losses."

Master chess coach and educator Bruce Pandolfini believes otherwise: too many losses at an early age might deter students from continuing to be interested in the game. For Pandolfini, who started the Chess in the Schools program in New York City, "one reason why early adolescence might be preferable to earlier instruction is that students ... are going to lose a lot, and at twelve or thirteen you can deal with defeat better." Furthermore, "If students start too early, and don't have good teaching, they can pick up very bad habits"; according to Pandolfini, "those habits will stay with them forever."

Supportive Contexts

In addition to personal traits related to motivation and persistence, a widening circle of support and resources (familial as well as cultural and societal) is critical to successful careers. In the case of musicians, parents, if not professionals, often are devotees who surround their children with music. Older siblings who play an instrument also influence careers, as was evident in the profile of Josef Gingold.

Supportive family contexts include listening habits, record and book collections, and leisure time activities. Harvey Phillips recalls that on Saturdays, especially in the winter when there was less farm work to do, family members with various instruments would get together and "just play music all night." In days past, records or radio programs inspired many budding musicians. Leonard Bernstein's TV appearances and book *The Joy of Music* had a profound impact on countless individuals, including symphony conductor Michael Morgan. A family visit to the opera or a symphony orchestra performance might be life changing, as it was for opera singers Virginia Zeani and Franz Grundheber.

Sometimes parents play a direct role in teaching their children. Jazz violinist Sara Caswell's mother, an adept organist with a Ph.D. in musicology, would sit next to Sara and play along with her: "She would write out each piece in decorative colors in order to make them more fun to learn.... As I grew older, she would continue to accompany me on concerti and sonatas while suggesting musical ideas to consider. She was one of my most influential teachers." Classical violinist Corey Cerovsek, who also has a master's degree in mathematics, describes long car rides with his father as music theory and history lessons. During those times his father would sometimes explain calculus and engineering to Corey.[12] The father of Russian Grandmaster Lev Alburt played chess with him until he was outmatched by his son, when he then sought out a colleague to provide more advanced coaching.

Parental support in finding appropriate teachers and taking their children to lessons turns out to be an important factor in sustaining years of practice of an art or sport. At the same time, overly demanding parents can stifle, if not crush, the willingness of a young talent to persist in a particular field.

In addition to family support, peers also may have a positive, or negative, impact on career interests. Among the featured artists who benefited from positive peer influence are Sylvia Waters, whose best friend encouraged her to attend concerts and ballet classes with her, and to apply to the Juilliard School. Michael Barrett recruited fellow university and conservatory instrumental students to play in ensembles he conducted. Students at the Liszt Academy, such as György Sebok and Janos Starker, drew on one another for ego support in the face of domineering giants in the field of Hungarian music. The competition of fellow chess players most likely served as a spur to chess standouts like Lev Alburt and Maurice Ashley to apply themselves even more diligently to excelling at the game.

On the other hand, negative peer pressure against students standing out and succeeding is also common. Mark Spitz had to cope with occasional negativity on the part of teammates, who may have resented his stardom. But it didn't deter Spitz. Peer culture at institutions like Harvard in fields such as mathematics may be both stimulating and daunting, or a turn-off, for gifted students, as noted by Daniel Biss.

Generally, what is evident in the careers of peak performers are supportive personal as well as institutional contexts as they progress to the highest skill levels.

Opportunities to excel, however, depend on what roles are available in a particular performance field.

Fields

For researchers like Howard Gardner who have studied the nature of different forms of intelligence and skilled performance, there are societal and cultural determinants at play concerning what is identified and rewarded as creativity.[13] As Mihaly Csikszentmihalyi has pointed out, "In order to understand 'talent' and 'giftedness,' it is just as important to understand social mechanisms of attribution as well as the special gifts of individuals."[14] These social mechanisms are known as domains or fields of endeavor and engagement.

Throughout this book, I have used the term "field" as it connotes the organized aspects of the more general term "domain." A field consists of a systematized body of knowledge and requisite skills, a codified vocabulary for defining the nature of ongoing work, organized roles of performance and intellectual endeavor, criteria for judging performance and achievement, constituted authorities who judge and reward what is considered to be exemplary performance, and specific norms embedded in a more diffuse and general cultural system that comprehends, for example, who is entitled to play what roles and what knowledge or skilled performance is most highly valued.

Various biographical sketches in *Talent Abounds* indicate that nontraditional individuals will have to persevere and strive harder if they are to be accepted by professionals in a determined field. David Baker, an African American trombonist, had to face racial discrimination in major symphony orchestras. Kay Stonefelt, a female percussionist, experienced similar obstacles. She also had to overcome initial reluctance to be taught the xylophone by Bernard Woma because, in Dagara culture and mythology, the instrument is not taught to or performed by women. In turn, Woma was initially limited in the musical genres he could learn and play by his ethnicity and regional identity.

Even where "isms" do not present barriers, the state of development of a particular field may not provide many opportunities for gainful employment. Among the distinguishing features of master teachers is the impact they have on extending the boundaries of a performance field. Saxophonist Eugene Rousseau, through his technical and artistic wizardry, has opened a respected place for the saxophone in symphony orchestras. Tubist Harvey Phillips has single-handedly commissioned new works (from popular to classical) and expanded performance opportunities for hundreds of tuba players through such marketing devices as "OCTUBAFEST," "TUBACHRISTMAS," "TUBASANTAS," and "TUBAJAZZ," thereby popularizing the instrument. Moreover, Rousseau and

Phillips have strengthened and extended a respected space for their instruments in university music programs and well beyond in venues ranging from concert halls to shopping malls.

The absence of compositions for even better known orchestral instruments such as cello may be a further hindrance to performance careers. But when such prodigious talents as Mstislav Rostropovich and Janos Starker appear on the concert scene, new works are created and previously neglected compositions brought to life.

Training programs in jazz have found a respected place in the halls of academia. Moreover, by publishing books on the teaching of jazz, when few existed, David Baker helped codify knowledge and institutionalize the systematic learning of a field by students who otherwise might depend on a hit-and-miss method of learning more intuitively by listening to records or attending live performances. According to Baker, "The attitude until the mid-60s, when the ball started rolling for jazz education, was 'Either you got it or you ain't,' or 'You'll hear it.'" He recounts how he would ask guitarist Wes Montgomery, while on a job: "'How does that go? What are those notes?' And he'd say, 'You'll hear it.' Usually it was the best indication that I didn't have the chance of a snowball in hell of hearing it. I may as well put up the white flag or call 911, because I knew it was over at that time."

Public Policy and Private Initiatives

The process of developing creative potential and skilled performance may start in families and communities, rely principally on the abilities of expert teachers, and depend on opportunities to express one's abilities, but ultimately public policy plays a leading role in ensuring the personal fulfillment and adult success of all of a society's members.

Public funding is critical to reaching the largest number of students with opportunities for acquiring new skills, developing interests, inquiring more deeply into different domains of knowledge, and being able to perform before audiences.

The valuable role of in-school and after-school special programs in the arts, chess, mathematics, and the sciences is evident in the biographies of the individuals featured in *Talent Abounds*. Students benefited, for example, from the existence of school orchestras as well as from citywide programs that enabled them to perform with students from other schools or, in the case of Michael Morgan, actually to conduct a youth orchestra. Chess in the Schools programs across the country have been instrumental in engaging otherwise turned off students in depressed urban areas, while developing sophisticated analytical skills and enhancing their self-esteem as they excel in a competitive game. Specialized schools, more recently magnet schools in the arts and sciences, provide opportunities for advanced training of those especially gifted or interested in a particular field.[15]

An outstanding example of a publicly funded music education program is Venezuela's State Youth Orchestra System. Founded in 1979 by José Antonio Abreau and supported by eight consecutive administrations (varying greatly in political orientation), the program has "put instruments and musical scores in the hands of 400,000 [mostly low-income, at-risk] children and young people."[16] More than two hundred youth orchestras have been formed across the country, with major ensembles, such as the Simon Bolivar Youth Orchestra, playing to rave reviews at the Royal Albert Hall and other major concert venues around the globe. This program, in developing musical talent and opening new vistas for some of the most marginalized populations, is viewed by its creators as a "pathway to social dignity."[17]

University programs that enable high school students to enroll in various college-level courses can play a key role in interesting and engaging students in scholarly disciplines. For those identified early as gifted in mathematics, such programs as the one headed by Sylvain Cappell at New York University provide a nurturing environment. University summer camps in mathematics and science, as well as the arts and athletics, have long been training grounds for countless professionals.

Where the state does not provide extensive after-school programs or specialized schools, private foundations play an important role in fostering talent in various ways, including providing funds for curriculum development. For example, the GRAMMY Foundation's Leonard Bernstein Center for Learning has developed a model, "Artful Learning," for all levels of public education based on the belief "that the arts and the artistic process reinforce teaching and learning in all subjects." The model is being implemented in schools from New York to California. Another example of private initiative is the Martina Arroyo Foundation, founded in 2003, with the mission of nurturing world-class operatic talent.[18]

Not-for-profit centers with arts programs, such as the New York City 92nd Street Y, figure prominently in the careers of many world-class talents. They provide courses as well as significant performance opportunities for young artists. The New Dance Group Studio in New York City, initially founded by the Works Progress Administration during the Great Depression, as Sylvia Waters described, was "a haven in the late 1950s for some of the most wonderful artists I had ever seen in my performance life." Waters, as a high school student, was able to take classes at the studio.

Normative and Institutional Constraints

Beyond public and private initiatives to identify and cultivate talent, there is a need to take into account predominant notions concerning the nature of talent and creativity. If elitist beliefs that only a few can be labeled as gifted prevail, fewer resources will be dedicated to identifying and developing high levels of skilled performance in all. Similarly, if a common notion holds that talent is inborn and there are only so many things instruction can do to raise performance to very high levels, then society will tend to discount efforts to do so. If "intelligence" is defined in terms of how well students score on standardized tests on a narrow range of skills and knowledge, many will be left behind—despite claims to the contrary. Cultural norms concerning what roles women can play, as well as those appropriate for children born outside specific hereditary families or clans, also restrict academic and career choices.

The bureaucratic organization and functioning of school systems pose further serious obstacles to effective education, hamstringing the autonomy and creativity of teachers—even more so with current governmental initiatives in education. Most of them are linked to the sets of skills considered essential to increasing the competitive position of a country in the global economy, rather than to such worthy goals as preparing individuals for the exercise of democratic citizenship rights, fostering social solidarity, strengthening tolerance of dissenting points of view, celebrating cultural diversity, and nurturing personal fulfillment. However, even within the impersonal conditions of large schools and classrooms that tend to batch-process students, there are educational strategies and pedagogies that provide meaningful instruction.

What Can Be Learned from Gifted Public School Teachers?

In attempting to draw parallels between the characteristics of master educators and public school teachers, a number of difficulties are immediately apparent. One obvious problem is being able to match the one-on-one teaching and coaching that occurs between master teachers and peak performers in the arts and athletics. Much of the instruction described in this volume occurs in music schools and conservatories, where teachers typically have fewer than twenty students, rather than the over one hundred students that is the norm for postprimary teachers. Yet, even under those daunting situations, gifted teachers are able to personalize instruction. Michael Morgan, for example, recalls how a junior high school teacher, Hermann Seush, took time after class to instruct him in music theory and history and the fundamentals of composition that were essential to conducting.

Getting to know students is easier in the smaller classrooms of elementary schools. Yet, even there teachers are overloaded with demanding schedules. Giving extra attention to a student may have a profound influence in determining individual futures. In the case of saxophonist Eugene Rousseau, his musical journey may have commenced in fourth grade, when Ms. Elda Jansen, who liked music, met him in the morning before school and started to encourage him in his interests.

As part of this study of master teachers, my research assistant, Margaret Clements, interviewed more than thirty public school teachers nominated by school superintendents from around the state of Indiana to be Armstrong Teacher Educators. As such, these public school teachers participate actively in the life of the Indiana University School of Education over a period of a year and more.

In discussing their approaches to teaching, the Armstrong Educators revealed many of the same distinguishing traits as the master teachers profiled throughout *Talent Abounds*. According to Clements, they are enthusiastic and passionate about learning and teaching, they have a deep respect for each of their students, believe that the potential of all students can be developed, find the means to provide the challenges and arrange the specific academic tasks that further their students' learning and personal growth, and are continually striving to increase their own mastery of subject matter and pedagogical knowledge as well as their effectiveness as educators. Typical of master teachers, they share their love of a particular field of study, provide safe learning environments, communicate honestly with students about their performances in a constructive manner, equip students to learn to move to progressively higher levels of understanding and skilled performance by presenting unfamiliar material as incremental problems to be solved, and have a wide repertoire of applications to demonstrate what they are trying to teach.[19]

What Can Be Done?

Talent Abounds began with an overriding question of what can be done to develop the potential of all students in public school systems. Can the types of personal instruction that occur in one-on-one instruction in private lessons or in special programs for the gifted and talented be extended to all students? For public schools to be able to provide a truly engaging quality education for all requires, as William Patterson notes, "Breaking out of Our Boxes."[20] This means reforming the way educational systems are organized and the ways in which teaching and learning occur. The recommendations made by Patterson are strongly reminiscent of the favorable conditions under which master teachers interact with their most prized pupils. In restructured schools, students would engage in meaningful activity, feel validated, and experience success. Schools would be smaller, more systematically providing opportunities for teachers to know their students on a personal basis and tailor instruction to their specific stages of development. The curriculum would be problem-oriented and provide longer blocks of time for in-depth instruction. Such structural arrangements would facilitate students acquiring the skills to more effectively manage their time and be self-directed learners.

These recommendations echo the work of Gardner, Csikszentmihalyi and colleagues, Robert Sternberg and Elena Grigorenko,[21] Theodore Sizer,[22] and Henry Levin with others,[23] who advocate educational policies and practices that take into account the multiple intelligences and talents of students; provide opportunities to engage in sustained, creative activity based on personal interests; and encourage a sense of personal efficacy. They further accord with writings of major educational theorists of the twentieth century, John Dewey[24] and L. S. Vygotsky,[25] concerning the philosophical and psychological underpinnings of democratic and effective schools.

Critical to the success of such endeavors is a corps of highly competent, committed, and caring teachers who are provided with the conditions that enable them to perform as responsible professionals. Recent policy trends in teacher education in the United States and elsewhere tend to emphasize subject matter competence almost exclusively, to the detriment of preparing teachers with the requisite pedagogical knowledge as to how to communicate content effectively. Such notions lead to state policies that facilitate contracting individuals with professional knowledge of subject matter, for example in mathematics and sciences, without any teaching experience. The role of teacher education in universities is downplayed in favor of on-site preparation. Courses in psychology, philosophy, history, sociology, and anthropology taught in university faculties of education are considered by many state authorities as irrelevant to the formation of teachers.

These trends run counter to the findings of this book: that truly gifted teachers need both subject master expertise and pedagogical expertise in order to effectively teach students of differing abilities, interests, and learning styles. Such pedagogical knowledge, skills, and value orientations are, in the judgment of this writer, best learned in higher-education teacher education programs that present reflective practitioners with a broad, humanistic education. At the same time, university faculties of education also have the responsibility of providing teachers with subject matter expertise and a desire for continuous learning and professional development.

Conclusions

Talent Abounds has examined the traits and interactions of gifted teachers and peak performers in different fields and societal contexts. It has explored the worlds of instrumental music, conducting opera, dance, chess, mathematics, the culinary arts, and sports. Among the principal findings of studying master teachers and their prodigies is that even the most innately gifted in various fields of endeavor benefited from a progression of teachers who intervened to raise their knowledge and performance skills to world-class levels. Both teachers and their extraordinary students manifested similar traits of passionate commitment to a particular field, and a driving persistence to excel, leading to new heights of skilled performance or extending the boundaries of knowledge.

Although it would appear that the teachers profiled in this book are extraordinary, that is not necessarily the conclusion I would reach. Public school teachers considered gifted by their colleagues share similar values and engage in many of the same practices as internationally renowned master teachers. That there are many such teachers in public education I do not doubt. Whether or not they are recognized and supported to work their magic is a critical issue. Ultimately, the challenge to educational policy and practice is not what extraordinary teachers can do to develop the potential of exceptional students, but what ordinary teachers can do to nurture the abilities of all students so that they can live fuller lives.[26] This study, it is hoped, has illustrated the set of conditions under which such an ideal goal is achievable.

Notes

1. In fact, DeLay, until her death in 2004, had a whole team of teachers working with her to instruct a number of students of varying ages and levels from different countries. Beginning in 1999, former protégé Perlman cotaught the most advanced students with her. In a documentary film on the Juilliard School, she noted that Perlman served as a source of inspiration and someone from whom she learned.

2. Generalizations about talent development are found in Benjamin S. Bloom, ed., *Developing Talent in Young People* (New York: Ballantine Books, 1985), 507–49.

3. See, for example, Anne Roe, *The Making of a Scientist* (New York: Dodd, Mead and Co, 1953); and R. Subotnik, "Talent Developed: Conversations with Masters in the Arts and Sciences," *Journal for the Education of the Gifted* 18(4) (1995): 440–66.

4. Particularly relevant here are the writings of educational theorists John Dewey and L. S. Vygotsky, as summarized in M. Glassman, "Dewey and Vygotsky: Society, Experience, and Inquiry in Educational Practice," *Educational Researcher* 30(4) (2001), 3–13, esp. 12.

5. On the master violin educator Suzuki, see, for example, S. Hersh and L. Peak, "Developing Character in Music Teachers: A Suzuki Approach," in *Learning in Likely Places*, ed. J. Singleton (Cambridge: Cambridge University Press, 1998), 153–71.

6. At the time of our 1998 interview, Piguet was concert master of L'Orchestre de la Suisse Romande de Geneva.

7. That is true even where artists are expected to work within a tradition but express their own subtle variations on it, as with the ancient apprenticeship *iemoto* system in Japan, or the extended musical apprenticeships in India.

8. Seshadri was interviewed for a chapter on music of the Indian subcontinent that is not included in this volume.

9. K. A. Ericsson, ed., *The Road to Excellence: The Acquisition of Expert Performance in the Arts, Sciences, Sports, and Games* (Mahwah, NJ: Lawrence Erlbaum Associates, 1996); and K. A. Ericsson and I. A. Faivre, "What's Exceptional about Exceptional Abilities?" in *The Exceptional Brain: Neuropsychology of Talent and Special Abilities*, ed. L. K. Obler and D. Fein (New York: Guildford Press, 1988), 436–73.

10. This is evident in the comments of mathematics educator Sylvain Cappell (in Chapter 10), who is particularly aware of these issues in working with gifted youngsters and the unreasonable expectations that parents may have for their children. Also pertinent are the comments of gifted mathematician Danny Biss (Chapter 10) with regard to the pressures to achieve a major breakthrough in his field as a young scholar.

11. Snider, M. "Always Remember Practice Makes Better." Newton Kansan Online (2000). http://thekansan.com/stories/082300/acc_0823000001.html. [The article was formerly available at this address. At press time, access could not be confirmed.]

12. A different relationship is that of performing with your parents in major concert halls, which is the case with pianist Jonathan Biss and his mother and father Miriam Fried and Paul Biss, both world-class violinists.

13. H. Gardner, *Frames of Mind: The Theory of Multiple Intelligences* (New York: Basic Books, 1993a; originally published in 1983); H. Gardner, *Creating Minds* (New York: Basic Books, 1993b); and H. Gardner, *Reframing Intelligence* (New York: Basic Books, 1999).

14. M. Csikszentmihalyi, "Solving a Problem Is Not Finding a New One: A Reply to Simon," *New Ideas in Psychology* 6(2) (1988): 186—summarized in the text by D. Pariser, "The Artistically Precocious Child in Different Cultural Contexts," *Journal of Multicultural and Cross-Cultural Research in Art Education* 10/11 (fall 1992/93): 50. Other works by Csikszentmihalyi include "Society, Culture and Person: A Systems View of Creativity," in *The Nature of Creativity: Contemporary Psychological Perspectives*, ed. R. Sternberg (New York: Cambridge University Press, 1988), 325–39; and his *Flow: The Psychology of Human Experience* (New York: Harper and Row, 1990); and M. Csikszentmihalyi, M. K. Rathunde, and S. Whalen, *Talented Teenagers: The Roots of Success and Failure* (New York: Cambridge University Press, 1993).

15. In socialist countries the state typically plays a much more direct role in establishing after-school programs in neighborhood centers. Frequently called "cultural palaces," they offer formal instruction in the arts as well as opportunities to pursue various hobbies. In addition to these programs, there are specialized schools in the arts and sports. A major concern with these schools, as well as magnet schools in the United States, is the danger of a curriculum that is too narrowly focused on a specific skills set or knowledge domain.

16. See Humberto Márquez, "Venezuela: A New Life for At-Risk Kids, and Music Too!" Caracas, August 24, 2007. http://www.changingthepresent.org/news/show/72771.

17. Ibid.

18. The foundation's very first summer program ("Performance") took place in June 2005 in New York City with students from the United States and Europe.

19. R. Arnove and M. Clements, "Master Teachers and the Development of World-Class Talent: A Comparative Study" (paper presented at the annual meeting of American Education Research Association, in Chicago, April 21–25, 2003); available by contacting R. Arnove at arnove@indiana.edu.

20. W. Patterson, "Breaking Out of Our Boxes," *Phi Delta Kappan*, 84(8) (2003): 569–74.

21. R. F. Sternberg and E. L. Grigorenko, *Teaching for Successful Intelligence: To Increase Student Learning and Achievement* (Arlington Heights, IL: Skylight Professional Development, 2000).

22. T. Sizer, *Horace's School* (Boston: Houghton Mifflin, 1992).

23. H. Levin, "Accelerated Schools: The Background," in *Accelerated Schools in Action: Lessons from the Field*, ed. C. Finnan, E. P. St. John, J. McCarty, and S. P. Slovacek (Thousand Oaks, CA: Corwin Press, 1996), 3–24.

24. J. Dewey, *Interest and Effort in Education* (Boston: Houghton Mifflin, 1900);

Democracy and Education (New York: Free Press, 1912).

25. L. S. Vygtosky, "Interaction between Learning and Development," in *Mind in Society: The Development of Higher Psychological Processes*, ed. M. Cole, V. John-Steiner, S. Scribner, and E. Souberman (Cambridge: Harvard University Press, 1978), 79–91 (original work published in 1935); *Educational Psychology*, trans. R. Silverman (Boca Raton, FL: CRC Press, 1997) (original work published in 1926).

26. This is not a unique finding. It accords with the conclusions of innumerable educators and researchers, commonly expressed in such leading education policy and practice journals as the *Phi Delta Kappan*.

Index

About the Author

Robert F. Arnove, Chancellor's Professor Emeritus at Indiana University–Bloomington, is a leading scholar of comparative and international education. Winner of many distinguished teaching awards, he has been a visiting scholar at universities in countries ranging from Argentina to Australia. His interest in education and social change and his commitment to combining scholarship with public service have led him to be president of a teacher's union, candidate for the U.S. Congress, and president of an experimental theater company.